THE PELICAN BOOK OF ENGLISH PROSE

GENERAL EDITOR : KENNETH ALLOTT

A 360

VOLUME I : ELIZABETHAN AND JACOBEAN PROSE

EDITED BY KENNETH MUIR

THE PELICAN BOOK OF ENGLISH PROSE

GENERAL EDITOR : KENNETH ALLOTT

VOLUME I

Elizabethan and Jacobean Prose

· 1550–1620 ·

EDITED BY KENNETH MUIR

PENGUIN BOOKS

Penguin Books Ltd, Harmondsworth, Middlesex

U.S.A.: Penguin Books Inc., 3300 Clipper Mill Road, Baltimore 11, Md

CANADA: Penguin Books (Canada) Ltd, 178 Norseman Street,
Toronto 18, Ontario

AUSTRALIA: Penguin Books Pty Ltd, 762 Whitehorse Road,
Mitcham, Victoria

SOUTH AFRICA: Penguin Books (S.A.) Pty Ltd, Gibraltar House,
Regent Road, Sea Point, Cape Town

—

First published 1956

Made and printed in Great Britain
by The Whitefriars Press Ltd
London and Tonbridge

CONTENTS

CONTENTS

2. THE MOVEMENT OF IDEAS:
REFLECTION, ARGUMENT, EXHORTATION, SATIRE

3. THE WORLD OF IMAGINATION, FEELING AND COMIC INVENTION: FICTION, HISTORICAL AND OCCASIONAL WRITING

CONTENTS

CONTENTS

4. THE CRITICISM OF THE ARTS

GENERAL INTRODUCTION

The Pelican Book of English Prose has the aim of bringing into focus for the ordinary reader nearly three hundred and fifty years of English prose: so that he may see for himself its variety and continuity in successive ages, the many purposes for which it has been employed (including the humbler ones), the prose styles thought expressive at different times, and the ruling interests and attitudes of particular periods with their associated changes of tone in the conduct of prose. This has involved some planning. An anthology is judged practically by what we can do with it. If it is to be read intelligently or used for study, not merely dipped into idly, it needs to support the reader's interest by a certain coherence and consistency of approach: that is to say, its contents must be properly arranged and introduced. The present anthology contains about 425,000 words of text exclusive of editorial matter and includes some three hundred writers who were at work between 1550 and 1880. These initial and terminal dates are plainly convenient: before 1550 prose cannot be read easily by the general reader without a glossary (and it will not be read, one suspects, with a glossary except by the serious student); after 1880 considerations of copyright become troublesome and begin to influence an editor's choice. The preliminary disposition of the material is in five volumes in chronological sequence, as follows:

I   Elizabethan and Jacobean prose (1550–1620)
II   Seventeenth-Century prose (1620–1700)
III   Eighteenth-Century prose (1700–80)
IV   Prose of the Romantic Period (1780–1830)
V   Victorian prose (1830–80).

Each volume is self-contained and independently edited, but

the unity of the whole anthology is preserved by a 'horizontal' classification which cuts across the 'vertical' chronological division just described. The anthology, then, is sub-divided both chronologically and, within each volume, by an arrangement of subject-matter in accordance with the following scheme:

1. The Picture of the Age: Scene, Personality, Event
2. The Movement of Ideas: Reflection, Argument, Exhortation, Satire
3. The World of Imagination, Feeling and Comic Invention: Fiction, Historical and Occasional Writing
4. The Criticism of the Arts

The editors of the separate volumes have found this scheme, which took its final form only after several revisions, sufficiently flexible; and it is hoped that it may provide a useful framework for the reader and enable him to grasp more rapidly the distinguishing characteristics of prose in each period. It was the general editor's task to see that the agreed scheme was followed and to act as a clearing-house for the suggestions and criticisms of his colleagues. The sharing among six editors of the task of reading and selecting pieces for the five volumes of the anthology has probably been an advantage. It has meant a wider and more accurate coverage of the enormous area of English prose between 1550 and 1880; and it has allowed particular sections of prose to be undertaken by editors whose interests are centred in the periods for which they are responsible. The disunity that might have resulted from the arrangement has been carefully guarded against: both by the adoption of the agreed scheme and by other means of ensuring a common approach which have still to be described.

Some of these means were mechanical. It was decided that a substantial proportion of the passages in each volume, usually selected from the more important writers, should be long enough to furnish material for an hour's discussion if the anthology should be used as a textbook. It was also thought desirable that the introductory essays to the five volumes should be mainly concerned with the discrimination of prose styles, and that they should all contain frequent references to the authors and extracts introduced. Again, it was proposed that in each volume passages should be chosen where possible to shed light on each other, and it was agreed that the value of the whole work would partly depend on the number of the relationships of this kind it was possible to establish. A good deal of effort lies behind whatever success has been achieved. For example, a dozen passages in Volume II bear on any discussion of political and theological attitudes in the Great Rebellion, Volumes III and IV have some nicely mixed specimens of political writing and also groups of passages which touch on marriage and the position of women, Volume I gives us Nashe and Gabriel Harvey on Nashe, Volume V Dickens and Walter Bagehot on Dickens. There are also links between the volumes – it is not an accident that a passage by Carlyle in Volume V should refer to an incident in Mungo Park's African travels which is reproduced in Volume IV. Some of these correspondences lie on the surface, as in the examples chosen, but many are more esoteric and will not be apparent until the anthology is actively used. In each volume the order of the passages in the first section, 'The Picture of the Age', is chronological, but the order in the other three sections – for the sake of these correspondences – offers what F. T. Palgrave calls 'gradations of feeling or subject'. Such gradations may or may not combine with a modified chronological plan.

More important than any of these means of ensuring singleness of approach has been the community of feeling among the editors about what an anthology of prose should be called on to illustrate. *The Pelican Book of English Prose* is not a collection of the best passages of English prose, or even, exclusively, of the best passages of the authors included in it – a collection on either principle would produce an effect less representative than the one aimed at. A common objection to prose anthologies is that their editors do not choose passages typical of the authors represented because they put an undue weight on 'fine writing'. From some anthologies one would naturally conclude that historians reserved all their energies for depicting battle-scenes, or that Lyly, Sir Thomas Browne and Landor were considerably more important as writers of prose than Hooker, Dryden and Gibbon. In contradistinction our working-hypothesis has been that prose should not be too self-conscious, that the writers of the best English prose usually had more on their minds than the problems of style, and that much respectable prose in every age is unmindful of the schoolmaster's ferula.[1] Consequently, in compiling this anthology, we have been guided by the following principles:

1. To choose passages primarily for the interest of their subject-matter (on the assumption, which has been justified, that such passages will inevitably illustrate all the prominent varieties of prose style).

2. To choose from a particular author not his most detachable pieces of fine writing, but passages which are typical of his normal manner when he is writing well.

3. To illustrate sparingly the 'purple passages' of English prose.

4. To include some prose at a pedestrian level of achievement for its documentary value (more particularly in the first section of each volume).

The editors consider that these methods of selection give a

1. The degree of self-conscious organization that is 'natural' varies, of course, from age to age, and, in any age, according to literary kind (for example, a declamatory style is more natural in a pulpit or from the hustings than in a diary or private letter).

more accurate cross-section of English prose than is obtained from most anthologies,[1] and that the loss in serious prose-artistry is negligible. Nothing that has been said should be taken to imply a settled antipathy to ornate prose, but it is fair to admit that the editors are suspicious of its self-conscious varieties after the Restoration (while recognizing with New-man that some 'verbiage' may be the natural expression of a generous 'fullness of mind').

The Text. Modernization has been rejected and passages are reproduced with the spelling and punctuation of the copy-texts (except for the silent correction of misprints and the conservative emendation of misleading punctuation). Thus Elizabethan prose retains its 'dramatic' or haphazard pointing except in special instances, and Keats's difficulties with spelling are left to appear. The only passages given in a modernized form are those first printed long after their original composition, e.g. an Elizabethan diary first pub-lished in the middle of the nineteenth century. Some un-familiar words and phrases, which are naturally more frequent in Volumes I and II, are glossed briefly in footnotes where the context seems to require it – this is a matter that has been left to the individual editor's discretion – but no attempt has been made to supply a sense for all unusual words or to explain the many allusions.

The source of each passage is given at its foot, and the abbreviation of titles has been indicated (wherever possible the extended title has been preserved if of interest). First editions have usually been employed, but many passages included in the anthology were added by their authors to editions later

1. *The London Book of Prose* (1932), compiled by Professor Dobrée and Sir Herbert Read, is an obvious exception. Its excellence sets a standard for this kind of work.

than the first, or were revised through several editions, so that the preferred form of a passage may be found, for example, in a fifth edition. On the other hand, the unrevised version of a passage has sometimes been preferred by an editor for its freshness and unfamiliarity. The apparent anomalies in the choice of copy-texts are mostly explicable on such grounds, but there were a few occasions when a first edition would have been used if it had been available. The use of certain copyright material is acknowledged in a note at the end of each volume.

K. A.

INTRODUCTION

I

ENGLISH prose did not, of course, begin with the Tudors; and some critics have argued that there has been an unbroken tradition of prose from the time of King Alfred. Others have gone further and claimed that at the Renaissance English writers were too much under the influence of classical models and that the prose with which this book is mainly concerned falls outside the native tradition – a tradition not restored until the age of Dryden. Only Sir Thomas More, it is argued, and the recusant writers in exile, adhered to the true tradition. There is surely here an element of special pleading. We can scarcely regard the prose of Hooker, Ralegh, Bacon, Donne and Taylor as a magnificent aberration. Anyone can point to passages written between 1560 and 1660 which are too obviously latinized in structure, but the peculiar vigour and variety of Elizabethan prose was largely due to the cross-fertilization of the two traditions, native and classical. It is true that Harding, Rastell and others who figure in Dr A. C. Southern's admirable book, *Elizabethan Recusant Prose*, are vigorous, plain and unaffected. But so too are the Protestant exiles Christopher Goodman and John Poynet, whose works, *How Superior Powers ought to be Obeyd* and *A Shorte Treatise of Politike Power*, are important in the history of political thought, Poynet's being reprinted in 1639 to stiffen opposition to Charles I. Yet one does not have to go to the exiles of either party for examples of the plain style. It is to be found in many travel narratives collected by the industrious Hakluyt, in Deloney's novels, and in countless pamphlets and sermons. This prose, although it often had freshness and vigour, was syntactically immature, and it was not a good medium for exact description or subtle argument.

Most of the authors included in this book learnt at school to write Latin prose, and when later they came to compose in English they were inevitably influenced by the classical models they had been bidden to study. Even two generations later Milton was to debate whether to write his *History of Britain* (c. 1650) not in the manner of Holinshed or Ralegh, but in the manner of Tacitus or Sallust. Furthermore a number of books, those intended to reach an international audience such as Bacon's *Novum Organum* (1620), were written in Latin.

At the beginning of the Elizabethan period the orthodox model was Cicero, and the Ciceronian influence remained strong until well into the next century. But during the same period there was a reaction.[1] As early as 1528 Erasmus had ridiculed the pedantry of the Ciceronians, who not only used collections of phrases from the master's works but also classified the rhythms and cadences to be found there. They were more concerned with reproducing these so as to make a colourable pastiche than they were with expressing their own views, or indeed with the matter at all.

There were several possible alternatives to the Ciceronian style. One was the artificial, highly antithetical, method of Isocrates; and some critics have believed that Lyly's style is ultimately derived from that model. The operative word is *ultimately*. Without going into the genetics of euphuism, the subject of debate for nearly half a century now, we should note that all the characteristics of euphuism (e.g. cross-alliteration, excessive use of similes drawn from natural history, various kinds of antithesis) may be found in writers before Lyly. If Lyly differs from certain of his predecessors it is in degree rather than in kind and by his concentration on a smaller repertoire of tricks. *Euphues* (1579) is as boring as it is clever, though when its influence had been properly assimilated it did more good than harm – it made writers more

1. See G. Williamson's *The Senecan Amble* (1951).

conscious of the structure of their prose. Lyly himself had written less affectedly in the Martin Marprelate controversy, and after *Euphues* he had the sense to modify his style to suit the requirements of the stage and even to vary it in accordance with the character speaking.

One example may be given here of euphuism in its pure and unpalatable state:

No no, it is the disposition of the thought, that altereth the nature of the thing. The Sunne shineth vpon the dounghill, and is not corrupted: the Diamond lyeth in the fire, and it is not consumed: the Christall toucheth the Toade and is not poysoned: the birde *Trochilus* lyueth by the mouth of the Crocodile and is not spoyled: a perfect wit is neuer bewitched with lewdnesse, neither entised with lasciuousnesse. Is it not common that the Holme Tree springeth amidst the Beech? That the Iuie spreadeth vpon the hard stones? That the soft fetherbed breaketh the hard blade?

Another example, from the early play *Campaspe* (1584), shows Lyle using his tricks with greater skill (p. 184), and the extract from *Mother Bombie* (1594) displays him as a successful writer of comic dialogue (p. 187). We need not, like Professor C. S. Lewis, rank him with Congreve; but we can recognize that Shakespeare learnt from him that witty prose requires a high degree of polish.

But by far the most popular alternative to Cicero was Seneca, whose more colloquial and aphoristic style gradually ousted Cicero's as the favourite model. This process is well described in Mr Peter Ure's introduction to Volume II of this anthology. We need observe here only that some Senecans, too, were more concerned with manner than with matter, as Bacon indeed complained.

It is arguable, however, that it was not by imitating the classics but by the actual process of translation that the Elizabethans learnt most on the nature of prose-structure. The great translators, from North and Adlington to Florio and translator-general' Holland, are strongly represented in this anthology, though Painter and Fenton and many others have had to be omitted. When all allowances have been made for their inaccuracies and misunderstandings, the Tudor translators of prose created masterpieces in their own language. No one now would wish to read Plutarch's life of Antonius in any other version than North's, which Shakespeare loved and used; it is difficult to imagine more attractive versions of Longus and Achilles Tatius than those of Day and Burton; and Florio's version of Montaigne (1603) has a gusto and liveliness which makes it unsurpassed. The immediate effect of such translations is to be found in the novels and romances of Greene and Lodge; and the *Arcadia* (1590) itself is clearly indebted to the *Diana* of Montemayor as well as to the Greek romances.

The Bible is a special case. The greatness of the Authorized Version was due not merely to the genius of Lancelot Andrewes and of the other members of the committee, and to their sense of the rhythms suitable to prose which had to be read in churches; nor was it due merely to the nature of the language, which for some thirty years possessed a unique power and freshness; it was due also to the quality of previous translations, from those of Wycliffe and Tyndale to the Bishops', the Geneva and Catholic versions, and to the conservatism of the 1611 revisers. This meant that the prose had its roots in medieval English and that it was influenced not at all by classical models. In concreteness, it might be argued, the Authorized Version is inferior to Wycliffe's; in its linking sentences together it is sometimes clumsy; in places the translators seem to have had no clear idea of the meaning of the original. But they triumphed by their unerring sense of diction and rhythm, as we can see by comparing the Geneva and Bishops' versions with the perfection achieved in 1611. The Authorized Version is not represented here as it will be accessible to all readers.

II

Elizabethan controversialists frequently complained of their opponent's style and they accused each other of using inkhorn terms – words that smelled of the lamp. Most writers coined words – especially from Latin, French and Italian – when they felt inclined; but it did not stop them from affecting horror at the coinages of others. The language was enormously expanded between 1580 and 1610, and although words were often still-born and were used only once, others are used to this day. The urge to experiment was partly held in check by education and tradition, but the impression one gets of Elizabethan prose is one of astonishing richness and freedom.

This richness and this freedom are displayed also in the metaphors used by the writers of prose as naturally as by the poets. Many of the prose-writers were, of course, poets; and they did not cease to be poets when they wrote prose. Sidney's *Arcadia* was regarded by many as a poem, or at least as the work of a poet. There was none of the feeling of later periods that poetic prose was in bad taste, or that the prose-writer should use only tame and domesticated metaphors. Indeed, what is true of imagery is true of nearly all the figures of rhetoric – they were used in prose as much as they were in verse.

Robert Greene was a typical professional writer of the period. Astonishingly prolific in spite of his irregular and apparently dissolute life, he turned out for the space of twelve years a vast quantity of work – plays, novels, exposures of the criminal underworld in which he lived, poems, autobiographies. He was an imitator of other men's work, but never merely an imitator. His early novels were written in the fashionable euphuistic style, but more palatable than Lyly's if only because he wrote in haste and was therefore unable to keep ordinariness from breaking in. Later on he was influenced by the Greek romances and by Sidney's *Arcadia* and his style became pastoral and limpid. In the last two years of his life he adopted yet another style, suitable to his realistic pictures of London life – a style as colloquial as Defoe's. Greene has been blamed for giving the public what it wanted, but it is only fair to say that after his earliest pamphlets he led the fashion. Between 1583 and 1590 three-quarters of the extant works of fiction came from his pen, and if he made a deliberate appeal to the new female public he never wrote down to it.

Greene and Lodge between them represent Elizabethan fiction at its most characteristic, and there were several others who wrote in roughly the same style – Warner and Breton, for example. Perhaps the masterpiece of this kind, in spite of its excessive euphuism, was *Rosalynd* (1590), a charming story which provided Shakespeare with more than the plot of *As You Like It*. These novels have some links with Sidney's unfinished *Arcadia* (1590) – the pastoral setting, the set speeches, the interspersed poems. But Sidney had a much more complicated plot, or rather an interwoven series of plots, he had a greater power of depicting character, and, above all, he had a profound sense of the moral issues involved. Almost every chapter, though Sidney is seldom directly didactic as Greene frequently is, has a moral lesson to teach the reader.

The prose of the *Arcadia* is free of affectation, but packed with artifice. Abraham Fraunce took many of the examples in his *Arcadian Rhetorike* (1588) from Sidney's then unpublished work. Yet we never feel, in reading it, that the manner is more important than the matter: the rhetoric is merely the means by which the matter is fully expressed. Sidney's powers of description, the pleasant balance of his clauses, and the delicate cadence of his prose are well illustrated by the famous passage describing Arcadia itself (p. 160); and his power of marshalling an argument, good in itself though evil in its context, is illustrated by Cecropia's temptation of Philoclea (p. 161). Even more remarkable, because of the rarity of good criticism in the Elizabethan age, is the quiet perfection of tone displayed in *The Defence of Poesie*. When this was written there was little contemporary poetry worth defending. He wrote before the university wits transformed the crude popular drama and when Spenser had published only *The Sheppeardes Calender*. But Sidney was able to express his love of poetry, his realization that it must teach delightfully, and the breadth of his tastes, as in his confession that the Ballad of Chevy Chase moved his heart more than a trumpet. He writes as a poet, a gentleman, and a scholar; and the natural ease of his style was unequalled before Dryden's prefaces. Daniel inherited some of Sidney's controversial manners and Jonson displayed considerable knowledge and intelligence in notes he collected during his later years, many of them adapted from previous critics and perhaps used by him as the basis of lectures. But most Elizabethan critics were pedants who repeated what previous pedants had said. Their views are conventional and their tone is illiberal. They occasionally spot a winner; they even praise Shakespeare – along with dozens of nonentities.

Greene at the end of his career became more realistic in his style and matter and he finally deserted fiction for autobiography and reportage. There were other writers who rebelled against the romantic conventions. There were, for example, many short stories, translated or adapted for the most part, which dealt with anti-romantic material – the tricks of unfaithful wives or of cunning rogues – but these are nearly all undistinguished in style. Gascoigne, before Greene began to write, had produced a comedy of manners ('The Aduentures of Master F. J.') which was apparently based on an actual scandal, and though the style is elaborate, the psychology of the characters is realistic. Chettle, Dickenson, and Breton also make use of realistic elements (see pp. 176, 179). But the outstanding writer of realistic fiction was Thomas Deloney. His 'novels' consist of a series of loosely connected episodes, and they show less structural skill than the best romances of the period; but his straightforward and colloquial prose, his bourgeois themes, and his use of significant detail, mark him out as a forerunner of Defoe. He was appealing to a less educated public than Sidney or Greene or Lodge, and this saved him from their defects, if their merits were beyond his reach. But some of his episodes are told with apparently artless mastery, and the narrative of the murder of Thomas of Reading is so admirable that the reader is in danger of forming too high an opinion of his merits as a novelist.

Thomas Nashe wrote one vigorous picaresque novel, *The Vnfortunate Traueller* (1594), only partially realistic. It is excellent in its satirical parts; but when he tries to be tragic or horrific, his cleverness spoils the effect, as in the murder of Esdras:

Eagerly I replied after this long suppliant oration: Though I knew God would neuer haue mercy vpon me except I had mercie on thee, yet of thee no mercy would I haue. Reuenge in our tragedies is continually raised from hell: of hell doe I esteeme better than heauen, if it afford me reuenge. There is no heauen but reuenge. I tel thee, I would not haue vndertoke so much toile to gaine heauen, as I haue done in pursuing thee for reuenge. Diuine reuenge, of which (as of the ioies aboue) there is no fulnes or satietie. Looke how my feete are blistered with following thee from place to place. I haue riuen my throat with ouer-straining it to curse thee. I haue ground my teeth to pouder with grating & grinding them together for anger when any hath namde thee. My tongue with vaine threates is bolne, and waxen too big for my mouth: my eyes haue broken their strings with staring and looking ghastly, as I stood deuising how to frame or set my countenance when I met thee. I haue neere spent my strength in imaginarie acting on stone wals, what I determined to execute on thee: intreate not, a miracle may not repriue thee, thus march I with my blade into thy bowels.

Similarly in his diatribe on the sins of London entitled *Christs*

Teares ouer Jerusalem (1593) he aimed at the sublime, but produced only turgid and inflated prose. It is inferior to Dekker's imitation, *The Seven Deadly Sinnes of London* (1606). Nashe was, in fact, an intermittently inspired hack. He wrote everything from moralizing to obscenity, from delicate lyrics to the violent invective of his tedious and protracted controversy with Gabriel Harvey. Much of his work, therefore, was ephemeral. He was at his best in *Pierce Penilesse* (1592), *The Terrors of the Night* (1594) and *Nashes Lenten Stuffe* (1599). In these works his cleverness and wit are appropriate to the subjects, he is not troubled by the necessity of telling a story, and the continuous brilliance of his phrasing, his high spirits and his originality all have plenty of scope. He determined to be lively at all costs, but in these three works the cost is not high. He never perpetrates a cliché, he delights in the use of language, coining words when he feels inclined, and he has a talent for vivid imagery.

John Eliot and Sir John Harington had something of Nashe's verve and wit and they were both conscious disciples of Rabelais as will be apparent from some of the passages given below (see pp. 91, 99). Eliot's *Ortho-Epia Gallica* (1593) was ostensibly a conversation-manual with French and English in parallel columns, but he introduced some delightful satire in the course of the lively conversation. Harington had a pretty wit and his letters were the best of the age.

Thomas Dekker followed in the footsteps of Harman and Greene in his books on vagabonds, but in general he owes more to Nashe. He lacks something of Nashe's wit and boisterousness, but he compensates for this by a greater range. He can achieve pathos and grandeur in his plague pamphlets; he is good-naturedly satirical in *The Gul's Horne-booke* (1609); and he is as good in his sincere and unaffected prayers as in his descriptions of natural beauty. His prose is nearly always lucid and unaffected, though to some critics there is some straining after effect in *The Seven Deadly Sinnes of London* (1606) and in *The Wonderfull Yeare* (1603). There is none in this prayer for coal-miners:

Out of my Bedde (the image of my graue) hast thou raised mee (O Lord), thy Angels sat vpon mine eye-liddes, like Centinels to guard me all the while I lay asleepe: O suffer thou the same watchmen to protect me now I am awake. I need thy help alwayes, (for what is man without thee?) but so neere the house of danger must I this day dwell, that on my knees I entreate thee to keepe side by side with mee in my goings. Saue my bodie, O Lord: for death is (at euery turning about) at my elbow. Saue my soule, whatsoeuer fals vpon my bodie. Which diuine part of me, that it may come into thy heauenly treasure-house, inspire mee with that wisedome which descendeth from aboue. Purifie my thoughts, & let them with spotles wings bee continually flying about thy throne. Purge my heart, that it may come before thee like a bridegroome, full of chaste loue. Refine my soule, that like siluer seuen times tried in the fire, it may beare the bright figure of Saluation. In vaine doeth the builder lay his foundation, vnlesse thy hand bee at the setting vp. Set therefore thy hand to this worke of mine; encourage mee to vndertake it, embolden mee to goe forward, and enable me to finish it.

The writers we have been discussing all used the language with freshness and vivacity, and they owed more to the native tradition than to a study of classical models. Compared with nearly all writers of the present century they are notably free from clichés, and if their sentences are sometimes clumsy in construction, and if they sometimes seem to be drunk with words, their language is always alive. They describe what they see and argue what they feel without falling back on worn phrases. This impression may partly be due to the unfamiliarity of the language they employ, and it may be admitted that they drew on a stock of commonplaces culled from various sources. But Mr Michael Roberts was right to emphasize that, whereas modern writing 'lacks the immediacy of a vigorous and direct appeal to the senses', when Nashe wrote 'it was the whole man speaking, not the retina and cerebral cortex'.

Yet Nashe, it may be said, was a Peter Pan – or a Moth – who never grew up; Greene wrote too often in forms which seem to us to be remote from reality; and much of Dekker's prose is ephemeral. With Bacon, Hooker and Ralegh we come to writers of whose greatness there can be no question. Bacon wrote more than one kind of prose. His *Essayes* (1597), particularly in their earliest form, were written in a style consisting of a mosaic of aphorisms and quotations which he had stored up in a commonplace-book. Individual sentences are brilliant, as in these superb openings:

> Revenge is a kind of wild justice.
> He that hath wife and children hath given hostages to fortune.
> Suspicions amongst thoughts are like bats amongst birds, they ever fly by twilight.

Frequently the effect is obtained by a homely but appropriate simile:

> Money is like muck, not good unless it be spread.

But, although the sentences are neatly arranged, there is no attempt to build them up into paragraphs. Moreover the wise saws and modern instances seem like the utterances of Mr Worldly Wiseman; 'good advice for Satan's kingdom' was Blake's comment.

For the greater Bacon we have to go to *The Advancement of Learning* (1605) in which the argument unrolls in noble and majestical periods. Here he found a style which was a fit vehicle for his breadth of vision and the amplitude of his mind. Lytton Strachey, commenting on Bacon's tragedy, remarked that 'it is probably always disastrous not to be a poet. His imagination, with all its magnificence, was insufficient; it could not see into the heart of things'. But perhaps, after all, Shelley was right to claim Bacon as a poet, though he was one who regarded words with suspicion and hostility and thought of poetry as 'submitting the shewes of things to the desires of the mind'. He believed that matter was more important than style, and he complained that both the Ciceronians and the Senecans neglected matter in pursuit of style. The travellers to New Atlantis are told that in Salomon's House:

We do hate all impostures and lies; insomuch as we have severely forbidden it to all our fellows, under pain of ignomiy and fines, that they do not show any natural work or thing adorned or swelling, but only pure as it is, and without all affectation of strangeness.

Professor L. C. Knights[1] and others have shown that the movement for a 'mathematical plainness' of expression, which culminated in the ideals of prose advocated by the Royal Society, may be traced back to Bacon, though the movement was assisted, as Mr Harold Fisch has recently reminded us,[2] by the Puritan idea of plain sermons. But, although Bacon's matter was more important to him than the excellence of his prose, he wrote *The Advancement of Learning* to persuade – James I among others – and happily he did not disdain to use the arts of rhetoric he regarded with such suspicion.

Hooker's style, too, is a reflection of the greatness of his mind. His masterpiece, *Of the Lawes of Ecclesiasticall Politie* (1594), is the finest intellectual monument to the Anglican *via media*, as superb in its way as the more emotive prose of Donne and Taylor, or as the angelic subtleties of Andrewes. Although Hooker has magnificently ornate passages – including a description of order in the macrocosm (see p. 115) as great as the speech in *Troilus and Cressida* which echoes it – the book should not be judged by isolated passages, but rather by the wonderful marshalling of the argument.

1. Cf. *Explorations* (1946), pp. 92–111.
2. Cf. ELH, *A Journal of English Literary History* xix (1952), pp. 229–248.

There is a great deal of Elizabethan prose dealing with religious controversy. The Martin Marprelate writers on both sides had a talent for lively invective; the recusants were often forceful and effective; Edmund Campion, when he wrote in the vernacular, displayed the magnanimity and courage of a saintly man; and Samuel Harsnet brought a rude humour and a boisterous talent for satire to the exposure of fraudulent exorcisms by Puritans and Papists. The age was, indeed, rich in satire and comparatively poor in serious argument, whether religious or philosophical; and the writers we have mentioned seem somewhat uncivilized beside the 'grave and judicious' Hooker, as Walton called him. He puts his case with moderation and serenity, arguing as a man who was both deeply religious and deeply civilized. He did not assume that his opponents were damned, he merely argued that they might be mistaken; and he refrained from wit because he preferred the conversion of one opponent to the applause of many friends.

Ralegh is more complex. The best of the many amateur poets, as well as a statesman and explorer, he was a daring speculator on matters of religion. Lord Acton regarded him as a villainous adventurer, but venerated him for his views on universal history, his belief that God reveals himself in human history and is not 'won to give his blessing in one age to that which He hath cursed in another'. With this conviction Ralegh surveyed the vanity of human wishes:

We find by dear and lamentable experience, and by the loss which can never be repaired, that of all our vain passions and affections past, the sorrow only abideth. . . . He shall find that all the art which his elder years have, can draw no other vapour out of these dissolutions, than heavy, secret and sad sighs. He shall find nothing remaining but those sorrows, which grow up after our fast-springing youth, overtake it, when it is at a stand; and overtop it utterly, when it begins to wither.

These characteristic cadences show that although Ralegh was

as a poet something of an amateur, as a prose-writer he was a consummate artist. Nor was it only the futility of human ambition which inspired this great music (see pp. 132, 250). His description of Guiana is picturesque and exciting; his account of the last fight of the *Revenge* has more of the true epic quality than Tennyson's poem:

> What became of the body, whether it was buried in the sea or on the land we know not: the comfort that remaineth to his friends is, that he hath ended his life honourably in respect of the reputation won to his nation and country, and of the same to his posterity, and that being dead, he hath not outlived his own honour.

Ralegh is equally effective when towards the end of *The Soule* he proclaims:

> The mind in searching causes is never quiet till it comes to God, and the will never is satisfied with any good till it comes to the immortal goodness.

Whether he is writing to his wife from the Tower (see p. 48), or meditating on the fate of empires, or analysing the nature of the soul, whenever he has a subject which calls forth his full powers, Ralegh's style is wonderful in its force and majesty.

More theological works and sermons were published during the period than any other kind of literature. At one end of the scale we have the sub-literary religious prose of such writers as William Perkins with over a hundred works to his credit, Edward Dering with about fifty, and Thomas Becon with more than sixty. One of the best of these writers was Arthur Dent whose *The Plaine-Mans Path-way to Heaven* (1601) went into twenty-five editions before 1640. Its earnest simplicity is impressive. At the other end of the scale is William Drummond's *A Cypresse Grove* (1623), a meditation on death in imaginative prose, more poetic, indeed, than any of Drummond's verse.

It may well be that amongst the thousands of sermons there are some written in admirable prose, but most of those known to me are hampered as literature by their conventional language. Latimer, however, at the beginning of the period wrote masterly, colloquial, heart-to-heart talks; and Bishop Lancelot Andrewes, although he analysed and dissected his texts in a formal and pedantic way, yet contrived to display his extraordinary intellectual and imaginative powers, his poetic feeling for language, his delicate sense of rhythm, and his genuine piety. Those who come fresh from Mr T. S. Eliot's famous essay to the sermons themselves are apt to be disappointed because the passages where Andrewes allows his imagination to take wing are few and far between. But they were not meant to be read as literature, even though at moments they are literature of a high order.

Dramatic prose developed comparatively late. It was rarely used in tragedy except for special purposes, such as comic relief or the presentation of madness. It is used superbly for mad scenes in *The Spanish Tragedy* (1587) and *Hamlet* (1601). Marlowe used it daringly near the end of *Doctor Faustus* (1592) to express the pathos and agony of the hero's farewell to his friends (p. 185); but this magnificently rhythmed prose obtains part of its effect from its juxtaposition with the great poetry which follows. Shakespeare used prose for the madness of Lear and for the antic disposition of Hamlet, though he also used it for the wit-contest with Rosencrantz and Guildenstern and the great meditation on the nature of man (see p. 215). He felt the need, we may suppose, after the prose of the later histories and of the mature comedies, to use it for exploring the complexities of human personality as well as for courtly conversation. Webster later used prose for the last scene between Bosola and the Duchess of Malfi (see p. 231).

In comedy prose became all-important. Lyly was the great innovator. Most of his comedies were written, apart from the songs, in his highly artificial prose – artificial even in *Mother Bombie*, though decreasingly euphuistic. It became an excellent vehicle for wit, as we have seen, and Beatrice and Rosalind, not to mention Falstaff, would have been impossible if Lyly had not shown the way.

It is sometimes forgotten that Shakespeare's prose, even at its most natural, is some way removed from the ordinary speech of the time. Middleton probably reproduces most accurately actual contemporary speech; Jonson in *Every Man in His Humour* is not far behind; but Shakespeare, quite deliberately, writes a literary prose which is never far enough from everyday speech to sound unnatural, and never near enough to be out of place in highly-wrought poetic dramas. There is, moreover, a great variety. The style is made to suit both the subject and the character, so that Henry V's grave discourse on war (p. 206) hardly seems to be by the same author as the poetic wit of Beatrice, the railings of Doll Tearsheet, or Falstaff's talk with Shallow (p. 197). If we omitted Shakespeare the period would still be rich in dramatic prose-dialogue from the racy realism of Middleton to the robust satire of Jonson, and from Lyly's delicate artificiality to the coarse outspokenness of Marston (p. 217), in which we seem to hear a crude forerunner of the Comedy of Manners.

III

After the civilized prose of Dryden, Addison, Swift and Berkeley, Elizabethan prose may appear to lack lucidity, ease and grace. It rambles pleasantly along, but with too little sense of direction. Sentences are often loosely joined together, and the rhythmical structure breaks down when a more elaborate period is attempted. Paragraphs are more often the convenience of the compositor than logical units. But in spite of these defects even the minor Elizabethan writer has a livelier vocabulary, a more concrete use of words, a greater freedom and daring than his Augustan successors. He is, no doubt, less civilized; but civilization is bought at a price. Johnson recommended that the young writer of his day should give his days and nights to the study of Addison, and certainly *The Spectator* is a better model than *Pierce Penilesse* or North's Plutarch or Florio's Montaigne. But the Elizabethan writers are not only valuable in themselves: they can, perhaps, teach us something about the use of language that has been over-looked since the advent of the age of reason. If our newspapers were written with some of the individuality of Nashe or Dekker, if our political pamphlets could have the vigour and concreteness of Elizabethan controversy, if our sermons could appeal as much to the intellect and to the imagination as those of Andrewes and Donne, if our popular novels did not appear to be written by efficient machines, we should have some cause for gratification. Whatever the faults of Elizabethan prose, it was never colourless.

KENNETH MUIR

THE PICTURE OF THE AGE:
SCENE, PERSONALITY, EVENT

Queen Elizabeth I

(1558)

Now, if ever any persone had eyther the gift or the stile to winne the hearts of people, it was this Queene; and if ever she did expresse the same, it was at that present, in coupling mildnesse with majesty as shee did, and in stately stouping to the meanest sort. All her facultyes were in motione, and every motione seemed a well guided actione; her eye was set upon one, her eare listened to another, her judgement ranne uppon a third, to a fourth shee addressed her speech; her spiritt seemed to be every-where, and yet so intyre in her selfe, as it seemed to bee noe where else. Some shee pityed, some shee commended, some shee thanked, at others shee pleasantly and wittily jeasted, contemning noe person, neglecting noe office; and distributing her smiles, lookes and graces, soe artificially, that thereupon the people againe redoubled the testimonyes of their joyes; and afterwards, raising every thing to the highest straine, filled the eares of all men with immoderate extolling their Prince.

Shee was a Lady, upon whom nature had bestowed, and well placed, many of her fayrest favores; of stature meane, slender, streight, and amiably composed; of such state in her carriage, as every motione of her seemed to beare majesty:

artificially] skilfully

her haire was inclined to pale yellow, her foreheade large and
faire, a seemeing sete for princely grace; her eyes lively and
sweete, but short-sighted; her nose somewhat rising in the
middest; the whole compasse of her countenance somewha
long, but yet of admirable beauty, not so much in that which
is tearmed the flower of youth, as in a most delightfull com-
positione of majesty and modesty in equall mixture. But without good qualityes of mynde, the gifts of nature are like
paynted floweres, without eyther vertue or sappe; yea, sometymes they grow horrid and loathsome. Now her vertue
were such as might suffice to make an Aethiopian beautifull
which, the more a man knowes and understands, the more he
shall admire and love. In life, shee was most innocent; in
desires, moderate; in purpose, just; of spirit, above credit and
almost capacity of her sexe; of divine witt, as well for depth
of judgement, as for quick conceite and speedy expeditione; of
eloquence, as sweete in the utterance, soe ready and easie to
come to the utterance: of wonderfull knowledge both in
learning and affayres; skilfull not only in the Latine and
Greeke, but alsoe in divers other forraine languages: none
knew better the hardest art of all others, that is, of com-
maunding men, nor could more use themselves to those care
without which the royall dignity could not be supported. She
was relligeous, magnanimous, mercifull and just; respective of
the honour of others, and exceeding tender in the touch of her
owne. Shee was lovely and loving, the two principall band
of duty and obedience. Shee was very ripe and measured in
counsayle and experience, as well not to lett goe occasiones
as not to take them when they were greene. Shee maintained
Justice at home, and Armes abroad, with great wisdome and
authority in eyther place. Her majesty seemed to all to shine
through courtesy: but as shee was not easy to receive any to
especiall grace, so was shee most constant to those whom she
received; and of great judgment to know to what point of

reatnesse men were fit to bee advanced. Shee was rather
berall than magnificent, making good choys of the recei-
oures; and for this cause was thought weake by some against
ie desire of money. But it is certaine that beside the want of
easure which shee found, her continuall affayres in Scotland,
rance, the Low Countries, and in Ireland, did occasione
reat provisione of money, which could not be better sup-
lyed, than by cutting off eyther excessive or unnecessary
xpence at home. Excellent Queene! what doe my words but
rrong thy worth? what doe I but guild gold? What but shew
ie sunne with a candle, in attempting to prayse thee, whose
onor doth flye over the whole world upon the two wings
f Magnanimity and Justice, whose perfection shall much
imme the lustre of all other that shall be of thy sexe?

Sir John Hayward

Annals, ed. J. Bruce (1840). Written 1612

FEMALE VAGRANT

HESE Doxes be broken and spoyled of their maydenhead by
ie vpright men, and then they haue their name of Doxes, and
ot afore. And afterward she is commen and indifferent for
iy that wyll vse her, as *homo* is a commen name to all men.
ich as be fayre and some what handsome, kepe company
ith the walkinge Mortes, and are redye alwayes for the
pright men, and are chiefely mayntayned by them, for
hers shalbe spoyled for their sakes; the other, inferior, sort
yll resorte to noble mens places, and gentlemens houses,
anding at the gate, eyther lurkinge on the backesyde about
ackehouses, eyther in hedge rowes, or some other thycket,
xpectinge their praye, whiche is for the vncomely company of
me curteous gest of whom they be refreshed with meate

vpright men] vagabonds of standing   *mortes*] loose women

and some monye, where eschaunge is made, ware for ware
this bread and meate they vse to carrye in their greate hoser
so that these beastlye bryberinge breeches scrue manye tyme
for bawdye purposes. I chaunced not longe sithens familiarl
to commen with a Doxe that came to my gate, and surelye
pleasant harlot, and not so pleasant as wytty, and not so wytt
as voyd of all grace and goodnes. I founde, by her talke, tha
shee hadde passed her tyme lewdlye eyghttene yeares i
walkinge aboute. I thoughte this a necessary instrument t
attayne some knowledge by, and before I woulde grope he
mynde, I made her bothe to eate and drynke well; that donc
I made her faythfull promisse to geue her some money, yf sh
would open and dyscouer to me such questions as I would
demaunde of her, and neuer to bee wraye her, neither to dis
close her name. And you shoulde, sayth she, I were vndon
feare not that, quoth I; but, I praye the, quoth I, say nothin
but trouth. I wyll not, sayth shee. Then, fyrste tell me, quot
I, how many vpright men and Roges dost thou knowe, o
hast thou knowne and byn conuersant with, and what the
names be? She paused a whyle, and sayd: why do you ask
me, or wherefore? For nothing els, as I sayde, but that
woulde knowe them when they came to my gate. Nowe, b
my trouth (quoth she) then are yea neuer the neare, for a
myne acquayntance, for the moste parte, are deade. Deac
quoth I, howe dyed they, for wante of cherishinge, or c
paynefull diseases? Then she sighed and sayde they wer
hanged. What, all? quoth I, and so manye walke abroade, a
I dayelye see? By my trouth, quoth she, I knowe not paste si
or seuen by their names, and named the same to me. Whe
were they hanged? quoth I. Some seuen yeares agone, som
three yeares, and some within this fortnight, and declared th
place where they weare executed, whiche I knewe well to be
true, by the reporte of others. Why (quoth I) dyd not th
sorrowfull and feareful sight much greeue the, and for th

tyme longe and euyll spent? I was sory, quoth shee, by the
Masse, for some of them were good louing men. For I lackt
not when they had it, and they wanted not when I had it, and
diuers of them I neuer dyd forsake, vntyll the Gallowes departed vs. O mercyfull God! quoth I, and began to bless me.
Why blesse ye? quoth she. Alas good gentleman, euery one
muste haue a lyuinge.

Thomas Harman

A Caueat or warening for Commen cursetors (1567)

'THE MAID THAT MILKS'

Queen Elizabeth discusses marriage

NOWE, touchinge daungers cheiflie feared, first to rehearce
my meaninge, latelie vnfolded to youe by my Lord Keeper:
Yt shall not be nedefull, though I must needs confes myne
owne mislike, soe mutch to striue against the matter, as, if I
wear a milke maide with a paile on my arme, whearby my
priuat person might be litle sett by, I wolde not forsake that
poore and single state to matche with the greatest Monarche;
not that I doe condemne the double knott, or iudge amisse of
suche as, forced by necessitie, cannot dispose theme selues to
another life; but wishe that none wear drawen to chaunge,
but suche as cannot keepe honest limitts. Yet, for yowr behalfe, there is no waie so difficulte, that maie towche my
priuat person, which I will not well content my selffe to take,
and, in this case, as willinglie to spoile my selffe quite of my
selffe, as yf I sholde put of my vpper garment when it weryes
me, yf the present state might not therbie be encombred. I
knowe I ame but mortall; which good lesson Mr Speaker, in
his thirde diuision of a vertuous Princes properties, had reason
to remembre; and so, their while, I prepair my selffe to welcome death, when soeuer it shall please God to send it. As yf

others wolde indeauour to performe the like, yt wolde not be soe bitter vnto manye, as yt hathe bene accompted. Myne owne experience teacheth me to be no fonder of those vaine delights then reason wolde; nor further to delight in thinges vncertaine, then maie seeme conuenient. But let good heed be taken, that, in reaching too farr after future good, youe perill not the present and beginn to quarrell, and fall by dispute together by the eares, before it be decyded whoe shall weare my Crowne. I will not denye but I might be thought the indifferentest iudge in this respect, that I shall not be when theise points are fullfilled, which none beside my selffe can speake in all this companye. Mysdeeme not my wordes, as thoughe I sought what heretofore hathe bene graunted. I entend it not; My braines be too thynn to carry soe tuffe a matter. Although, I trust, God will not in suche haste cutt of my daies, but that, accordinge to yowr owne desart and my desier, I maie prouide some goode waie for yowr full securitie. And thus, as one that yeeldeth yow moe thanks, both for youre zeale vnto my selffe, and saruice in this Parlament, then my tonge can vttre, I recomend youe vnto the assured guarde and best keepinge of the Almightie; who will preserue youe safe, I truste, in all felicitie; and wissh with all, that each of youe had tasted some dropes of Lethes floode, to cancell and deface those speaches owt of yowr remembraunce.   Queen Elizabeth

'Oration in the Parliament House' (1576)
from *Nugae Antiquae* (1775)[1]

1. With a copy of this speech to Sir John Harington:
Boye Iacke, I haue made a Clerke wryte faire my poore wordes for thyne vse, as it cannot be suche striplinges haue entrance into Parliamente Assemblyes as yet. Ponder them in thy howres of leysure, and plaie wythe them tyll they enter thyne vnderstandinge; so shallt thou hereafter, perchance, fynde some good frutes hereof when thy godmother is oute of remembraunce; and I do thys, because thy father was readye to sarue and loue vs in trouble and thrall.

English Gardens

WE haue in like sort such workemen as are not onelie excellent in graffing the naturall fruits, but also in their artificiall mixtures, whereby one tree bringeth foorth sundrie fruits, and one and the same fruit of diuers colours and tasts, dallieng as it were with nature and hir course, as if hir whole trade were perfectlie knowne vnto them: of hard fruits they will make tender, of sowre sweet, of sweet yet more delicate, beereuing also some of their kernels, other of their cores, and finallie induing them with the sauour of muske, ambre, or sweet spices at their pleasures ... Whereby and sundrie other circumstances not here to bee remembred, I am persuaded, that albeit the gardens of the *Hesperides* were in times past so greatlie accounted of because of their delicacie: yet if it were possible to haue such an equall iudge, as by certaine knowledge of both were able to pronounce vpon them, I doubt not but he would giue the price vnto the gardens of our daies, and generallie ouer all Europe, in comparison of those times, wherein the old exceeded. *Plinie* and other speake of a rose that had three score leaues growing vpon one button: but if I should tell of one which bare a triple number vnto that proportion, I know I shall not be beleeued, and no great matter though I were not, howbeit, such a one was to be seene in Antwarpe 1585, as I haue heard, and I know who might haue had a slip or stallon thereof, if he would haue ventured ten pounds vpon the growth of the same, which should haue bene but a tickle hazard, and therefore better vndoone, as I did alwaies imagine. For mine owne part, good reader, let me boast a litle of my garden, which is but small, and the whole *Area* thereof little aboue 300 foot of ground, and yet, such hath beene my good lucke in purchase of the varietie of simples, that notwithstanding my small abilitie, there are verie neere three hundred of one sort and other conteined therein,

7

no one of them being common or vsuallie to bee had. If therefore my little plot, void of all cost in keeping be so well furnished, what shall we thinke of those of Hampton Court, Nonesuch, Tibaults, Cobham garden, and sundrie other apperteining to diuerse citizens of London, whom I could particularlie name, if I should not seeme to offend them by such my demeanour and dealing?

William Harrison

'An Historicall Description of Britayne'
from Holinshed's *Chronicles* . . . (1587)

A Day at Kenilworth

A mornings I rize ordinarily at seauen a clok: Then reddy, I go intoo the Chappell: soon after eyght, I get me commonly intoo my Lords Chamber, or intoo my Lord's prezidents. Thear, at the cupboord, after I haue eaten the manchet, serued ouer night for liuery, (for I dare be az bolld, I promis yoo, az any of my freends the seruaunts thear: and indeed, coold I haue fresh if I woold tary; but I am of woont iolly & dry a mornings) I drink me vp a good bol of Ale: when in a sweet pot it iz defecated by al nights standing, drink iz the better; take that of me: & a morsell in a morning, with a sound draught, iz very holsome and good for the eysight. Then I am az fresh all the forenoon after, az had I eaten a hole pees of beef. Noow, syr, if the Councell sit, I am at hand, wait at an inch, I warrant yoo. If any make babling, "peas!" (say I) "woot ye whear ye ar?" if I take a lystenar, or a priar in at the chinks or at the lokhole, I am by & by in the bones of him; but now they keep good order; they kno me well inough: If a be a freend, or such one az I lyke, I make him sit dooun by me on a foorm, or a cheast: let the rest walk, a Gods name!

manchet] white bread   *defecated*] allowed to clear

And heer doth my langagez now and than stond me in good sted, my French, my Spanish, my Dutch, & my Latten: sumtime amoong Ambassadours men, if their Master be within with the Councel, sumtime with the Ambassadour himself, if hee bid call hiz lacky, or ask me whats a clok: and I warrant ye I aunswer him roundly, that they maruell to see such a fello thear: then laugh I, & say nothing. Dinner & supper I haue twenty placez to go to, & hartly prayd to: And sumtime get I too Master Pinner, by my faith a worshipfull Gentleman, and az carefull for his charge az ony hir highnez hath: thear find I alway good store of very good viaunds: we eat and bee merry, thank God & the Queene! Himself in feeding very temperat & moderat az ye shall see ony: and yet, by your leaue, of a dish – az a colld pigeon or so, that hath cum to him at meat, more then he lookt for, – I haue seen him een so by and by surfit, az he hath pluct of hiz napkin, wyept his knife, & eat not a morsell more: lyke ynoough to stik in hiz stomake a too dayz after: (Sum hard message from the higher officers, perceiue ye me?) Vpon search, hiz faithfull dealing and diligens hath found him fautles. In afternoons & a nights, sumtime am I with the right worshipfull Sir George Howard, az good a Gentleman as ony liuez: And sumtime at my good Lady Sidnies chamber, a Noblewooman that I am az mooch boound vntoo, as ony poore man may bee vnto so gracyous a Lady: And sumtime in sum oother place; But alwayez among the Gentlwemen by my good will (O, yee kno that cum alweyez of a gentle spirite); & when I see cumpany according, than can I be az lyuely to; sumtyme I foote it with daunsing: noow with my Gittern, and els with my Cittern, then at the Virgynalz: – Ye kno nothing cums amisse to mee: – then carroll I vp a song withall, that by and by they com flocking about me lyke beez too hunny: and euer they cry, "anoother, good Langham, anoother!" Shall I tell yoo? when I see Misterz — (A! see a madde knaue! I had almost tollde all!) that shee gyuez onz but an ey or an ear: why, then man, am I blest! my grace, my corage, my cunning iz doobled: She sayz sumtime she likez it, & then I like it mooch the better; it dooth me good to heer hoow well I can doo. And, too say truth: what, with myne eyz, az I can amoroously gloit it, with my spanish sospires, my french heighes, mine Italian dulcets, my Dutch houez, my doobl releas, my hy reachez, my fine feyning, my deep diapason, my wanton warblz, my running, my tyming, my tuning, and my twynkling, I can gracify the matters az well az the prowdest of them; and waz yet neuer staynd, I thank God. By my troth, cuntreman, it iz sumtim by midnight ear I can get from them. And thus haue I told ye most of my trade, al the leeue long daye: what will ye more? God saue the Queene and my Lord! I am well, I thank yoo.

Robert Langham

A Letter: Whearin part of the entertainement
vnto the Queenes Maiesty . . . (1575)

A FRANK LETTER

To Edmund Molyneux

MR MOLLINEAX:

Few woordes are beste. My lettres to my Father have come to the eys of some. Neither can I condemne any but yow for it. If it be so yow have plaide the very knave with me; and so I will make yow know if I haue good proofe of it. But that for so muche as is past. For that is to come, I assure yow before God, that if euer I know you do so muche as reede any lettre I wryte to my Father, without his commandement, or my consente, I will thruste my Dagger into yow. And truste to it,

gloit] cast admiring glances   *sospires*] sighs

for I speak it in earnest. In the meane time farwell. From Courte this laste of May 1578.

By me

Philippe Sidney

Sir Philip Sidney

Complete Works, ed. A. Feuillerat (1923)

THE EVILS OF PLAYGOING

IN our Assemblies at playes in *London*, you shall see suche heauing, and shoouing, suche ytching and shouldring, too sitte by women; Suche care for their garments, that they bee not trode on: Such eyes to their lappes, that no chippes light in them: Such pillowes to ther backes, that they take no hurte: Such masking in their eares, I knowe not what: Such giuing them Pippins to passe the time: Suche playing at foote Saunt without Cardes: Such ticking, such toying, such smiling, such winking, and such manning them home, when the sportes are ended, that it is a right Comedie, to marke their behauiour, to watche their conceites, as the Catte for the Mouse, and as good as a course at the game it selfe, to dogge them a little, or followe aloofe by the print of their feete, and so discouer by slotte where the Deare taketh soyle. If this were as well noted, as ill seene: or as openly punished, as secretly practised: I haue no doubte but the cause would be feared to dry vp the effect, and these prettie Rabbets very cunningly ferretted from their borrowes. For they that lack Customers al the weeke, either because their haunte is vnknowen, or the Constables and Officers of their Parishe, watche them so narrowly, that they dare not queatche; To celebrate the Sab-

slotte] track   *soyle*] pool where hunted animal takes refuge
queatche] stir

both, flock to Theaters, and there keepe a generall Market of Bawdrie: Not that any filthynesse in deede, is committed within the compasse of that grounde, as was doone in *Rome*, but that euery wanton and his Paramour, euery man and his Mistresse, euery John and his Joan, euery knaue and his queane, are there first acquainted and cheapen the Merchandise in that place, which they pay for elsewhere as they can agree. These wormes when they dare not nestle in the Pescod at home, finde refuge abrode and are hidde in the eares of other mens Corne. Euery Vawter in one blinde Tauerne or other, is Tenant at will, to which shee tolleth resorte, and playes the stale to vtter their victualls, and helpe them to emptie their mustie caskes. There is she so intreated with wordes, and receiued with curtesie, that euery back roome in the house is at her commaundement.

Stephen Gosson
The Schoole of Abuse (1579)

FASHIONS

GENTLE Reader, now thou hast perused these Histories to the ende, I doubte not but thou wilte deeme of them as thei worthely deserue, and thinke suche vanities more fitter to bee presented on a Stage (as some of theim haue been) then to bee published in Printe (as till now they haue neuer been) but to excuse myself of the follie that here might bee imputed vnto me, that my self beyng the first that haue put them to the print, should like-wise be the first that should condemne them as vaine. For mine owne excuse herein I aunswere, that in the writyng of them I haue vsed the same maner that many of our yong Gentlemen vseth now adaies in the wearing of their

Vawter] vaulter, hence whoremonger

apparell, which is rather to followe a fashion that is newe (bee it neuer so foolishe) then to bee tied to a more decent custome, that is cleane out of vse; Sometyme wearyng their haire freeseled so long, that makes theim looke like a water Spaniell: sometymes so shorte, like a newe shorne Sheepe; their Beardes sometymes cutte round, like a Phillipes Doler, sometymes square, like the Kynges hedde in Fishstreate: Sometymes so neare the skinne, that a manne might iudge by his face the Gentleman had had verie pilde lucke: their Cappes and Hattes sometymes so bigge, as will hold more witte then three of them haue in their heddes; Sometymes so little, that will hold no witte at all. Their Ruffes sometymes so huge, as shall hang aboute their neckes like a Carte wheele; sometymes a little fallyng bande, that makes theim looke like one of the Queenes silke women. Their Clokes sometymes so long, as it shall trippe on their heeles, sometymes so shorte, as will not hang ouer their elbowes: their Jerkinnes sometymes with hye collors, buttoned close vnder their chinne, sometymes with no collars at all aboute their neckes, like a wenche in a redde wastcoate that were washyng of a bucke: Sometymes with long, sausie sleeues, that will be in euery dishe before his maister, sometymes without sleeues, like Scogins manne, that vsed to run of sleeuelesse errandes: Their Dublettes sometymes faggotte wasted aboue the Nauill, sometymes Cowe-beallied belowe the flanckes, that the Gentleman must vndoe a button when he goes to pisse.

In their hoose so many fashions as I can not describe; sometymes Garragascoynes, breached like a Beare, sometymes close to the docke, like the Deuill in a Plaie (wantyng but a taile); sometymes rounde, like to Sancte Thomas Onions, sometymes petite Ruffes, of twoo ynches long, with a close stockyng cleane aboue the nocke of his taile; sometymes after the Italian maner; and many tymes thei imitate the Frenche fashion so

Garragascoynes] gaskins, loose breeches   *nocke*] cleft

neare, that all their haire is readie to fall of their heddes.

Now I am sure, if any of theim were asked why he vsed suche varietie in his apparell, he would aunswere, because he would followe the fashion. Lette this, then, suffice likewise for myne excuse.

Barnaby Riche

His Farewell to Militarie Profession (1581)

A QUEER DELUSION

But the notablest example heereof is, of one that was in great perplexitie, imagining that his nose was as big as a house; insomuch as no freend nor physician could deliuer him from his conceipt, nor yet either ease his greefe, or satisfie his fansie in that behalfe: till at the last, a physician more expert in this humor than the rest, vsed this deuise following. First, when he was to come in at the chamber doore being wide open, he suddenlie staied and withdrew himselfe; so as he would not in any wise approch neerer than the doore. The Melancholike person musing heereat, asked him the cause why he so demeaned himselfe? Who answered him in this maner: Sir, your nose is so great, that I can hardlie enter into your chamber but I shall touch it, and consequentlie hurt it. Lo (quoth he) this is the man that must doo me good; the residue of my freends flatter me, and would hide mine infirmitie from me. Well (said the physician) I will cure you, but you must be content to indure a little paine in the dressing: which he promised patientlie to susteine, and conceiued certeine hope of his recouerie. Then entred the physician into the chamber, creeping close by the walles, seeming to feare the touching and hurting of his nose. Then did he blindfold him, which being doone, he caught him by the nose with a paire of pinsors, and threwe downe into a tub, which he had placed before his patient, a great quantitie of blood, with many peeces of bul-

locks liuers, which he had conueied into the chamber, whilest
the others eies were bound vp, and then gaue him libertie to
see and behold the same. He hauing done thus againe twoo or
three times, the melancholike humor was so qualified, that the
mans mind being satisfied, his greefe was eased, and his
disease cured.

Reginald Scot
The Discouerie of Witchcraft (1584)

AT TILBURY 1588

MY LOVING PEOPLE,

We have been persuaded by some that are careful of our
safety, to take heed how we commit ourselves to armed multi-
tudes, for fear of treachery; but I assure you, I do not desier to
live to distrust my faithful and loving people.

Let tyrants fear; I have always so behaved myself, that,
under God, I have placed my chiefest strength and safeguard
in the loyal hearts and good will of my subjects, and therefore
I am come amongst you, as you see, at this time, not for my
recreation and disport, but being resolved in the midst and
heat of the battle, to live or die amongst you all, to lay down
for my God, and for my kingdoms, and for my people, my
honour and my blood, even in the dust.

I know I have the body but of a weak and feeble woman;
but I have the heart and stomach of a king, and of a king of
England too; and think foul scorn that Parma or Spain, or any
prince of Europe should dare to invade the borders of my
realm; to which rather than any dishonour shall grow by me,
I myself will take up arms, I myself will be your general,
judge, and rewarder of every one of your virtues in the field.

I know already, for your forwardness you have deserved
rewards and crowns; and we do assure you on the word of a

prince, they shall be duly paid you. In the mean time my lieutenant-general shall be in my stead, than whom never prince commanded a more noble or worthy subject; not doubting but by your obedience to my general, by your concord in the camp, and your valour in the field, we shall shortly have a famous victory over those enemies of my God, of my kingdoms, and of my people.

Queen Elizabeth

A Collection of Scarce and Valuable Tracts (1809), ed. W. Scott

THE ARMADA (I)

MOST HONOURABLE:

I am commanded to send these prisoners ashore by My Lord Admiral, which had ere this been long done, but that I thought their being here might have done something which is not thought meet now ...

We have the army of Spain before us and mind, with the grace of God, to wrestle a pull with him. There was never anything pleased me better than the seeing the enemy flying with a southerly wind to the northwards. God grant you have a good eye to the Duke of Parma; for with the grace of God, if we live, I doubt it not but ere it be long so to handle the matter with the Duke of Sidonia as he shall wish himself at St Mary Port among his orange trees.

God give us grace to depend upon him; so shall we not doubt victory, for our cause is good.

Humbly taking my leave this last day of July 1588

Your Honour's faithfully to be commanded ever

Francis Drake

Sir Francis Drake

Letter to Sir F. Walsingham (1588) from *The Defeat of the Spanish Armada* (1894) by J. K. Laughton

THE ARMADA (II)

... I WILL deliver your Honour mine opinion, wherein I beseech your pardon if it fall out otherwise. I verily believe great extremity shall force them if they behold England in sight again. By all that I can gather, they are weakened of eight of their best sorts of shipping, which contained many man; as also many wasted in sickness and slaughter. Their masts and sails much spoiled; their pinnaces and boats, many cast off and wasted; wherein they shall find great wants when they come to land and water, which they must do shortly or die; and where or how, my knowledge cannot imagine. As the wind serveth, no place but between the Foreland and Hull. Considering the shallows and sands not greatly to be doubted, the hugeness and great draught of water in their ships considered, and otherwise the wind as it is at North-West, they have no place to go withal, but for the Scaw in Denmark, which were an hard adventure as the season of the year approacheth. If the wind by change suffer them, I verily believe they will pass about Scotland and Ireland to draw themselves home; wherein, the season of the year considered, with the long course they have to run and their sundry distresses and – of necessity – the spending of time by watering, winter will so come on as it will be to their great ruin.

God hath mightily protected her Majesty's forces with the least losses that ever hath been heard of, being within the compass of so great volleys of shot, both small and great. I verily believe there is not three score men lost of her Majesty's forces.

Thomas Fenner

Letter to Sir F. Walsingham (1588) from *The Defeat of the Spanish Armada* (1894) by J. K. Laughton

A Domestic Tragedy

1590. Aug. 22nd, Ann my nurse has long byn tempted by a wycked spirit: but this day it was evident how she was possessed of him. God is, hath byn, and shall be her protector and deliverer! Amen.

Aug. 26th, at night I anoynted (in the name of Jesus) Ann Frank her brest with the holy oyle.

Sept. 8th, Nurse Anne Frank wold have drowned hirself in my well, but by divine Providence I came to take her up befor she was overcome of the water.

Sept. 29th, Nurse Anne Frank most miserably did cut her owne throte, afternoone abowt four of the clok, pretending to be in prayer before her keeper, and suddenly and very quickly rising from prayer, and going toward her chamber, as the mayden her keper thowght, but indede straight way down the stayrs into the hall of the other howse, behinde the doore, did that horrible act; and the mayden who wayted on her at the stayr-fote followed her, and missed to fynde her in three or fowr places, tyll at length she heard her rattle in her owne blud.

John Dee

Private Diary, ed. J. O. Halliwell (1842). Written 1590

Witchcraft

Item, the saide *Agnis Tompson* was after brought againe before the Kings Maiestie and his Counsell, and being examined of the meetings and detestable dealings of those witches, she confessed that vpon the night of *Allhollon* Euen last, she was accompanied aswell with the persons aforesaide, as also with a great many other witches, to the number of two hundreth: and that all they together went by Sea each one in a Riddle or

Ciue, and went in the same very substantially with Flaggons
of wine making merrie and drinking by the waye in the same
Riddles or Ciues, to the Kerke of North Barrick in Lowthian,
and that after they had landed, tooke handes on the land and
launced this reill or short daunce, singing all with one voice.

Commer goe ye before, commer goe ye,
Gif ye will not goe before, commer let me.

At which time she confessed, that this *Geilles Duncane* did
goe before them playing this reill or daunce vpon a small
Trump, called a Iewes Trump, vntill they entred into the
Kerk of north Barrick.

These confessions made the King in a wonderful admiration,
and sent for the said *Geillis Duncane*, who vpon the like
Trump did playe the said daunce before the Kings Maiestie,
who in respect of the strangenes of these matters, tooke great
delight to bee present at their examinations.

Item, the said *Agnis Tomson* confessed that the *Diuell* being
then at North Barrick Kerke attending their coming in the
habit or likenes of a man, and seeing that they tarried ouer
long, he at their comming enioyned them all to a pennance,
which was, that they should kisse his Buttockes, in signe of
duetye to him: which being put ouer the Pulpit barre, euerye
one did as he had enioyned them: and hauing made his vn-
godly exhortations, wherein he did greatlye inveighe against
the King of Scotland, he receiued their oathes for their good
and true seruice towards him, and departed: which doone,
they returned to Sea, and so home againe.

At which time the witches demaunded of the Diuel why he
did beare such hatred to the King, who answered, by reason
the King is the greatest enemy he hath in the worlde: all
which their confessions and depositions are still extant vpon
record.

Item, the saide *Agnis Sampson* confessed before the Kings

Maiestie sundrye thinges which were so miraculous and strange, as that his Maiestie saide they were all extreame lyars, wherat she answered, she would not wishe his Maiestie to suppose her woords to be false, but rather to beleeue them, in that she would discouer such matter vnto him as his maiestie should not any way doubt off.

And therupon taking his Maiestie a little aside, she declared vnto him the verye woordes which passed betweene the Kings Maiestie and his Queene at Vpslo in Norway the first night of their mariage, with their answere eache to other: whereat the Kinges Maiestie wondered greatlye, and swore by the liuing God, that he beleeued that all the Diuels in hell could not haue discouered the same: acknowledging her woords to be most true, and therefore gaue the more credit to the rest which is before declared.

Anon

Newes from Scotland (1591)

RUSSIA

THE whole countrie differeth very much from it selfe, by reason of the yeare: so that a man would marueile to see the great alteration and difference betwixte the winter, and the sommer *Russia*. The whole countrie in the winter lyeth vnder snow, which falleth continually, and is sometime of a yarde or two thicke, but greater towardes the north. The riuers and other waters are all frosen vp a yarde or more thicke, how swift or broade so euer they bee. And this continueth commonly fiue moneths, viz, from the beginning of Nouember till towardes the ende of March, what time the snow beginneth to melte. So that it would breede a frost in a man to looke abroad at that time, and see the winter face of that countrie. The sharpenesse of the ayre you may iudge of by this: for that

20

water dropped downe or cast vp into the ayre, congealeth into Ise before it come to the ground. In the extremitie of winter, if you holde a pewter dishe or pot in your hand, or any other mettall (except in some chamber where their warme stoaues bee) your fingers will friese faste vnto it, and draw off the skinne at the parting. When you passe out of a warme roome into a colde, you shall sensibly feele your breath to waxe starke, and euen stifeling with the colde, as you drawe it in and out. Diuers not onely that trauell abroad, but in the very markets, and streats of their townes, are mortally pinched and killed withall: so that you shall see many drop downe in the streates, many trauellers brought into the townes sitting dead and stiffe in their sleddes. Diuers lose their noses, the tippes of their eares, and the bals of their cheekes, their toes, feete, &c. Many times (when the winter is very harde and extreame) the beares and woolfes issue by troupes out of the woodes driuen by hunger, and enter the villages, tearing and rauening all they can finde: so that the inhabitants are faine to flie for safegard of their liues. And yet in the Sommer time you shall see such a new hew and face of a countrie, the woods (for the most part which are all of fir and birch) so fresh and so sweet, the pastures and medowes so greene and well growen, (and that vpon the sudden) such varietie of flowres, such noyse of birdes (specially of Nightingales, that seeme to be more lowde and of a more variable note then in other countries) that a man shall not lightly trauell in a more pleasant countrie.

Giles Fletcher

Of the Russe Common Wealth (1591)

POLITE CONVERSATION

(*Giordano and Edward*)

G. Why do you stand barehedded? you do your self wrong.

E. Pardon me good sir, I doe it for my ease.

G. I pray you be couered, you are too ceremonious.

E. I am so well, that me thinks I am in heauen.

G. If you loue me, put on your hat.

E. I will doe it to obay you, not for any pleasure that I take in it.

G. What? will you rather stand than sit?

E. I am very well. Good lord what dainty knacks you haue here?

G. I haue nothing, but a few trifles.

E. What deuice is this, if a man may knowe?

G. It is a kinde of sweete water, verie far fetcht.

E. What doo you with it, if it be lawfull to knowe?

G. I vse it to wash mine eyes, and my face.

E. In good truth it is verie good, and verie sweete.

G. I praie you take that little that I haue, for my sake.

E. Not for anie thing in the world.

G. I haue some more, take it if you loue me.

E. I would rather please you in any other thing.

G. You shall doe mee an vnspeakable fauour, to accept this little bottle.

E. It will be an exceeding fauor to me, if you please to keep it your selfe.

G. I beseeche you take it as a guift from me.

E. I accept it vpon condition, that you will vouchsafe to weare this rapier and dagger for my sake.

G. I shall be gladder if you keepe it your selfe, and doo not depriue you of so goodlie a thing.

E. I praie you doo not denie me so smale a boone.

G. It were pittie to depriue you of it.

E. So shall I be resolued that I am in your fauour, and that
   you loue me, if you will take it in good parte.

G. See whether I loue you, that euen in vnlawfull things I am
   content to obay you, now imagine what I would do in
   things lawful.

E. I doo not present it vnto you for the value, for that is little,
   but you must esteeme my good will.

E. I accuse the cause of this.

G. And I commend the effect.

John Florio
Second Frutes . . . (1591)

CARD-SHARPERS

THE Conny-catchers, apparalled like honest ciull gentlemen,
or good fellows, with a smooth face, as if butter would not
melt in their mouthes, after dinner when the clients are come
from Westminster hal and are at leasure to walke vp and
downe Paules, Fleet-street, Holborne, the sttrond, and such
common hanted places, where these cosning companions
attend onely to spie out a praie: who as soone as they see a
plaine cuntry felow well and cleanly apparelled, either in a
coat of home spun russet, or of freeze, as the time requires,
and a side pouch at his side, there is a connie, saith one. At that
word out flies the Setter, and ouertaking the man, begins to
salute him thus: Sir, God saue you, you are welcom to London, how doth all our good friends in the countrie, I hope
they be all in health? The countrie man seeing a man so
curteous he knowes not, halfe in a browne studie at this
strange salutation, perhaps makes him this aunswere. Sir, all
our friends in the countrie are well thankes bee to God, but
truly I know you not, you must pardon me. Why sir, saith

the setter, gessing by his tong what country man hee is, are you not such a cuntry man, if he say yes, then he creeps vpon him closely; if he say no, then straight the setter comes ouer him thus: In good sooth sir, I know you by your face and haue bin in your companie before, I praie you (if without offence) let me craue your name, and the place of your abode. The simple man straight tels him where he dwels, his name, and who be his next neighbors, and what Gentleman dwell about him. After he hath learned all of him, then he comes ouer his fallowes kindly: sir, though I haue bin somwhat bold to be inquisitiue of your name, yet holde me excused, for I tooke you for a friend of mine, but since by mistaking I haue made you slacke your busines, wele drinke a quart of wine, or a pot of Ale together: if the foole be so readie as to go, then the Connie is caught: but if he smack the setter, and smels a rat by his clawing, and will not drinke with him, then away goes the setter, and discourseth to the verser the name of the man, the parish hee dwels in, and what gentlemen are his near neighbours, with that away goes he, & crossing the man at some turning, meets him ful in the face, and greetes him thus.

What goodman Barton, how fare al our friends about you? you are will met, I haue the wine for you, you are welcome to town. The poore countryman hearing himselfe named by a man he knows not, maruels and answers that he knowes him not, and craues pardon. Not me goodman Barton, haue you forgot me? why I am such a mans kinsman, your neighbor not far off: how doth this or that good gentleman my friend? good Lord that I should be out of your remembrance, I haue beene at your house diuers times. Indeede, sir, saith the farmer, are you such a mans kinsman, surely sir if you had not chalenged acquaintance of me, I should neuer haue knowen you, I haue clean forgot you, but I know the good gentleman your cosin well, he is my very good neighbor: and for his sake

smack] suspect

saith the verser, weel drink afore we part; haply the man thanks him, and to the wine or ale they goe, then ere they part, they make him a cony, & so feret-claw him at cardes, that they leaue him as bare of mony, as an ape of a taile. . .

Robert Greene

A Notable Discouery of Coosnage (1591)

CONVERSION

LIVING thus a long time, God (who suffereth sinners to heape coles of fire vpon their owne heads, and to bee fed fat with sinne against the day of vengeance) suffered me to go forward in my loose life: many warninges I had to draw me from my detestable kind of life, and diuers crosses to contrary my actions: but all in vaine, for though I were sundry times afflicted with many foule and greeuous diseases, and thereby scourged with the rod of Gods wrath, yet when by the great labor and frendship of sundry honest persons, they had (though to their great charges) sought and procured my re-couery, I did with the Dog *Redire in vomitum*, I went again with the Sow to wallow in the mire, and fell to my former follies as frankly, as if I had not tasted any iot of want, or neuer been scourged for them. *Consuetudo peccandi tollit sen-sum peccati*; my daily custome in sinne had cleane take away the feeling of my sinne: for I was so giuen to these vices afore-saide, that I counted them rather veniall scapes & faults of nature, than any great and greeuous offences: neither did I care for death, but held it onely as the end of life. For com-ming one day into Aldersgate street to a welwillers house of mine, hee with other of his friendes perswaded me to leaue my bad course of life, which at length would bring mee to vtter destruction, whereupon I scoffingly made them this answer. Tush, what better is he that dies in his bed than he that endes his life at Tyburne, all owe God a death: if I may haue my desire while I liue, I am satisfied, let me shift after death as I may. My friends hearing these words, greatly greeued at my gracelesse resolution, made this reply: If you feare not death in this world, nor the paines of the body in this life, yet doubt the second death, and the losse of your soule, which without hearty repentance must rest in hell fire for euer and euer.

Hell (quoth I) what talke you of hell to me? I know if I once come there, I shal haue the company of better men than my selfe, I shal also meete with some madde knaues in that place, & so long as I shall not sit there alone, my care is the lesse. But you are mad folks (quoth I) for if I feared the Iudges of the bench no more than I dread the iudgements of God, I would before I slept diue into one Carles bagges or other, and made merrie with the shelles I found in them so long as they would last. And though some in this company were Fryers of mine owne fraternitie to whom I spake the wordes: yet were they so amazed at my prophane speeches, that they wisht them-selues foorth of my company. Whereby appeareth, that my continuall delight was in sinne, and that I made my selfe drunke with the dregges of mischiefe. But beeing departed thence vnto my lodging, and now grown to the full, I was checked by the mightie hand of God: for *Sicknes* (the mes-senger of death) attached me, and tolde me my time was but short, and that I had not long to liue: whereupon I was vexed in mind, and grew very heauy. As thus I sate solempnly think-ing of my end, and feeling my selfe waxe sicker and sicker, I fell into a great passion, and was wonderfully perplexed, yet no way discouered my agony, but sate still calling to mind the lewdnes of my former life: at what time sodainly taking the booke of *Resolution*[1] in my hand, I light vpon a chapter there-

[1] See note on p. 224.

in, which discouered vnto mee the miserable state of the
reprobate, what Hell was, what the worme of Conscience was,
what tormentes there was appointed for the damned soules,
what vnspeakable miseries, what vnquenchable flames, what
intollerable agonies, what incomprehensible griefs; that there
was nothing but feare, horrour, vexation of mind, depriua-
tion from the sight and fauour of God, weeping and gnashing
of teeth, and that al those tortures were not termined or
dated within any compasse of yeares, but euerlasting world
without end; concluding all in this of the Psalmes: *Ab inferis
nulla est redemptio.*

After that I had with deepe consideration pondered vpon
these points, such a terrour stroke into my conscience, that for
very anguish of minde my teeth did beate in my head, my
lookes waxed pale and wan, and fetching a great sigh, I cried
vnto God, and said: If all this be true, of what shall become of
me? If the rewarde of sinne be death and hell, how many
deaths and hels do I deserue, that haue beene a most miserable
sinner? If damnation be the meed for wickednes, then am I
damned? for in all the world there neuer liued a man of
worser life. Oh what shall I doe? I cannot call to God for
mercie; for my faultes are beyond the compasse of his fauour:
the punishment of the body hath an ende by death, but the
paines of the soule by death are made euerlasting. Then what
a miserable case am I in if I die? yet if my death might re-
deeme my offences, and wash away my sinnes, oh might I
suffer euery day twentie deathes while seuen yeares lasteth, it
were nothing: but when I shall end a contempt to the world,
I shal enioy the disdaine of men, the displeasure of God, and
my soule (that immortall creature) shall euerlastingly bee
damned: Oh woe is mee, why doe I liue? nay rather why was
I borne? Cursed be the day wherein I was born, and haplesse
be the brests that gaue me sucke. Why did God create me to
bee a vessell of wrath? Why did hee breath life into me, thus

to make me a lost sheepe? Oh I feele a hell already in my conscience, the number of my sinnes do muster before my eies, the poore mens plaints that I haue wronged, cries out in mine eares and saith, *Robin Greene* thou art damned; nay, the iustice of God tels mee I cannot be saued.

Robert Greene

The Repentance of Robert Greene (1592)

A LAST LETTER

SWEET Wife, as euer there was any good will or friendship betweene thee and mee, see this bearer (my Host) satisfied of his debt, I owe him tenne pound, and but for him I had perished in the streetes. Forget and forgiue my wronges done vnto thee, and Almighty God haue mercie on my soule. Fare-well till we meet in heauen, for on earth thou shalt neuer see me more. This 2. of September, 1592. Written by thy dying Husband.

Robert Greene

The Repentance of Robert Greene (1592)

ROBERT GREENE

I WAS altogether vnacquainted with the man, & neuer once saluted him by name: but who in London hath not heard of his dissolute, and licentious liuing; his fonde disguisinge of a Master of Arte with ruffianly haire, vnseemely apparell, and more vnseemelye Company: his vaineglorious and Thrasoni-call brauinge: his piperly Extemporizing, and Tarletonizing: his apishe counterfeiting of euery ridiculous and absurd toy: his fine coosening of Iuglers, and finer iugling with cooseners:

Tarletonizing] behaving like Tarleton, a famous clown

28

hys villainous cogging, and foisting; his monstrous swearinge, and horrible forswearing; his impious profaning of sacred Textes: his other scandalous and blasphemous rauinge; his riotous and outragious surfeitinge; his continuall shifting of lodginges: his plausible musteringe, and banquetinge of roysterly acquaintaunce at his first comminge; his beggarly departing in euery hostisses debt; his infamous resorting to the Banckeside, Shorditch, Southwarke, and other filthy hauntes: his obscure lurkinge in basest corners: his pawning of his sword, cloake, and what not, when money came short; his impudent pamphletting, phantasticall interluding, and desperate libelling, when other coosening shifts failed: his imployinge of Ball (surnamed, cuttinge Ball) till he was intercepted at Tiborne, to leauy a crew of his trustiest companions, to guarde him in daunger of Arrestes: his keping of the foresaid Balls sister, a sorry ragged queane, of whome hee had his base sonne, *Infortunatus Greene:* his forsaking of his owne wife, too honest for such a husband: particulars are infinite: his contemning of Superiours, deriding of other, and defying of all good order?

Gabriel Harvey
Foure Letters . . . (1592)

PERILOUS VOYAGE

(1592)

THE tenth of October being by the accompt of our Captaine and Master very neere the shore, the weather darke, the storme furious, and most of our men hauing giuen ouer to trauell, we yeelded our selues to death, without further hope of succour. Our captaine sitting in the gallery very pensiue, I came and brought him some *Rosa Solis* to comfort him; for he was so cold, that hee was scarce able to mooue a ioint. After he had drunke, and was comforted in heart, hee began for the ease of his conscience to make a large repetition of his fore-passed time, and with many grieuous sighs he concluded in these words: Oh most glorious God, with whose power the mightiest things among men are matters of no moment, I most humbly beseech thee, that the intollerable burthen of my sinnes may through the blood of Jesus Christ be taken from me: and end our daies with speede, or shew vs some mercifull signe of thy loue and our preseruation. Hauing thus ended, he desired me not to make knowen to any of the company his intol-lerable griefe and anguish of minde, because they should not thereby be dismayed. And so suddenly, before I went from him, the Sunne shined cleere; so that he and the Master both obserued the true eleuation of the Pole, whereby they knew by what course to recouer the Streights. Wherewithall our captaine and Master were so reuiued, and gaue such com-fortable speeches to the company, that euery man reioyced, as though we had receiued a present deliuerance.

The next day being the 11 of October, we saw *Cabo Deseado* being the cape on the South shore (the North shore is nothing but a company of dangerous rocks, Isles, and sholds). This cape being within two leags to leeward of vs, our master greatly doubted, that we could not double the same: wher-upon the captain told him: You see there is no remedy, either we must double it, or before noon we must die: therfore loose your sails, and let vs put it to Gods mercy. The master being a man of good spirit resolutely made quicke dispatch and set saile. Our sailes had not bene halfe an houre aboord, but the footrope of our foresaile brake, so that nothing held but the oylet holes. The seas continually brake ouer the ships poope, and flew into the sailes with such violence, that we still expected the tearing of our sayles, or ouersetting of the ship, and withall to our vtter discomfort, wee perceiued that wee fell still more and more to leeward, so that wee could not double the cape: wee were nowe come within halfe a mile of the cape, and so neere the shore, that the counter-suffe of the sea would rebound against the shippes side, so that wee were much dismayed with the horror of our present ende. Beeing thus at the very pinch of death, the winde and Seas raging beyond measure, our Master veared some of the maine sheate; and whether it was by that occasion, or by some current, or by the wonderfull power of God, as wee verily thinke it was, the ship quickened her way, and shot past that rocke, where wee thought shee would haue shored. Then betweene the cape and the poynt there was a little bay; so that wee were somewhat farther from the shoare: and when we were come so farre as the cape, wee yeelded to death: yet our good God the Father of all mercies deliuered vs, and wee doubled the cape about the length of our shippe, or very little more. Being shot past the cape, we presently tooke in our sayles, which onely God had preserued vnto vs: and when we were shot in betweene the high lands, the wind blowing trade, without any inch of sayle, we spooned before the sea, three men being not able to guide the helme, and in sixe houres wee were put fiue and twenty leagues within the Streights, where wee found a sea answerable to the Ocean.

In this time we freed our ship from water, and after wee had rested a little, our men were not able to mooue; their sinewes were stiffe, and their flesh dead, and many of them (which is most lamentable to bee reported) were so eaten with lice, as that in their flesh did lie clusters of lice as big as peason, yea, and some as big as beanes. Being in this miserie we were constrained to put into a cooue for the refreshing our men. Our Master knowing the shore and euery cooue very perfectly, put in with the shore, and mored to the trees, as beforetime we had done, laying our ankor to the seaward.

Here we continued vntil the twentieth of October; but not

being able any longer to stay through the extremitie of famine, the one and twentieth we put off into the chanell, the weather being reasonable calme: but before night it blew most extreamely at Westnorthwest. The storme growing outragious, our men could scarcely stand by their labour; and the Streights being full of turning reaches we were constrained by discretion of the Captaine and Master in their accounts to guide the ship in the hell-darke night, when we could not see any shore, the chanell being in some places scarce three miles broad.

John Jane

From Richard Hakluyt's *The Principal Nauigations, Voiages, Traffiques and Discoueries of the English Nation* (1600)

POET'S PETITION

MOST gratious and dread soueraigne, tyme cannot worke my peticions, nor my peticions the tyme. After many years seriuce yt pleased your Maiestie to except against Tents and Toyles, I wish that for Teants I might putt in Tenements, so should I be eased of some toyles. Some landes, some goodes, fines, or forfeitures that should fall by the iust fall of these most false traitors, that seeing nothing will come by the Reuells, I may pray vppon the Rebells. Thirteene years your highnes seruant but yet nothing, Twenty freinds that though they saye they wilbe sure I find them sure to be slowe. A thowsand hopes but all nothing, a hundred promises but yet nothing. Thus casting vpp the Inventary of my freinds, hopes, promises, and tymes, the *summa totalis* amounteth to iust nothing. My last will is shorter than myne invencion: but three legacies, patience to my Creditors, Melancholie without measure to my friends, and beggerie without shame to my family ... In all humilitie I entrete that I may dedicate to your sacred Maiestie

Lillie de tristibus wherein shalbe seene patience, labours and misfortunes ... The last and the least, that if I bee borne to haue nothing, I may haue a protection to pay nothinge, which suite is like his that haueing folloued the Court tenn years for recompence of his seruis committed a Robberie and took it out in a pardon.

John Lyly

'John Lillies Second Peticion to the Queene' (? 1598)
from *Euphues*, ed. E. Arber (1868)

GUIANA

AFTER we departed from the port of these *Ciawani*, we passed vp the riuer with the flood, and ancored the ebbe, and in this sort we went onward. The third daie that we entred the riuer, our Galley came on ground, and stuck so fast, as we thought that euen there our discouery had ended, and that we must haue left 60 of our men to haue inhabited like rookes vpon trees with those nations: but the next morning, after we had cast out all her ballast, with tugging and hawling to and fro, we got her afloate, and went on: At fower daies ende wee fell into as goodly a riuer as euer I beheld, which was called the great *Amana*, which ran more directly without windings and turnings then the other. But soone after the flood of the sea left vs, and we enforced either by maine strength to row against a violent currant, or to returne as wise as we went out, we had then no shift but to perswade the companies that it was but two or three daies worke, and therefore desired them to take paines, euery gentleman and others taking their turns to row, and to spell one the other at the howers end. Euerie day we passed by goodlie branches of riuers, some falling from the west, others from the east into *Amana*, but those I leaue to the description in the *Chart* of dis-

couerie, where euerie one shall be named with his rising and
descent. When three daies more were ouergone, our companie:
began to despaire, the weather being extreame hot, the
riuer bordered with verie high trees, that kept away the aire
and the currant against vs euery daie stronger then other: Bu
we euer more commanded our Pilots to promise an end the
next daie, and vsed it so long, as we were driuen to assure
them from fower reaches of the riuer to three, and so to two
and so to the next reach: but so long we laboured, that many
daies were spent, and so driuen to draw our selues to harder
allowance, our bread euen at the last, and no drinke at all
and our men and our selues to wearied and scorched, and
doubtfull withall whether we should euer performe it or no
the heat encreasing as we drew towards the line; for wee
were now in fiue degrees.

The farther we went on (our victuall decreasing and the aire
breeding great faintnes) we grew weaker and weaker, when
wee had most need of strength and abilitie, for howerlie the
riuer ran more violently then other against vs, and the barge
wheries, and ships bote of Captaine *Giffard* and Captaine
Calfield, had spent all their prouisions, so as wee were
brought into despaire and discomfort, had we not perswaded
all the companie that it was but onelie one daies worke more
to attaine the lande where we should be releeued of all we
wanted, and if we returned, that we were sure to starue by the
way, and that the worlde would also laugh vs to scorne. On the
banks of these riuers were diuers sorts of fruits good to eate,
flowers and trees of that varietie as were sufficient to make ter
volumes of herbals, we releeued our selues manie times with the
fruits of the countrey, and somtimes with foule and fish: We
saw birds of all colours, some carnation, some crimson, orenge-
tawny, purple, watchet, and of all other sorts both simple and
mixt, as it was vnto vs a great good passing of the time to
beholde them, besides the reliefe we found by killing some

34

store of them with our fouling peeces, without which, hauing little or no bread, and lesse drink, but onely the thick and troubled water of the riuer, we had been in a very hard case.

*

When we ronne to the tops of the first hils of the plaines adioyning to the riuer, we behelde that wonderfull breach of waters, which ranne downe *Caroli*: and might from that mountaine see the riuer how it ran in three parts, aboue twentie miles off, and there appeared some ten or twelue ouerfals in sight, euery one as high ouer the other as a Church-tower, which fell with that fury, that the rebound of waters made it seeme, as if it had beene all couered ouer with a great shower of rayne: and in some places we tooke it at the first for a smoke that had risen ouer some great towne. For mine owne part I was well perswaded from thence to haue returned, being a very ill footeman, but the rest were all so desirous to goe neere the saide strange thunder of waters, as they drew me on by little and little, till we came into the next valley, where we might better discerne the same. I neuer saw a more beawti-full countrey, nor more liuely prospectes, hils so raised heere and there ouer the vallies, the riuer winding into diuers braunches, the plaines adioyning without bush or stubble, all faire greene grasse, the ground of hard sand easy to march on, eyther for horse or foote, the deare crossing in euery path, the birds towards the euening singing on euery tree with a thousand seueral tunes, cranes and herons of white, crimson, and carnation pearching on the riuers side, the ayre fresh with a gentle easterlie wind, and euery stone that we stooped to take vp, promised eyther golde or siluer by his complexion.

Sir Walter Ralegh
The Discouerie of Guiana (1596)

A Private Skirmish

(1599)

About nine aclocke in the morning, Sir Charles Candish being at his new building, which is some quarter of a mile from his little house where he and his Lady do lie, and going from thence to a bricke kill, as far distant from that building as that is from his house, being attended by these three persons only, Henry Ogle, Launcelot Ogle his page, and one horse-keeper, he discerned to the number of about 20 horse on the side of a hill, which he thought to be Sir John Biron with companie hunting, but sodainly they all gallopping apace towards him, he perceved he was betrayed; wherupon, being upon a litle nagge, he put spurres to him, thincking to recover the new building, but the titt fell with him, and before he could recover out of the stirrop, he was overtaken, and before he could drawe his sworde, two pistolls were discharged upon him, and one of them with a round bullet hit him in the inner side of the thighe, but missed the bone and lies yet in the flesh nere the point of his buttocke. He hath also divers small shot in severall parts of his thighe and body thereabouts, which are thought came out of the same pistoll. Notwithstanding, so stronge was the hande of God with him as, after this wound receved, he and his two poore men and boy unhorsed sixe of them and killed two in the place, a third fell downe in the forrest and is thought dead also, and the fourth was left behinde in the same place, so sore hurt as it is not thought he can recover, and lieth in the village adjoining. Upon this some of the workmen came towards them, being without weapons. John Stanhope, who was the hindmost during all the fight, was now the formost in running away, carieng all the rest of his hirelings with him. Sir Charles is hurt also in the head and in the hand, but those two are but small hurtes, and the

kill] kiln

surgeons do assuredly hope that there is no great daunger in the other wounds with the pistoll, though by incision they intend to take out the bullet, which is within an inch and a half of the skinne. Sir Charles and his three had rapiers and daggers only. They left behinde them six goode geldings, whereof some are worth twenty pounds a peece, two or three cloakes, two rapiers, two pistolls, one sword and dagger, and some of theire hattes, all of which are safely kept by Sir Charles. All this companie did all the morning before lie in the forrest, seming as though they had ben a hunting; one of them that were killed was a keper, whome Stanhope that morning tooke with him, as he found him in his parke without bootes or weapon, but a pike staffe which he had, and, as the fellow confessed before he died, he knew not whether he was caried, or what to do, untill he came to the hill-side where they staide so longe. This is the truth of that accident.

John Chamberlain
Letters, ed. Sarah Williams (1861)

THE DYING QUEEN

(17 *December* 1602)

SWEET MALL,

I herewith send thee, what I woud God none did know, some ill bodings of the realme and its welfare. Our deare Queene, my royale godmother, and this state's natural mother, dothe now bear shew of human infirmitie, too faste for that evil which we shall get by her dethe, and too slowe for that good which shee shall get by her releasement from pains and miserye.

Deare Mall, how shall I speake what I have seene, or what I have felt? – Thy good silence in these matters emboldens my pen. For, thanks to the swete god of silence! thy lips do not wanton out of discretion's path, like the many gossipping dames we coud name, who lose their husband's fast hold in good friends, rather than hold fast their own tongues. Nowe I will truste thee with greate assurance, and whilst thou doste broode over thy young ones in the chamber, thou shalte reade the doinges of thy grieving mate in the cowrte.

I finde some lesse mindfull of whate they are soone to lose, than of what they may perchance hereafter get. Nowe, on my owne parte, I cannot blote from my memorie's table, the goodnesse of our Sovereigne Ladie to me, even (I will saie) before borne; her affectione to my mother who waited in privie chamber, her betterring the state of my father's fortune (which I have, alass! so much worsted,) her watchings over my youthe, her likinge to my free speech, and admiration of my little learninge and poesy, which I did so muche cultivate on her commande, have rootede such love, suche dutyfull remembraunce of her princelie virtues, that to turne askante from her condition withe tearlesse eyes, woud staine and foule the springe and founte of gratitude.

It was not manie daies since I was bidden to her presence. I bleste the happy momente; and founde her in moste pitiable state. She bade the archbishope aske me if I had seene Tyrone: I replied, with reverence, that "I had seene him withe the Lord Deputie." She lookede up, with much choler and griefe in her countenance and saide, "Oh, nowe it mindeth me that you was *one* who sawe this manne *elsewhere*:" – and hereat, she droppede a teare, and smote her bosome. She helde in her hande a goldene cuppe, whiche she often put to her lippes; but, in soothe, her hearte seemethe too fulle to lacke more fillinge. This sighte movede me to thinke on whate paste in Irelande; and I truste she did not lesse thinke on *some* who were busier there than myselfe. She gave me a message to the Lord Deputie, and bade me come to the chamber at seven o'clocke. Hereat some who were aboute her did marvel, as I do not

holde so highe a place as those she did not chuse to do her com-
mandes. Deare Mall, if I gette no profitte, I shall gette some
envie, and this businesse may turne to some accounte withe
the Lord Deputie. Her Majestie enquirede of some matters
whiche I had written; and as she was pleasede to note my
fancifulle braine, I was not unheedfull to feede her humoure,
and reade some verses, whereat she smilede once, and was
pleasede to saie; – "When thou doste feele creepinge tyme at
thye gate, these fooleries will please thee lesse; I am paste my
relishe for suche matters: thou seeste my bodilie meate dothe
not suite me well; I have eaten but one ill tastede cake since
yesternighte." She rated moste grievouslie, at noone, at some
who minded not to bringe uppe certaine matters of accounte.
Several menne have been sente to, and when readie at hande,
her Highnesse hathe dismissede in anger; but who, dearest
Mall, shall saye, that *"youre Highnesse hathe forgotten"* ...

Nexte monthe I will see thie swete face, and kiss my boys
and maids, which I praie thee not to omitte on my accounte.
Send me up, by my manne Combe, my Petrarche. Adieu,
swete Mall.

I am thine ever lovinge
John Harington.

Sir John Harington
Letter to Lady Mary Harington (1602)
from *Nugae Antiquae* (1804)

END OF AN EPOCH

(1603)

23 *Marche.* I dyned with Dr. Parry in the Priuy Chamber, and
vnderstood by him, the Bishop of Chichester, the Deane of
Canterbury, the Deane of Windsore, &c. that hir Majestie

hath bin by fitts troubled with melancholy some three or four monethes, but for this fortnight extreame oppressed with it, in soe much that shee refused to eate anie thing, to receiue any phisike, or admit any rest in bedd, till within these two or three dayes. Shee hath bin in a manner speacheles for two dayes, verry pensiue and silent; since Shrouetide sitting sometymes with hir eye fixed vpon one obiect many howres togither, yet shee alwayes had hir perfect senses and memory, and yesterday signified by the lifting vp of hir hand and eyes to heauen, a signe which Dr. Parry entreated of hir, that shee beleeued that fayth which shee hath caused to be professed, and looked faythfully to be saued by Christes merits and mercy only, and noe other meanes. She tooke great delight in hearing prayers, would often at the name of Jesus lift vp hir handes and eyes to Heauen. Shee would not heare the Archbishop speake of hope of hir longer lyfe, but when he prayed or spake of Heauen, and those ioyes, shee would hug his hand &c. It seemes shee might haue liued yf she would haue vsed meanes; but shee would not be persuaded, and princes must not be forced. Hir physicians said shee had a body of a firme and perfect constitucion, likely to haue liued many yeares. A royall Maiesty is noe priuiledge against death. 24 *March*. This morning about three at clocke hir Majestie departed this lyfe, mildly like a lambe, easily like a ripe apple from the tree.

3 *Aprill*. Dr. Parry told me the Countess Kildare assured him that the Queene caused the ring wherewith shee was wedded to the crowne, to be cutt from hir finger some six weekes before hir death, but wore a ring which the Earl of Essex gave hir vnto the day of hir death.

John Manningham
Diary, ed. John Bruce (1868)

Plague

WHAT an vnmatchable torment were it for a man to be bard vp euery night in a vast silent Charnell-house? hung (to make it more hideous) with lamps dimly & slowly burning, in hollow and glimmering corners: where all the pauement should in stead of greene rushes, be strewde with blasted Rosemary: withered Hyacinthes, fatall Cipresse and Ewe, thickly mingled with heapes of dead mens bones: the bare ribbes of a father that begat him, lying there: here the Chaplesse hollow scull of a mother that bore him: round about him a thousand Coarses, some standing bolt vpright in their knotted winding sheetes: others halfe mouldred in rotten Coffins, that should suddenly yawne wide open, filling his nosthrils with noysome stench, and his eyes with the sight of nothing but crawling wormes. And to keepe such a poore wretch waking, he should heare no noise but of Toads croaking, Screech-Owles howling, Mandrakes shriking: were not this an infernall prison? would not the strongest-harted man (beset with such a ghastly horror) looke wilde? and runne madde? and die? And euen such a formidable shape did the diseased Citie appeare in: For he that durst (in the dead houre of gloomy midnight) haue bene so valiant, as to haue walkt through the stil and melancholy streets, what thinke you should haue bene his musicke? Surely the loude grones of rauing sicke men; the strugling panges of soules departing: In euery house grief striking vp an Allarum: Seruants crying out for maisters: wiues for husbands, parents for children, children for their mothers: here he should haue met some frantickly running to knock vp Sextons; there, others fearfully sweating with Coffins, to steale forth dead bodies, least the fatall hand-writing of death should seale vp their doores. And to make this dismall consort more full, round about them Bells heauily tolling in one place, and ringing out in another. The dreadfulnesse of such an houre, is in-vtterable: let vs goe further.

If some poore man, suddeinly starting out of a sweete and golden slumber, should behold his house flaming about his eares, all his family destroied in their sleepes by the mercilesse fire; himself in the very midst of it, wofully and like a madde man calling for helpe: would not the misery of such a distressed soule, appeare the greater, if the rich Vsurer dwelling next doore to him, should not stirre, (though he felt part of the danger) but suffer him to perish, when the thrusting out of an arme might haue saued him? O how many thousands of wretched people haue acted this poore mans part? how often hath the amazed husband waking, found the comfort of his bedde lying breathlesse by his side! his children at the same instant gasping for life! and his seruants mortally wounded at the hart by sicknes! the distracted creature beats at death doores, exclaimes at windowes, his cries are sharp inough to pierce heauen, but on earth no eare is opend to receiue them.

And in this maner do the tedious minutes of the night stretch out the sorrowes of ten thousand: It is now day, let vs looke forth and try what Consolation rizes with the Sun: not any, not any: for before the Iewell of the morning be fully set in siluer, a hundred hungry graues stand gaping, and euery one of them (as at a breakfast) hath swallowed downe ten or eleuen liuelesse carcases: before dinner, in the same gulfe are twice so many more deuoured: and before the sun takes his rest, those numbers are doubled: Threescore that not many houres before had euery one seuerall lodgings very delicately furnisht, are now thrust altogether into one close roome: a litle noisome roome: not fully ten foote square. Doth not this strike coldly to the hart of a worldly mizer? To some, the very sound of deaths name, is in stead of a passing-bell: what shall become of such a coward, being told that the self-same bodie of his, which now is so pampered with superfluous fare, so perfumed and bathed in odoriferous waters, and so gaily apparelled in varietie of fashions, must one day be throwne (like stinking carion) into a rank and rotten graue; where his goodly eies, that did once shoote foorth such amorous glances, must be beaten out of his head: his lockes that hang wantonly dangling, troden in durt vnderfoote: this doubtless (like thunder) must needs strike him into the earth. But (wretched man!) when thou shalt see, and be assured (by tokens sent thee from heauen) that to morrow thou must be tumbled into a Mucke-pit, and suffer thy body to be bruisde and prest with three-score dead men, lying slouenly vpon thee, and thou to be vndermost of all! yea and perhaps halfe of that number were thine enemies! (and see howe they may be reuenged, for the wormes that breed out of their putrifying carkasses, shall crawle in huge swarmes from them, and quite deuoure thee) what agonies will this strange newes driue thee into? If thou art in loue with thy selfe, this cannot choose but possesse thee with frenzie. But thou art gotten safe (out of the ciuill citie Calamitie) to thy Parkes and Pallacès in the Country, lading thy asses and thy Mules with thy gold, (thy god), thy plate, and thy Iewels: and the fruites of thy wombe thriftily growing vp but in one onely sonne, (the young Landlord of all thy carefull labours) him also hast thou rescued from the arrowes of infection; Now is thy soule iocund, and thy sences merry. But open thine eyes, thou Foole! and behold that darling of thine eye, (thy sonne) turnde suddeinly into a lumpe of clay; the hand of pestilence hath smote him euen vnder thy wing: Now doest thou rent thine haire, blaspheme thy Creator, cursest thy creation, and basely descendest into bruitish & vnmanly passions, threatning in despite of death and his Plague, to maintaine the memory of thy childe, in the euerlasting brest of Marble: a tombe must now defend him from tempests: and for that purpose, the swetty hinde (that digs the rent he paies thee out of the entrailes of the earth) he is sent for, to conuey foorth that burden of thy sorrow:

But note how thy pride is disdained: that weather-beaten sun-burnt drudge, that not a month since fawnd vpon thy worship like a Spaniell, and like a bond-slaue, would haue stoopt lower than thy feete, does now stoppe his nose at thy presence, and is readie to set his Mastiue as hye as thy throate, to driue thee from his doore: all thy golde and siluer cannot hire one of those (whom before thou didst scorne) to carry the dead body to his last home: the Country round about thee shun thee, as a Basiliske, and therefore to *London* (from whose armes thou cowardly fledst away) poast vpon poast must be gal-loping, to fetch from thence those that may performe that Funerall office: But there are they so full of graue-matters of their owne, that they haue no leisure to attend thine: doth not this cut thy very heart-strings in sunder? If that doe not, the shutting vp of the Tragicall Act, I am sure will: for thou must be inforced with thine owne handes, to winde vp (that blasted flower of youth) in the last linnen, that euer he shall weare: vpon thine owne shoulders must thou beare part of him, thy amazed seruant the other: with thine owne hands must thou dig his graue, (not in the Church, or common place of buriall,) thou hast not fauour (for all thy riches) to be so happie, but in thine Orcharde, or in the proude walkes of thy Garden, wringing thy palsie-shaking hands in stead of belles, (most miserable father) must thou search him out a sepulcher.

Thomas Dekker

The Wonderfull Yeare (1603)

GOSSIP AFTER CHILDBIRTH

THEN euery day after her lying downe will sundry dames visit her, which are her neighbours, her kinsewomen, or other her speciall acquaintance, whom the goodman must welcome

with all cheerefulnesse, and be sure there be some dainties in
store to set before them: where they about some three or
foure houres (or possibly halfe a day) will sit chatting with the
Child-wife, and by that time the cups of wine haue merily
trolde about, and halfe a dosen times moystned their lips with
the sweet ioyce of the purpled grape: They begin thus one
with another to discourse; Good Lord neighbor, I meruaile
how our gossip *Free:* doth, I haue not seene the good soule
this many a day. Ah God help her quoth another, for she hath
her hands full of worke, and his heart full of heauinesse: While
she drudges all the weake at home, her husband like an vn-
thrift neuer leaues running abroad, to the Tennis court, and
Dicing houses, spending all that euer he hath in such lewd
sort: yea, and if that were the worst it is well: But heare ye
Gossip, there is another matter spoiles all, he cares no more for
his wife, then for a dog, but keepes queanes euen vnder her
nose. Iesu sayth another, who would thinke he were such a
man, he behaues himselfe so orderly and ciuilly, to all mens
sightes. Tush, holde your peace Gossip (sayth the other) it is
commonly seene, the still sowe eates vp all the draffe, hee
carries a smooth countenance, but a corrupt conscience: That
I know F. well enough, I will not say he loues mistresse G.
goe-too gossip I drink to you. Yea and saith another, there
goes foule lies if G. himselfe loues not his maid N. I can tell
you their mouthes will not be stopt with a bushell of wheat
that speak it. Then the third fetching a great sigh, saying, by
my truth such another bold Bettresse haue I at home: for
neuer giue me credit gossip, if I tooke her not the other day
in close conference with her maister, but I thinke I beswad-
deld my maid in such sort, that she will haue small list to do so
againe. Nay gossip (saith another) had it bene to me, that
should not haue serued her turne, but I would haue turnd the
queane out of doors to picke a Sallet: for wot ye what gossip?

bold Bettresse] brazen hussy

45

it is ill setting fire and flax together: but I pray you tell me one thing, when saw you our friend mistresse C.? now in good soothe she is a kind creature, and a very gentle Peat: I promise you I saw her not since you and I dranke a pinte of wine with her in the fish market. O gossip (saith the other) there is a great change since that time, for they haue bene faine to pawne all that euer they haue, and yet God knowes her husband lies still in prison. O the passion of my heart (saith another) is all their great and glorious shew come to nothing? good Lord what a world is this. Why gossip (saith another) it was neuer like to be otherwise, for they loued euer to goe fine, and fare daintily, and by my fay gossip, this is not a world for those matters, and therupon I drinke to you. This is commonly their communication, where they find cheare according to their choice.

Robert Tofte (?)

The Batchelars Banquet (1603). Translated from the French

JAMES I

(1603)

WHEN I came to the presence-chamber, and had gotten goode place to see the lordlie attendants, and bowede my knee to the Prince, I was orderde by a specyal messenger, and that in secrete sorte, to waite a whyle in an outwarde chamber, whence, in near an houre waitinge, the same knave ledde me up a passage, and so to a smale roome, where was good order of paper, inke, and pens, put on a boarde for the Prince's use. Soon upon this, the Prince his Highnesse did enter, and in muche good humour askede, "If I was cosen to lorde Haryngton of Exton?" I humblie repliede, – "His Majestie did me

Peat] lass

some honour in enquiringe my kin to one whome he had so late honourede and made a barone;" and moreover did adde, "wee were bothe branches of the same tree." Then he enquyrede muche of lernynge, and showede me his owne in suche sorte, as made me remember my examiner at Cambridge aforetyme. He soughte muche to knowe my advances in philosophie, and utterde profounde sentences of Aristotle, and suche lyke wryters, which I had never reade, and which some are bolde enoughe to saye, others do not understand: but this I must passe by. The Prince did nowe presse my readinge to him parte of a canto in "Ariosto"; praysede my utterance, and said he had been informede of manie, as to my lernynge, in the tyme of the Queene. He asked me "what I thoughte pure witte was made of; and whom did it best become? Whether a Kynge shoulde not be the beste clerke in his owne countrie; and, if this lande did not entertayne goode opinion of his lernynge and good wisdome?" His Majestie did much presse for my opinion touchinge the power of Satane in matter of witchcraft; and askede me, with muche gravitie, – "If I did trulie understande, why the devil did worke more with anciente women than others?" I did not refraine from a scurvey jeste, and even saide (notwithstandinge to whom it was saide) that – "we were taught hereof in scripture, where it is tolde, that the devil walketh in dry places." His Majestie, moreover, was pleasede to saie much, and favouredelye, of my good report for merth and good conceite: to which I did covertlie answer; as not willinge a subjecte should be wiser than his Prince, nor even appeare so.

More serious discourse did next ensue, wherein I wantede roome to continue, and sometime roome to escape, for the Queene his mother was not forgotten, nor Davison neither. His Highnesse tolde me her deathe was visible in Scotlande before it did really happen, being, as he said, "spoken of in secrete by those whose power of sighte presentede to them a bloodie heade dancinge in the aire." He then did remarke muche on this gifte, and saide he had soughte out of certaine bookes a sure waie to attaine knowledge of future chances. Hereat, he namede many bookes, which I did not knowe, nor by whom written; but advisede me not to consult some authors which woulde leade me to evile consultations. I tolde his Majestie, "the power of Satan had, I muche fearede, damagede my bodilie frame; but I had not farther will to cowrte his friendshipe, for my soules hurte." – We nexte discoursede somewhat on religion, when at lengthe he saide: "Now, Sir, you have seen my wisdome in some sorte, and I have pried into yours. I praye you, do me justice in your reporte, and in good season, I will not fail to add to your understandinge, in suche pointes as I maye find you lacke amendemente." I made courtesie hereat, and withdrewe downe the passage, and out at the gate, amidst the manie varlets and lordlie servantes who stoode around.

Sir John Harington

From *Nugae Antiquae* (1804)

CONDEMNED CELL

(1603)

YOU shall nowe receive (my deare wife) my last words, in these my last lynes, my Love I send you, that you may keepe itt, when I am dead, and my Counsell that you may remember itt, when I am noe more; I would not by my will present you with Sorrowes (Deare Besse). Lett them goe into the grave with mee; and bee buried in the dust. And seeing itt is not the will of God, that I shall see you any more in this life, beare itt patiently, and with an heart like thy selfe.

First I send you all the thankes, which my heart can conceive, or my words can expresse for your many travailes, and care taken for mee, which though they have not taken effect, as you wished, yett my debt to you, is not the lesse, but pay itt I never shall, in this world.

Secondly I beseech you, for the love you bare mee liveing, doe not hide your selfe many dayes, after my death, but by your Travailes seeke to help your miserable fortunes, and the Right of your poore Child, Thy mournings cannot availe mee, I am but dust.

Thirdly you shall understand, that my Land was conveyed Bona fide to my Childe. The writeings weere drawne att Midsommer twelve monthes, my honest Cosen Brett, can testifie soe much, and Dalberrie too cann remember some-what therein, And I trust my blood, will quench their Malice, that have thus cruelly murthered mee, And that they will not seeke alsoe to kill thee and thine with extreame povertie.

To what freind to direct thee, I knowe not, for all mine have left mee, in the true tyme of triall; and I plainely per-ceive, that my death was determyned from the first day.

Most sorrie I am (God knowes) that being thus surprised with death, I can Leave you in noe better estate, God is my wittnesse, I meant you all my office of wynes,[1] or all that I could have purchased by sellinge itt, halfe my stuffe, and all my Jewells, But some on't for the Boy, but god hath pre-vented all my Resolutions, and even that great god that ruleth all in all; But if you can live free from want, Care for noe more; the rest is but vanitie.

Love God, and beginn betymes, to repose your selfe on him, and therein shall you find true and lasting Riches, and endlesse Comfort, For the rest when you have travailled and wearied all your thoughts, over all sorts of wordly Cogitations, you shall but sitt downe by sorrowe in the end.

1. The power to grant licences for the sale of wines, held by Ralegh since 1584.

Teach your sonne alsoe to love and feare god whilst hee is yett younge, that the feare of god may growe upp with him; and the same God will bee a husband to you, and a Father to him, A husband, and a Father, which Cannot bee taken from you.

Baylie oweth mee £200 and Adrian Gilbert £600. In Jersey, I have alsoe much monye oweing mee, Besides the Arrerages of the Wynes will pay my debts. And howsoever you doe, for my soules sake, pay all poore men.

When I am gone, noe doubt you shall bee sought by many; for the world thinks, that I was very rich. But take heed of the pretences of men, and theire affections; For they last not but in honest, and worthie Men; And noe greater misery can befall you in this life, then to become a prey, and afterwards to bee dispised: I speake not this (god knowes) to disswade you from marriage, for itt will bee best for you, both in respect of the world and of God.

As for mee, I am noe more yours, nor you mine, Death hath Cutt us a sunder; and God hath devided mee from the world, and you from mee.

Remember your poore Child, for his Fathers sake, who chose you, and Loved you, in his happiest tymes.

Gett those Letters (if it bee possible) which I writt to the Lords, wherein I sued for my life, God is my wittnesse, Itt was for you and yours I desired life. Butt itt is true that I disdaine my selfe for begging itt, For knowe it (deare wife) that your sonne, is the sonne of a true man, and one, whoe in his owne respect, dispiseth Death, and all his mishapen and ouglye shapes.

I cannot write much: God hee knowes, howe hardly, I steale this tyme, while others sleepe; and itt is alsoe high tyme, that I should seperate my thoughts from the world.

Begg my dead body, which Liveinge was denyed thee; and either Laye itt att Shirbourne (if the Land Continue) or in Excester Church by my Father and Mother.

I can say noe more, tyme and death call me away.

The everlasting, powerfull, infinite and omnipotent god, that Almightie God, whoe is goodnesse itt selfe, the true life, and true light, keepe thee, and thine; have mercye on mee, and teach mee to forgive my persecutors and Accusers, and send us to meete in his glorious kingdome.

My deare wife farewell, Blesse my poore Boye, Pray for mee, and Lett my Good god hold you both in his armes.

Written with the dyeing hand of sometyme thy Husband, but now (alasse) overthrowne Wa: Raleigh.

Yours that was, But nowe not
my owne.

W.R.

Sir Walter Ralegh

Selections, ed. G. E. Hadow (1917)[1]

MATERNAL ANXIETY

Lady. Good morrowe Nurce.

Nurce. God giue you good morrowe Madame.

Lady. How now, how doth the childe?

Nurce. He is fayre and plumpe, and doth very wel thanks be to God, sauing that he hath bin somwhat waiward the last night.

Lady. Hath he so? What shold aile him? It may be he hath some tooth a growing, is he in his cradle? see if he sleepeth.

Nurce. He is full awaken Madame.

Lady. He is not yet made readie is he?

Nurce. No Madame, I haue let him sleepe all this morning.

1. The original of this letter is in the British Museum (Sloane Ms. 3520).

Lady. Unswaddle him, vndoe his swadling bands, giue him his
breakefast whilst I am heere, make his pappe, take away that
fierbrand which smoketh for it will taste of the smoke,
where is his little spoone? wash him before me, haue you
cleane water? O my little hart! God blesse thee, Rub the
crowne of his head, wash his eares, and put some fine clout
behinde them to th'end to keepe them drye and cleane,
wash his face: Lift vp a little his haires. Is not that some dust
that I see vpon his forehead? His browes are very round.
What hath he vpon his ey-lids? me thinks that his eyes are
somewhat watrish, make them cleane: how quick is his
ey-ball, hath he not a pimple vpon his nose? His little
cheekes are wet, I bileeue you did leaue him alone to crye
and weepe: picke his nosthrils, wipe his mouth and his lips.
How many teeth hath he? his gummes be sore, Showe me
his tongue, let me see the pallet of his mouth, he hath a
prettie chin, What a faire necke he hath! pull off his shirt,
thou art prety and fat my little darling, wash his armepits:
what ayleth his elboe? O what an arme he hath! his hand-
wrist is very small: open his right hand: the palme of his
left hand is all on water, did he sweat? how he spreadeth his
small fingers! his thumbe and little finger are Flea-bitten,
for the blacke spots are there yet, is there any Fleas in your
Chamber? ... Now swadle him againe, But first put on his
biggin and his little band with an edge, where is his little
petticote? giue him his coate of changeable taffata, and his
sattin sleeues: Where is his bibbe? Let him haue his gathered
Aprone with stringes, and hang a Muckinder to it: you
need not yet to giue him his Corall with the small golden
chayne, for I beleeue it is better to let him sleepe vntill the
after noone, giue him some sucke, I pray you take heed to
wipe well the nipple of your dugge before you put it in his
mouth, for feare that there be any haire or other thing

biggin] cap   *muckinder*] bib

which may hurt him. You mayd, goe fetch the childes cradle, make his bed, where is his pillowe? seeke a cleane pillow-bere, Set on the couerlet, now put him in his cradle and rocke him till he sleepe, but bring him to me first that I may kisse him: God send thee good rest my little boykin. I pray you good Nurce haue a care of him.

Nurce. Dout not of it Madame with the grace of God.

Lady. Well then, God be with you till anon.

Peter Erondell

The French Garden (1605)

THE KING OF DENMARK VISITS ENGLAND

Sir John Harington to Mr Secretary Barlow (1606)

I CAME here a day or two before the Danish King came, and from the day he did come untill this hour, I have been well nigh overwhelmed with carousal and sports of all kinds. The sports began each day in such manner and such sorte, as well night persuaded me of Mahomets paradise. We had women, and indeed wine too, of such plenty, as woud have astonished each sober beholder. Our feats were magnificent, and the two royal guests did most lovingly embrace each other at table. I think the Dane hath strangely wrought on our good English nobles; for those, whom I never could get to taste good liquor, now follow the fashion, and wallow in beastly delights. The ladies abandon their sobriety, and are seen to roll about in intoxication. In good sooth, the parliament did kindly provide his Majestie so seasonably with money, for there hath been no lack of good livinge; shews, sights, and ban-quetings, from morn to eve.

One day, a great feast was held, and, after dinner, the representation of Solomon his Temple, and the coming of the

Queen of Sheba was made, or (as I may better say) was meant to have been made, before their Majesties, by device of the Earl of Salisbury and others. – But, alass! as all earthly thinges do fail to poor mortals in enjoyment, so did prove our presentment hereof. The Lady who did play the Queens part, did carry most precious gifts to both their Majesties; but, forgetting the steppes arising to the canopy, overset her caskets into his Danish Majesties lap, and fell at his feet, tho I rather think it was in his face. Much was the hurry and confusion; cloths and napkins were at hand, to make all clean. His Majestie then got up and woud dance with the Queen of Sheba; but he fell down and humbled himself before her, and was carried to an inner chamber and laid on a bed of state; which was not a little defiled with the presents of the Queen which had been bestowed on his garments; such as wine, cream, jelly, beverage, cakes, spices, and other good matters. The entertainment and show went forward, and most of the presenters went backward, or fell down; wine did so occupy their upper chambers. Now did appear, in rich dress, Hope, Faith, and Charity: Hope did assay to speak, but wine rendered her endeavours so feeble that she withdrew, and hoped the King would excuse her brevity. Faith was then all alone, for I am certain she was not joyned with good works; and left the Court in a staggering condition. Charity came to the Kings feet, and seemed to cover the multitude of sins her sisters had committed: In some sorte she made obeysance and brought giftes, but said she would return home again, as there was no gift which Heaven had not already given his Majesty; she then returned to Hope and Faith, who were both sick and spewing in the lower hall. Next came Victory, in bright armour, and presented a rich sword to the King, who did not accept it, but put it by with his hand; and, by a strange medley of versification, did endeavour to make suit to the King; but Victory did not tryumph long, for, after much lamentable utterance, she was led away like a silly captive, and laid to sleep in the outer steps of the anti-chamber. Now did Peace make entry, and strive to get foremoste to the King; but I grieve to tell how great wrath she did discover unto those of her attendants, and, much contrary to her own semblance, most rudely made war with her olive branch, and laid on the pates of those who did oppose her coming. I have much marvalled at these strange pageantries, and they do bring to my remembrance what passed of this sort in our Queens days; of which I was sometime an humble presenter and assistant; but I neer did see such lack of good order, discretion, and sobriety, as I have now done. I have passed much time in seeing the royal sports of hunting and hawking, where the manners were such as made me devise the beasts were pursuing the sober creation, and not man in quest of exercise or food. I will now, in good sooth, declare to you, who will not blab, that the Gunpowder fright is got out of all our heads, and we are going on, hereaabouts, as if the Devil was contriving every man shoud blow up himself, by wild riot, excess, and devastation of time and temperance. The great ladies do go well-masked, and indeed it be the only show of their modesty, to conceal their countenance; but, alack, they meet with such countenance to uphold their strange doings, that I marvel not at ought that happens.

Sir John Harington

From *Nugae Antiquae* (1775)

LETTER TO HIS WIFE

(16 *February* 1617)

THIS is now the 8th day that I have kept my bedd. Yesterday I tooke a purge by Doctor Giffords advise ... There are but 3 ways: eyther this suddayn obstruccon will bringe death which is most welcom of all and to speake the truth I most earnestly desire it. First to enjoy my saviour; secondly I have seene enough and known enough and too much of this world; thirdly God hath led me by his hand past the difficulties of malice, misery, and debt, there is but one enemy to conquer, death, whom my saviour hath conquered for me, and I longe to step over his backe. And when I am gone an old objection will be ended, whether I wanted others or other wanted me. I shall synne no more; I shalbe reprehended no more. The second way is yf this be but a cold it cannot be longe, my strength or physicke will break it. The third is yf it grow to be a consumption I shall have the longer tyme to repent but that will be the most miserable of all ... It were best dye now, and best dye heere where no body dares interrupt my thoughts. To be a true Judge of myselfe I thincke the greatest part of this is Melancholy, yet god graunt never worse melancholy possesse my mynde ...

The losse of my pracktise makes me sadde. I know you could be contented to endure me longer with money. Yf I scape this and come home be not froward, be not crosse, withdraw not your hart nor counsayle from me, pracktise not upon me, reprehend me no more. For then my next sicknes I will certaynly dy yf I can; and would now yf I could. The reason may be guessed; doe you thincke that I see not what I doe amisse. Doe you thincke I speak not more bitterly to my own hart for every offence then you can? Doe you thincke it can be pleasinge to me to see you suffer such things under your eys and authority as you doe in others and reserve your gale for me? This hath made me ask, I have been somtymes stunge a fortenight to break out in a rage. But God and your soule knows who begyns. Selfe and sudden will and presumtion above your sex in you: riot and misdiet in me must be amended. I by the laws of God am your governor. You are not mine. Yf you desire a sole supremacy marry no

gale] gall

more when I am dead: there be enough that can speake you fair and undoe you, and you shall fynd none to deale with myne as I have dealt with yours. Chaunge that wicked axiom which you repeat so often, that you desire to be kyndly used though it be by a dissembler. For I dreamt I saw a dissembler pawninge your plate, sellinge your leases, feastinge in your house, and putting my boy to keepe his hawks and dogges and you makinge much of hym. I will leve you all and therefore give me leve to leve you this, and I pray you make better use of it then to grieve. For God knows I desire your health and contentment rather then my own lyfe.

John Hoskyns

From The Life, Letters, and Writings of
John Hoskyns (1937) by L. B. Osborn

THE MOVEMENT OF IDEAS: REFLECTION, ARGUMENT, EXHORTATION, SATIRE

The Rate for the Job

AND because founders of Colledges doe plant, and founders of Lectures doe water: it followeth wel in order to speake of the defect, which is in Publique Lectures: Namely, in the smalnesse and meanesse of the salary or reward which in most placcs is assigned vnto them: whether they be Lectures of Arts, or of Professions. For it is necessary to the progression of Scyences, that Readers be of the most able and sufficient men; as those which are ordained for generating, and propagating of Scyences, and not for transitorie vse. This cannot be, except their condition, and endowment be such, as may content the ablest man to appropriate his whole labour, and continue his whole age in that function and attendance, and therefore must haue a proportion answerable to that mediocritie or competencie of aduancement, which may be expected from a Profession, or the Practize of a Profession: So as, if you will haue Scyences flourish, you must obserue *Dauids* military lawe, which was, *That those which staied with the Carriage, should haue equall part with those which were in the Action:* else will the carriages be ill attended: So Readers in scyences are indeede the Gardyans of the stores and prouisions of Scyences, whence men in actiue courses are furnished, and therefore ought to haue equall entertainment with them; otherwise if the fathers in Scyences be of the weakest sort, or be ill maintained

      Et Patrum invalidi referent ieiunia nati ...

Francis Bacon

*The Twoo Bookes ... of the Proficience and
Aduancement of Learning ...* (1605)

THE VALUE OF LEARNING

To proceede now from imperiall and militarie vertue, to morall and priuate vertue; first, it is an assured truth, which is contained in the verses;

    Scilicet ingenuas didicisse fideliter artes,
    Emollit mores nec sinit esse feros.

It taketh away the wildnesse and barbarisme and fiercenesse of mens minds: but indeed the accent had need be vpon, *fideliter*. For a little superficiall learning doth rather worke a contrary effect. It taketh away all leuitie, temeritie, and insolencie, by copious suggestion of all doubts and difficulties, and acquainting the minde to ballance reasons on both sides, and to turne backe the first offers and conceits of the minde, and to accept of nothing but examined and tryed. It taketh away vaine admiration of any thing, which is the roote of all weakenesse. For all things are admired, either because they are new, or because they are great. For nouelty, no man that wadeth in learning or contemplation throughly, but will find that printed in his heart, *Nil novi super terram:* Neither can any man maruaile at the play of Peppets, that goeth behinde the curtaine, and aduiseth well of the Motion. And for magnitude, as *Alexander* the Great, after that he was vsed to great Armies, and the great Conquests of the spatious Prouinces in *Asia,* when hee receiued Letters out of *Greece,* of some fights

nd seruices there, which were commonly for a passage, or a
ʳort, of some walled Towne at the most, he sayd; *It seemed
ɔ him, that he was aduertised of the battailes of the Frogs, and the
Mise, that the ould tales went of.* So certainely, if a man medi-
ate much vppon the vniuersall frame of nature, the earth
with men vppon it (the diuinesse of soules except) will not
eeme much other, than an Ant-hill, whereas some Ants
arrie corne, and some carrie their young: and some goe
mptie, and all too and fro, a little heape of dust. It taketh
way, or mitigateth feare of death, or aduerse fortune: which
s one of the greatest impediments of vertue, and imperfections
ɔf manners ...

It were too long to goe ouer the particular remedies, which
earning doth minister, to all the diseases of the minde, some-
imes purging the ill humours, sometimes opening the
ɔbstructions, sometimes helping digestion, sometimes en-
reasing appetite, somtimes healing the wounds and exulcera-
ions thereof, and the like; and therefore I will conclude with
hat which hath *rationem totius*; which is, that it disposeth the
onstitution of the minde, not to be fixed or setled in the
lefects thereof; but still to be capable, and susceptible of
rowth and reformation. For the vnlearned man knowes not,
vhat it is to descend into himselfe, or to cal himselfe to account,
ɪor the pleasure of that *Suauissima vita, indies sentire se fieri
ɪeliorem*: The good parts hee hath, hee will learne to shew to
he full, and vse them dexterously, but not much to encrease
hem: The faults he hath, he will learne how to hide and
ɔlour them, but not much to amend them; like an ill Mower,
hat mowes on still, and neuer whets his Syth: whereas, with
he learned man, it fares otherwise, that he doth euer intermix
he correction and amendment of his minde, with the vse and
mployment thereof: Nay further in generall and in sum:
ertain it is that *Veritas*, and *Bonitas* differ, but as the Seale and
he Print: for Truth prints Goodnesse, and they be the clouds

of Error, which descend in the stormes of passions and perturbations ...

Lastly, leauing the vulgar arguments, that by learning, man excelleth man in that, wherein man excelleth beasts; that by learning man ascendeth to the heauens and their motions, where in bodie he cannot come; and the like; let vs conclude with the dignitie and excellency of knowledge and learning in that whereunto mans nature doth most aspire; which is immortalitie or continuance; for to this tendeth generation and raysing of houses and families; to this buildings, foundations, and monuments, to this tendeth the desire of memorie, fame, and celebration; and in effect, the strength of all other humane desires; wee see then howe farre the monuments of wit and learning, are more durable, than the monuments of power, or of the hands. For haue not the verses of *Homer* continued 25 hundred yeares, or more, without the losse of a sillable, or letter: during which time, infinite Pallaces, Temples, Castles, Cities haue been decayed, and demolished. It is not possible to haue the true pictures or statuaes of *Cyrus, Alexander, Cæsar,* no nor of the Kings, or great personages of much later yeares; for the originals cannot last, and the copies cannot but leese of the life and truth. But the Images of mens wits and knowledges remaine in Bookes, exempted from the wrong of time, and capable of perpetual renouation: Neither are they fitly to be called Images, because they generate still, and cast their seedes in the mindes of others, prouoking and causing infinit actions and opinions, in succeeding ages. So that if the inuention of the Shippe was thought so noble, which carryeth riches, and commodities, from place to place, and consociateth the most remote regions in participation of their fruits: how much more are letters to bee magnified, which as Shippes, passe through the vast Seas of time, and make ages so distant, to participate of the wisedome, illuminations, and inuentions the one of the other? Nay further wee see, some of the Philosophers which were least diuine, and most immersed in the sences, and denyed generally the immortality of the soule; yet came to this point, that whatsoeuer motions the sprite of man could act, and perfourme without the Organs of the bodie, they thought might remaine after death; which were only those of the vnderstanding, and not of the affection; so immortall and incorruptible a thing did knowledge seeme vnto them to be: But we that know by diuine reuelation, that not onely the vnderstanding, but the affectious purified, not onely the spirite, but the bodie changed shall be aduanced to immortalitie, doe disclaime in these rudiments of the sences.

Francis Bacon
The Twoo Bookes . . . of the Proficience and
Aduancement of Learning . . . (1605)

ADVICE TO A TEACHER

IF your scholer do misse sometimes, in marking rightlie these foresaid six thinges, chide not hastelie: for that shall, both dull his witte, and discorage his diligence: but monish him gentelie: which shall make him, both willing to amende, and glad to go forward in loue and hope of learning.

I hauc now wished, twise or thrise, this gentle nature, to be in a Scholemaster: And, that I haue done so, neither by chance, nor without some reason, I will now declare at large, why, in mine opinion, loue is fitter then feare, ientlenes better then beating, to bring vp a childe rightlie in learninge.

With the common vse of teaching and beating in common scholes of England, I will not greatlie contend: which if I did, it were but a small grammaticall controuersie, neither belonging to heresie nor treason, nor greatly touching God nor the Prince: although in very deede, in the end, the good or ill

bringing vp of children, doth as much serue to the good or il
seruice, of God, our Prince, and our whole countrie, as any
one thing doth beside.

I do gladlie agree with all good Scholemasters in these
points: to haue children brought to good perfitnes in learning:
to all honestie in manners: to haue all faultes rightlie amended
to haue euerie vice seuerelie corrected: but for the order and
waie that leadeth rightlie to these pointes, we somewhat
differ. For commonlie, many scholemasters, some, as I haue
seen, moe, as I haue heard tell, be of so crooked a nature, as,
when they meete with a hard witted scholer, they rather
breake him, than bowe him, rather marre him, then mend
him. For whan the scholemaster is angrie with some other
matter, then will he sonest faul to beate his scholer: and
though he him selfe should be punished for his folie, yet must
he beate some scholer for his pleasure: though there be no
cause for him to do so, nor yet fault in the scholer to deserue
so. These ye will say, be fond scholemasters, and fewe they be,
that be found soch. They be fond in deede, but surelie ouer-
many soch be found euerie where. But this will I say, that euen
the wisest of your great beaters, do as oft punishe nature, as
they do correcte faultes. Yea, many times, the better nature, is
sorer punished: For, if one, by quicknes of witte, take his
lesson readelie, an other, by hardnes of witte, taketh it not so
speedelie: the first is alwaies commended, the other is commonlie punished: whan a wise scholemaster, should rather
discretelie consider the right disposition of both their natures,
and not so moch way what either of them is able to do now,
as what either of them is likelie to do hereafter. For this I
know, not onelie by reading of bookes in my studie, but also
by experience of life, abrode in the world, that those, which
be commonlie the wisest, the best learned, and best men also,
when they be olde, were neuer commonlie the quickest of
witte, when they were yonge. The causes why, amongst

ther, which be many, that moue me thus to thinke, be these ewe, which I will recken. Quicke wittes commonlie, be apte o take, vnapte to keepe: soone hote and desirous of this and hat: as cold and sone wery of the same againe: more quicke o enter spedelie, than hable to pearse farre: euen like other harpe tooles, whose edges be verie soone turned. Soch wittes delite them selues in easie and pleasant studies, and neuer passe arre forward in hie and hard sciences. And therefore the uickest wittes commonlie may proue the best Poetes, but ot the wisest Orators: readie of tonge to speak boldlie, not eepe of iudgement, either for good counsell or wise writing. Also, for maners and life, quicke wittes commonlie be, in esire newfangled, in purpose, vnconstant, light to promise ny thing, readie to forget euery thing: both benefite and niurie: and therby neither fast to frend, nor fearefull to foe: nquisitiue of euery trifle, not secret in greatest affaires: bolde, with any person: busie, in euery matter: soothing, soch as be resent: nipping any that is absent: of nature also, alwaies, attering their betters, enuying their equals, despising their nferiors: and, by quicknes of witte, verie quicke and readie, o like none so well as them selues.

Roger Ascham
The Scholemaster (1570)

THE CARE OF HOUNDS

A GOOD keeper of Houndes should be gratious, curteous, and entle, louing his dogges of a naturall disposition, and he ught to be both well footed and well winded, aswell to fill is horne as his bottell: the first thing whiche he ought to do vhen he riseth, is to go see his Houndes, to make their odging cleane, and to dresse them as the case shall require: fter he hath so clensed them, he ought to take his horne and

sounde three or foure tymes the call, to the ende he may com-
forte them and call them to him: and when he shall see then
all aboute hym, then shall he couple them, and in couplyng
them he muste take good heede that he couple not the Dogge
together, for feare least they fight one with another, and i
there be any yong houndes, it shalbe good to couple then
with the olde bitches, to teache them to followe: when they
are all well coupled, the keeper muste fill two great bagges o
pockets with small bones, and other good morsels, as fishe, o
horse feete fried, fatte roste meates, and such like, then h
shall breake all into small gobbets into his bagges, and hang
one bagge about his owne necke, and giue another vnto on
of his companions, that done, he must take two wispes o
cleane straw and put them vnder his gyrdell, with a littl
brush or duster to rubbe and duste his houndes when they
shall come into the fielde: the other Huntesmen or varlette
whiche shalbe with him ought to do asmuch. Afterward
euery man shal take a fayre wande in his hande, and let on
go before to call the houndes vnto him, another shall com
behind which shall ierke them forwardes, and if there be two
others, they shall go on eche side, and so all foure togithe
shall go leade the houndes through the greene Corne fielde
and through the medowes, aswell to feede them, as for to
teach them to knowe theyr voyce, making them to pass
through the heardes of sheepe and other suche like beastes, to
accustome them, and to make them to know them: and i
there be any dogge that is so il taught as he would runne at
sheepe or any such tame beast, you must couple him with
ramme or a stoute Sheepe, and with your wande you must
all to pay him and beate him a good while, crying and
threatening to the ende that another time he may know th
rate of suche as vse it.

George Turberville

The Noble Arte of Venerie or Hunting (1576)

GESTURE

Guazzo and Anniball

Guaz. It is muche in my opinion to keepe a certaine maiestie in the iesture, which speaketh as it were by vsing silence, and constraineth as it were by way of commaundement, the hearers to haue it in admiration and reuerence.

Annib. Yet herein is required such a moderation, that a man with too litle be not immoueable like an image, neither with too much, too busie like an Ape: and as the one stirring no parte, thinking to get the opinion of grauitie, incurreth the suspition of folly, and is taken for a feigned person, brought in to speake, hauing of him selfe no life, so the other by the libertie of his iestures, thinking to vse a plausible kinde of curtesie, whereby to winne fauour, speaketh a playerlike kinde of lightnesse, whereby hee getteth discommendation. I will not in this place aduise him that speaketh to holde his head vpright, to take heede of licking or byting the lippes, and to see the woordes agree to the iesture, as the daunce doeth to the sowne of the instrument: neither likewise doe I thinke it meete to admonishe the hearer to take heede of rude lowtishe lookes, of wrying the bodie aside, of too set a grauitie in lookes, of too sower a countenaunce, of gazing about him, of whispering in any others eare, of laughing without occasion, of gaping too wide, of shewing him selfe greeued at the speakers wordes, and of all those thinges whereby you may either amaze him that spekeath, or els seeme to bee wearie of his talke. I will not, I say, speake of these thinges, for I should but make a recitall of *Galatee*,[1] and those bookes, whiche the morall Philosophers and Rhetoritians haue written vppon this matter. These are thinges whiche are

1. Giovanni della Casa's *Galateus* (tr. as *Galateo*), a treatise on manners.

learned, not so muche by readyng, as by vsing company, for when an other speaketh, wee marke what liketh and what disliketh, and by that wee knowe what we ought to auoyde and what to followe: as when wee our selues speake, and that wee see some of the hearers litle attentiue, or some other way to vse some yll behauiour, wee learne by his inciuilitie how we ought to behaue our selues in hearing others. It shall suffice then to say for this time, that touching this action, wee must frame all the bodie in suche sort, that it seeme neither to bee of one whole immooueable lumpe, neither yet to bee altogether loosely disioynted.

Guaz. That is, wee must imitate those which neither Saintlike are too ceremonious, neither Iugglerlike are too quicke and too full of action.

Annib. Just. But aboue all, it behooueth him, which by his action is willing to mooue an other, to feele first some motions in him selfe, and to drawe foorth the affections of his heart, in suche sort, that the hearers seeing them shew without the eyes, may be mooued by the verie countenance of him that speaketh.

Guaz. This same in my iudgement is one of the best and necessariest aduertisementes which you haue hythervnto giuen: for that the ende of the speaker, being to stirre vp the affections of others, hee ought to take paine in it. And it can not be that you shoulde bee sorowfull for my mishap, if while I recount it vnto you, you perceiue not me to be sorowfull. Neither can I possibly wring the teares from your eyes, vnlesse I first wipe them from mine owne.

George Pettie

The Civile Conuersation of M. Steeven Guazzo (1581)

DANCING

IT is diligently to be noted that the associatinge of man and woman in daunsing, they bothe obseruinge one nombre and tyme in their meuynges, was nat begonne without a speciall consideration, as well for the necessarye coniunction of those two persones, as for the intimation of sondry vertues, whiche be by them represented. And for as moche as by the associacion of a man and woman in daunsinge may by signified matrimonie, I coulde in declarynge the dignitie and commoditie of that sacrament make intiere volumes, if it were nat so communely knowen to all men, that almoste euery frere lymitour carieth it writen in his bosome. Wherfore, lest in repetyng a thinge so frequent and commune my boke shulde be as fastidious or fulsome to the reders as suche marchaunt preachours be nowe to their custumers, I wyll reuerently take my leue of diuines. And for my parte I wyll endeuour my selfe to assemble, out of the bokes of auncient poets and philosophers, mateř as well apte to my purpose as also newe or at the lest waies infrequent, or seldome herde of them that haue nat radde very many autours in greke and latine.

But nowe to my purpose. In euery daunse, of a moste auncient custome, there daunseth to gether a man and a woman, holding eche other by the hande or the arme, which betokeneth concorde. Nowe it behouethe the daunsers and also the beholders of them to knowe all qualities incident to a man, and also all qualities to a woman lyke wyse appertaynynge.

A man in his naturall perfection is fiers, hardy, stronge in opinion, couaitous of glorie, desirous of knowledge, appetityng by generation to brynge forthe his semblable. The good nature of a woman is to be milde, timerouse, tractable, benigne, of sure remembrance, and shamfast. Diuers other

frere lymitour] friar licensed to beg within certain limited areas

qualities of eche of them mought be founde out, but these be moste apparaunt, and for this time sufficient.

Wherfore, whan we beholde a man and woman daunsinge to gether, let us suppose there to be a concorde of all the saide qualities, beinge ioyned to gether, as I haue set them in ordre And the meuing of the man wolde be more vehement, of the woman more delicate, and with lasse aduancing of the body signifienge the courage and strenthe that oughte to be in a man and the pleasant sobrenesse that shulde be in a woman And in this wise *fiersenesse* ioyned with *mildenesse* maketh *Seueritie*; *Audacitie* with *timerositie* maketh *Magnanimitie* wilfull opinion and *Tractabilitie* (which is to be shortly persuaded and meued) makethe *Constance* a vertue; *Couaitise* of *Glorie*, adourned with *benignitie* causeth honour; *desire of knowlege* with *sure remembrance* procureth *Sapience*; *Shamfastnes* ioyned to *Appetite of generation* maketh *Continence* whiche is a meane betwene *Chastitie* and *inordinate luste*. These qualities, in this wise beinge knitte to gether, and signified in the personages of man and woman daunsinge, to expresse or sette out the figure of very nobilitie; whiche in the higher astate it is contained, the more excellent is the vertue in estimation.

Sir Thomas Elyot

The Boke named the Gouernour (1531)

LOVE

I SAYE therefore that accordinge as it is defined of the wise menn of olde time, *Loue is nothinge elles but a certein coueting to enioy beawtie*, and forsomuch as *coueting* longeth for nothinge, but for thinges knowen, it is requisite that knowleage go euermore before couetinge, which of his owne nature willeth the good, but of him self is blind, and knoweth it not. Therfore hath nature so ordeined, that to euery vertue of knowleag ther is annexed a vertue of longing. And bicause in oure soule there be three maner wayes to know, namelye, by sense, reason, and vnderstandinge: of sense, there arriseth appetite or longinge, which is commune to vs with brute beastes: of reason arriseth election or choise, which is proper to man: of vnderstanding, by the which man may be partner with Aungelles, arriseth will. Euen as therfore the sense knoweth not but sensible matters and that which may be felt, so the appetyte or *couetinge* onlye desireth the same: and euen as the vnderstanding is bent but to bechouldc thinges that may be vnderstoode, so is that wil only fead with spirituall gooddes. Man of nature indowed with reason, placed (as it were) in the middle beetwene these two extremities, may through his choise inclinynge to sense, or reachynge to vnderstandynge, come nigh to the *couetinge* sometime of the one somtime of the other part. In these sortes therfore may *beawtie be coueted*, the general name wherof may be applied to al thinges, eyther naturall or artificiall, that are framed in good proportion, and due tempre, as their nature beareth. But speakynge of the *beawtie* that we meane, which is onlie it, that appeereth in bodies, and especially in the face of mann, and moueth thys feruent *couetinge* which we call *Loue*, we will terme it *an influence of the heauenlie bountifulness*, the whiche for all it stretcheth ouer all thynges that be created (like the light of the Sonn) yet whan it findeth out a face well proportioned, and framed with a certein liuelie agreement of seuerall colours, and set furth with lightes and shadowes, and with an orderly distaunce and limites of lines, therinto it distilleth it self and appeereth most welfauoured, and decketh out and lyghtneth the subiect where it shyneth wyth a marueylous grace and glistringe (like the Sonne beames that strike against beawtifull plate of fine golde wrought and sett wyth precyous iewelles) so that it draweth vnto it mens eyes with pleasure, and percing through them imprinteth him selfe in the soule, and wyth an vnwonted sweetenesse all to stirreth her and delyteth, and settynge her on fire maketh her to couett him. Whan the soule then is taken wyth *couetynge to enioye thys beawtie* as a good thynge, in case she suffre her selfe to be guyded with the iudgement of sense, she falleth into most deepe erroures, and iudgeth the bodie in whyche *Beawtye* is descerned, to be the principall cause thereof: wherupon to enioye it, she reckeneth it necessarye to ioigne as inwardlye as she can wyth that bodye, whyche is false: and therefore who so thynketh in possessynge the bodye to inioye *beawtie*, he is farr deceiued, and is moued to it, not wyth true knowleage by the choise of reason, but wyth false opinyon by the longinge of sense. Wherupon the pleasure that foloweth it, is also false and of necessytye full of erroures. And therefore into one of the two vyces renn all those louers that satisfye theyr vnhonest lustes with the women whom they loue: For eyther assone as they be come to the coueted ende, they not onely feele a fulnesse and lothesomnesse, but also conceyue a hatred against the wyght beloued, as thoughe longinge repented hym of hys offence and acknowleaged the deceite wrought hym by the false iudgement of sense, that made hym beleaue the yll to be good: or elles they contynue in the verye same couetynge and greedynesse, as thoughe they were not in deede come to the ende, whyche they sought for. And albeit throughe the blynde opynyon that hath made them dronken (to their seeminge) in that instante they feele a contentation, as the deseased otherwhile, that dreame they drinke of some cleare spring, yet be they not satisfied, nor leaue of so. And bicause of possessing coueted goodnes there arriseth alwayes quietnesse and satisfaction in the possessors minde, in case this were the true and righte end of their couetinge, whan they possesse it they would be at quietnesse and throughlye satisfied, whiche they be not: but rather deceyued through that likenesse, they furthwith retourn again to vnbridled couetinge, and with the very same trouble which they felt at the first, they fall again into the raginge and most burninge thirst of the thinge, that they hope in vaine to possesse perfectlye. These kind of louers therefore loue most vnluckely, for eyther they neuer comebye their couetinges, which is a great vnluckinesse: or elles if they do comebye them, they finde they comebye their hurt, and ende their myseryes with other greater miseries, for both in the beginninge and middle of this loue, there is neuer other thinge felt, but afflictions, tourmentes, greefes, pining, trauaile, so that to be wann, vexed with continuall teares, and sighes, to lyue with a discontented minde, to be alwaies dumbe, or to lament, to couet death, in conclusion to be most vnlucky are the propreties which (they saye) beelonge to louers. The cause therfore of this wretchednesse in mens mindes, is principally *sense*, whiche in youthfull age bereth moste swey, bicause the lustinesse of the fleshe and of the bloode, in that season addeth vnto him euen so much force, as it withdraweth from reason: therfore doeth it easelye traine the soule to folowe appetite or longinge, for when she seeth her selfe drowned in the earthly prison, bicause she is sett in the office to gouern the body, she can not of her self vnderstand plainly at the first the truth of spirituall behouldinge. Wherfore to compasse the vnderstanding of thinges, she must go begg the beginning at the senses, and therfore she beleaueth them, and giueth ear to them, and is contented to be lead by them, especiallye whan they haue so much courage, that (in a maner) they enforce her and bicause they be deceitfull they fyll her with errours and false opinions. Wherupon most communlye it happeneth, that yonge men be wrapped in this sensual loue, which is a very rebell against reason, and therefore thei make them selues vnwoorthy to enioy the fauoures and benefites, which loue bestoweth vpon his true subiectes, neither in loue feele they any other pleasures, then what beastes without reason do, but much more greuous afflictions. Setting case therfore this to be so, which is most true, I say, that the contrary chaunseth to them of a more ripe age. For in case they, whan the soule is not nowe so much wayed downe with the bodyly burdein, and when the naturall burning asswageth and draweth to a warmeth, if thei be inflamed with beawty, and to it bend their coueting guided by reasonable choise, they be not deceiued, and possesse beawtye perfectly, and therefor through the possessing of it, alwaies goodnes ensueth to them; bicause beauty is good and consequently the true loue of it is most good and holy, and euermore bringeth furth good frutes in the soules of them, that with the bridle of reason restraine the yll disposition of sense, the which old men can much sooner do then yong. Yt is not therfore out of reason to say, that olde men may also loue without sclaunder and more happily, then yong men: taking notwithstanding this name *Olde*, not for the age at the pittes brincke, nor when the canelles of the body be so feble, that the soule can not through them worke her feates, but when knowleage in vs is in his right strength. And I wil not also hide this from you: namely, that I suppose, where sensuall loue in euery age is naught, yet in yonge men it deserueth excuse, and perhappes in some case lefull: for although it putteth them in afflictions, daungeres, trauailes, and the vnfortunatenes that is said, yet are there many that to winne them the good will of their Ladies practise vertuous thinges, which for all they be not bent to a good end, yet are they good of them selues, and so of that much bitternesse they pike out a litle sweetnesse, and through the aduersities which they susteine, in the ende they acknowleage their errour. As I iudge therfore those yong men that bridle their appetites, and loue with reason, to be godlye: so do I houlde excused suche as yelde to sensuall loue, wherunto they be so inclined through

canelles] channels   *lefull*] lawful

the weakenesse and frailtie of man: so they showe therin meekenesse, courtesie, and prowesse, and the other worthie condicions that these Lordes haue spoken of, and whan those youthfull yeeres be gone and past, leaue it of cleane, keapinge alouf from this sensuall couetinge as from the lowermost steppe of the stayers, by the whiche a man may ascende to true loue. But in case after they drawe in yeeres once they reserue still in their colde hart the fire of appetites, and brynge stoute reason in subiection to feeble sense, it can not bee said how much they are to be blamed: for lyke men without sense they deserue with an euerlastinge shame to be put in the numbre of vnreasonable liuing creatures, bicause the thoughtes and wayes of sensuall loue be farr unfittinge for ripe age.

Sir Thomas Hoby
The Courtyer of Count Baldesar Castilio (1561)

A FOOLISH LOVER

THIS Ieronimo you knew him well fat slaue, cherrie cheeked, faire and well liking, merry, with a slicke face, pleasant disposed, and a tratling companion: Now he is leane, wan, pale, looking like one halfe dead, weake, vgly, dreaming, louing to be alone, and cares for no bodies company: so that none of those that had seene him before, could now knowe him againe.

O the poore and wretched yoong man! Of what proceeds his griefe?

Of loue.

Of loue? Tell troth.

Now he is mad: he is foolish: oftentimes he walketh alone.

tratling] tattling

but will neuer speake to any bodie: alwaies mumbling or recording some thing in English verse, that he hath made to his sweete-heart and minion.

O caitiffe boye!

One while you shall see him faine a sea of teares, a lake of miseries, wring his hands and weep, accuse the heauen, curse the earth, make an anatomie of his heart, to freeze, to burne, to adore, to plaie the Idolater, to admire, to faine heauens, to forge hels, to counterfait Sisyphus, to play the Tantalus, to represent Titius Tragedie. And by and by he exalteth in his verse, that Diana whom he loueth best: her haire is nothing but gold wire, her browes arches and vautes of Ebenus: her eies twinckling starres like Castor and Pollux, her lookes lightnings: her mouth Corall: her necke Orient-Pearle: her breath Baulme, Amber, and Muske: her throat of snow: her necke milke-white: her dugs that she hath on her brest, Mountains or Apples of Alablaster. All the rest of her body is but a prodigalitie and treasure of heauen and of nature, that she had reserued to work the perfection of his mistres and dear.

Tis great danger least he fall beside himselfe in the end.

O the poore passionate is cruelly eclipsed! One while you shall see him drownd in teares and lamentations, to make the aire eccho with his sighs, complaints, murmurings, rages, imprecations: otherwhiles if he haue got but a glaunce of his goddesse, you shall see him gay, glistering like an Emerawd, and pleasant, sometime you shall see him crosse, passe and repasse fiue or six times a day through a street that he may haue but one friendly looke of her eye that he loueth best.

What will you giue me if I shoew you a letter that he wrot to his sweet-hart.

I pray thee my minion do me this fauour that I may see it.

I will read it out aloud, hearken.

Mistresse your beautie is so excellent, so singular, so

celestiall, that I beleeue Nature hath bestowed it on you as a
sampler to shew how much she can do when she will imploy
her full power and best skill. All that is in your selfe is but
honie, is but sugar, is but heauenly ambrosia. It was to you to
whom Paris should haue iudged the golden apple, not to
Venus, no, nor to Iuno, nor to Minerua, for neuer was there
so great magnificence in Iuno, so great wisedome in Minerua,
so great beautie in Venus, as in you. O heauens, gods and
goddesses, happie shall he be to whom you grant the fauour
to col you, to kisse you, and to lie with you. I cannot tell
whether I am predestinated by the Fairies, wherefore I commend me to your good grace, and kissing your white hands,
humbly I take my leaue without Adieu.

John Eliot

Ortho-Epia Gallica (1593)

MARRIAGE IN UTOPIA

FURTHERMORE in cheusynge wyfes and husbandes they obserue earnestly and straytelye a custome whiche semed to vs
very fonde and folysh. For a sad and an honest matrone shew-
eth the woman, be she maide or widdowe, naked to the
wower. And lykewyse a sage and discrete man exhibyteth the
wower naked to the woman. At this custome we laughed,
and disalowed it as foolyshe. But they on the other part doo
greatlye wonder at the follye of all other nations, whyche in
byinge a colte, where as a lytle money is in hassarde, be so
charye and circumspecte, that though he be almoste all bare,
yet they wyll not bye hym, oneles the saddel and all the
harneys be taken of, leaste vnder those couerynges be hydde
som galle or soore. And yet in chewsynge a wyfe, whyche
shalbe either pleasure or dyspleasure to them all theire lyfe

col] neck, hug   *wower*] wooer

after, they be so recheles, that al the resydewe of the woomans bodye beinge couered with cloothes, they esteme her scaselye be one handebredeth (for they can se no more but her face) and so do ioyne her to them not without greate ieoperdie of euell agreing together, if any thynge in her body afterwarde should chaunce to offend and myslyke them. For all man be not so wyse as to haue respecte to the vertuous condicions of the partie. And the endowmentes of the bodye cause the vertues of the mynde more to be estemed and regarded: yea euen in the mariages of wyse men. Verely so fowle deformitie maye be hydde under thoes coueringes, that it maye quite alienate and take awaye the mans mynde from his wyfe, when it shal not be lawfull for their bodies to be seperate agayne. If suche deformitie happen by any chaunce after the mariage is consummate and finyshed: well, there is no remedie but patience. Euery man muste take his fortune wel a worthe. But it were wel done that a lawe were made wherebye all suche deceytes myghte be eschewed, and aduoyded before hand.

Raphe Robynson

A Fruteful and Pleasaunt Worke . . . of the New Yle called Utopia (1551)
translated from the Latin of Sir Thomas More's *Utopia* (1516)

DISCONTENTED WIFE

NOW if to these greeuous and insupportable behauiours, we shall adde the heauie crosses of their continuall alarums of discontentments and brawles; why then these be ordinarily the crosses of these miserable men: and these iangling peales do they ring continually vnto them.

Well (saith Dame *Parnell*) yet happie is such a Gentlewoman, for she hath a husband that maketh much of her indeed: O what a fine gowne she had vpon her this morning, the very lace and fringe about it, is worth more then any three of the best that euer I yet wore, since I was first borne: And what rich iewels and great orient pearle had shee about her necke? but her Rings, her Girdle, her Purse, her rich Furres, so sweetely perfumed, they past, and were the richest of all that euer I saw. Well may she shew her selfe amongst the proudest, and walke where she pleaseth, not a litle vnto her credit: but I poore soule, cannot with mine honor looke out of doores, nor suffer any to come and visit me, so much am I fallen out of reparations, for want of good apparell. Besides, happie is my Lady such a one, for she is vsed with all respect and compliments, of Courtly ceremonies, befitting a right wife, where I am scarce made account of as they doo a common seruant, for she may goe abroade here and there as best liketh her, without needing either to giue account where she hath bin, or asking any leaue to take her pleasure: whilest I all the day long sit wearing out my fingers ends with sowing and working, as if I were a litle gyrle set to my taske, or else like a base skullion, must attend on my kitchinstuffe and cookerie in the Kitchin, and scarce can I go to Church to serue God, but that at my returne, I am so baited at, that a dogge would neuer endure such a life as I do. But what want all the rest of my neighbours and kindred? Marrie nothing at all, they can but aske and haue: but demand and straight it is brought vnto them. For haue not they all their houses furnished with all such stuffe as is requisite for the same? haue they not Gentlemen to attend vpon them, wayting women to follow them? haue they not theyr Coches, to take the aire when they list? and may they not, if they so like, go for their recreation vnto their gardens of pleasure, and banquetting houses in the Summer time? yes, yes, they haue but what they will. But I (I thinke I am accurst) what haue I? what want I? who attends on me? and what followers haue I? where are my seruants? nay rather vnto whom am not I a seruant? Well well I say no more, I see there is not any woman in al our Citie worse vsed then I am, so I am, and yet I know no reason why I should be thus dealt withall: for though I say it my selfe that should not say so, I am as young as they are, as well fauoured as they, as well borne and as rich: nay then I will say more then I euer thought to haue done: They haue many faultes that I haue not, and want those good qualities that I enjoy: I by Gods body do they want them, that they do.

And hauing so said, and wringing out two or three little little tinie teares (and those God he knoweth with much ado) they begin a fresh skirmish as their fashion is, and proceed with theyr second peale of rayling in this sort.

But it is no matter; for I must needs say, I haue rightly deserued to be vsed thus, and worse too if it were possible; seeing I haue plaid the foole so grosely as I haue done, who might haue married with such a Noble man, and with such a Countie, and such a Cauellier would very faine haue had me, if I had bene willing, all these three being the brauest and gallantest Gentlemen of all our Citie: and yet like a beast as I was (I thinke I was bewitcht, that I was) I woulde haue none of them, onely because I woulde match with him that knoweth not how to vse such a one as I am according vnto my estate and woorthinesse.

And thus talking idlely and going from one vaine and tedious discourse vnto an other, shee concludeth at the last, that thou art not scarce worthie to wipe her shooes, and that the very dust and filth that commeth out of her fathers house, is more woorth then all thy reuenewes, and all the money thou spendest for house-keeping in thy house.

Robert Tofte

Of Mariage and Wiuing (1599). Translated
from the Italian of Ercole Tasso

Countie] Count

MAN AND BEAST

PRESUMPTION is our naturall and originall infirmitie. *Of all creatures man is the most miserable and fraile, and therewithall the proudest and disdainfullest.* Who perceiueth and seeth himselfe placed here, amidst their filth and mire of the world, fast tied and nailed to the worst, most senselesse, and drooping part of the world, in the vilest corner of the house, and farthest from heauens coape, with those creatures, that are the worst of the three conditions; and yet dareth imaginarily place himselfe aboue the circle of the Moone, and reduce heauen vnder his feet. It is through the vanity of the same imagination, that he dare equall himselfe to God, that he ascribeth diuine conditions vnto himselfe, that he selecteth and separateth himselfe from out the ranke of other creatures; to which his fellow-brethren and compeers, he cuts out and shareth their parts, and allotteth them what portions of meanes or forces he thinkes good. How knoweth he by the vertue of his vnderstanding the inward and secret motions of beasts? By what comparison from them to vs doth he conclude the brutish-nesse, he ascribeth vnto them? When I am playing with my Cat, who knowes whether she haue more sport in dallying with me, than I haue in gaming with her? We entertaine one another with mutuall apish trickes, If I haue my houre to begin or to refuse, so hath she hers. *Plato* in setting forth the golden age vnder *Saturne*, amongst the chiefe aduantages that man had then, reporteth the communication he had with beasts, of whom enquiring and taking instruction, he knew the true qualities, and differences of euery one of them: by, and from whom he got an absolute vnderstanding and perfect wisedome, whereby he led a happier life than we can doe. Can we haue a better proofe to iudge of mans impudency, touching beasts? This notable Author was of opinion, that in the greatest part of the corporall forme, which nature hath bestowed on them, she hath onely respected the vse of the Prognostications, which in his daies were thereby gathered. That defect which hindreth the communication betweene them and vs, why may it not as well be in vs, as in them? It is a matter of diuination to guesse in whom the fault is, that we vnderstand not one another. For, we vnderstand them no more then they vs. By the same reason, may they as well esteeme vs beasts, as we them. It is no great maruell if we vnderstand them not: no more doe we the Cornish, the Welch, or Irish. Yet haue some boasted that they vnderstood them, as *Apollonius Thyaneus, Melampus, Tiresias, Thales* and others. And if it be (as Cosmographers report) that there are Nations, who receiue and admit a Dogge to be their King, it must necessarily follow, that they giue a certaine interpretation to his voice and mouing. We must note the parity that is between vs. We haue some meane vnderstanding of their senses, so haue beasts of ours, about the same measure. They flatter and faune vpon vs, they threat, and entreat vs, so doe we them. Touching other matters, we manifestly perceiue, that there is a full and perfect communication amongst them, and that not onely those of one same kinde vnderstand one another, but euen such as are of different kindes.

John Florio
The Essayes of Michael, Lord of Montaigne (1603)

CLOTHES

MEE thinkes this same Vanity of cloathes hath done Vertue wrong, for wee discry great men as much by their cloathes as action, which is very improper. For we allow not houses by their plaistering and gainesse, but by their roomes and conueniency. Hath it not also weakened our best force and made vs call in outward helpes? For not of our heades but of our

gainesse] bright colouring

Taylors wee aske aide. Where power languisheth with enter-taining these baudes of pleasure, sedition comes in. For when Pouertie finds her endlesse labours end with powring her gaines into excesse, Mutinie counsailes want against this too much plenty. Thus to these miserable ones speakes a seditious fellow in the *Florentine* state, "Strip vs all naked (saith he) and you shall perceiue no difference; cloth vs with their garments and they with ours, and doubtles we shall look like noblemen, they looke like vassals; for it is onely Pouerty and riches that makes the disparity betweene vs." It is the lustre of greatnes and yet the most daungerous – daungerous, for it feeds enuie; daungerous, for it makes vs vnapt for any other estate, to which mortalitie being euer subiect should neuer bee vnfit to entertaine it. *Cleopatrae's* misery looked much more deformed, because men's memories could ioyne her present state to the state shee put vpon her when shee would resemble the Goddesse *Isis*. It is like a face vsed to look through a ruffe, when put in a falling band, lookes as if looking through a halter. But this is a common curse vpon greatnesse, that it can nothing so well defend it selfe from misfortune as mis-fortune from fortunate. To become great of little indures much better then to become little of great. I cannot thinke it a lawfull excuse to say, "The minde still aimes vpward." No, the minde of Vertue is still it selfe; and is it selfe, let fortune's Arithmetick be either adding or subtracting. Shee can ioyne no more earth to her then the body, and rather would shee bee rid of that then receiue more. It is disputable whether these robes of greatnesse should at all bee allowed, but to bee in them alwayes, without question, is disallowed. There are some that can see and not iudge. Know these. It is necessary for greatnes to shew them somewhat which they may vnder-stand. Now for the light changes of attire – mee thinkes they go like a singing catch; some are beginning when others are ending, others in the middest when another begins againe.

Let another bee absent from this mint and without the discipline of a Taylor but a few monthes, and at his next appearance, his friends shall not know whether hee bee a man or a Ghost of times past or a spirite mouing a Westminster Statue. They money-masters haue not ingrossed all vanitie though they haue money; for these people haue a chaunge where to bee out of fashion is to bee banquerupt; and as the one's billes are protested, so the other's discretion. This is not to haue a head but a Hatte buttond vp on the side. It is no matter what soule, so a body in fashion, of which, though I doe dispise it enough, yet I wish it no other mischiefe then the painter's Shoppe, where a picture of seauen yeares since lookes more like an Anticke Dauncer than a man. But thus shall I bee if I speake more of them, for I draw them, and Time drawes them, out of fashion, and they, if I lay any more holde on them, draw mee.

But now the motions of man, by reason of his reason called Actions – what an Ecclipse doe they suffer with Vanitie's darke body getting betweene them and the cleanesse of reason?

Sir William Cornwallis

Essayes (1601)

Of Studies

Studies serue for Delight, for Ornament, and for Ability. Their Chiefe Vse for Delight, is in Priuatenesse and Retiring; For Ornament, is in Discourse; And for Ability, is in the Iudgement and Disposition of Businesse. For Expert Men can Execute, and perhaps Iudge of particulars, one by one; But the generall Counsels, and the Plots, and Marshalling of Affaires, come best from those that are *Learned*. To spend too much Time in *Studies*, is Sloth; To vse them too much for Ornament, is Affectation; To make Iudgement wholly by their Rules is the Humour of a Scholler. They perfect Nature, and are perfected by Experience: For Naturall Abilities, are like Naturall Plants, that need Proyning by *Study*: And *Studies* themselues, doe giue forth Directions too much at Large, except they be bounded in by experience. Crafty Men Contemne *Studies*; Simple Men Admire them; And Wise Men Vse them; For they teach not their owne Vse; But that is a Wisdome without them, and aboue them, won by Obseruation. Reade not to Contradict, and confute; Nor to Beleeue and Take for granted; Nor to Finde Talke and Discourse; But to weigh and Consider. Some *Bookes* are to be Tasted, Others to be Swallowed, and Some Few to be Chewed and Digested: That is, some *Bookes* are to be read onely in Parts; Others to be read but not Curiously; And some Few to be read wholly, and with Diligence and Attention. Some *Bookes* also may be read by Deputy, and Extracts made of them by Others: But that would be, onely in the lesse important Arguments, and the Meaner Sort of *Bookes*: else distilled *Bookes*, are like Common distilled Waters, Flashy Things. Reading maketh a Full Man; Conference a Ready Man; And Writing an Exact Man. And therefore, If a Man Write little, he had need have a Great memory; If he Conferre little, he had need haue a Present wit; And if he Reade litle, he had need haue much Cunning, to seeme to know that, he doth not. *Histories* make Men Wise; *Poets* Witty; The *Mathematicks* Subtill; *Naturall Philosophy* deepe; *Morall* Graue; *Logick* and *Rhetorick* Able to Contend. *Abeunt studia in Mores.* Nay there is no Stond or Impediment in the Wit, but may be wrought out by Fit *Studies*: Like as Diseases of the Body, may haue Appropriate Exercises. Bowling is good for the Stone and Reines; Shooting for the Lungs and Breast; Gentle Walking for the Stomacke; Riding for the Head; And the Like. So if a Mans Wit be Wandring, let him Study the *Mathematicks*; For in Demonstrations, if his Wit be called away neuer so

little, he must begin again: If his Wit be not Apt to distinguish
or find differences, let him *Study* the *Schoole-men*; For they are
Cymini sectores. If he be not Apt to beat ouer Matters, and to
call vp one Thing, to Proue and Illustrate another, let him
Study the *Lawyers Cases*: So euery Defect of the Minde, may
haue a Speciall Receit.

Francis Bacon

Essayes . . . (1597). Text from the enlarged edition of 1625

HOW TO BEHAVE AT THE THEATRE

PRESENT not your selfe on the Stage (especially at a new play)
vntill the quaking prologue hath (by rubbing) got cullor into
his checkes, and is ready to giue the trumpets their Cue that
hees vpon point to enter: for then it is time, as though you
were one of the *Properties*, or that you dropt out of the
Hangings, to creepe from behind the Arras, with your *Tripos*
or three-footed stoole in one hand, and a teston mounted
betweene a forefinger and a thumbe in the other: for if you
should bestow your person vpon the vulgar, when the belly
of the house is but halfe full, your apparell is quite eaten vp,
the fashion lost, and the proportion of your body in more
danger to be deuoured then if it were serud vp in the Counter
amongst the Powltry: avoid that as you would the Bastome.
It shall crowne you with rich commendation to laugh alowd
in the middest of the most serious and saddest scene of the
terriblest Tragedy: and to let that clapper (your tongue) be
tost so high, that all the house may ring of it: your Lords vse
it; your Knights are Apes to the Lords, and do so too: your
Inne-a-court-man is Zany to the Knights, and (marry very
scuruily) comes likewise limping after it: be thou a beagle to

teston] sixpence   *Bastome*] cudgel
Counter . . . Powltry] a prison in the Poultry, a street near Cheapside

them all, and neuer lin snuffing till you haue sented them: for by talking and laughing (like a Plough-man in a Morris) you heap *Pelion* vpon *Ossa*, glory vpon glory: As first, all the eyes in the galleries will leaue walking after the Players, and onely follow you: the simplest dolt in the house snatches vp your name, and when he meetes you in the streetes, or that you fall into his hands in the middle of a Watch, his word shall be taken for you, heele cry, *Hees such a gallant*, and you passe. Secondly, you publish your temperance to the world, in that you seeme not to resort thither to taste vaine pleasures with a hungrie appetite, but onely as a Gentleman, to spend a foolish houre or two, because you can doe nothing else. Thirdly you mightily disrelish the Audience, and disgrace the Author: marry, you take vp (though it be at the worst hand) a strong opinion of your owne iudgement and inforce the Poet to take pity of your weakenesse, and, by some dedicated sonnet, to bring you into a better paradice, onely to stop your mouth. Now Sir, if the writer be a fellow that hath either epigramd you, or hath had a flirt at your mistris, or hath brought either your feather or your red beard, or your little legs &c. on the stage, you shall disgrace him worse then by tossing him in a blancket, or giuing him the bastinado in a Tauerne, if in the middle of his play, (bee it Pastorall or Comedy, Morall or Tragedie) you rise with a screud and discontented face from your stoole to be gone: no matter whether the Scenes be good or no, the better they are the worse do you distast them: and, beeing on your feete, sneake not away like a coward, but salute all your gentle acquaintance, that are spred either on the rushes, or on stooles about you, and draw what troope you can from the stage after you: the *Mimicks* are beholden to you, for allowing them elbow roome: their Poet cries, perhaps, a pox go with you, but care not for that, theres no musick without frets.

lin] leave off

87

Mary if either the company, or indisposition of the weather binde you to sit it out, my counsell is then that you turne plain Ape, take vp a rush, and tickle the earnest eares of your fellow gallants, to make other fooles fall a laughing: mewe at passionate speeches, blare at merrie, finde fault with the musicke, whew at the childrens Action, whistle at the songs: and aboue all, curse the sharers, that whereas the same day you had bestowed forty shillings on an embrodered Felt and Feather, (Scotch-fashion) for your mistres in the Court, or your punck in the Cittie, within two houres after, you encounter with the very same block on the stage, when the haberdasher swore to you the impression was extant but that morning.

Thomas Dekker

The Guls Horne-Booke (1609)

In Praise of Tobacco

TABACCO that excellent plant, the vse whereof (as of fift element) the world cannot want, is that little shop of Nature, wherein her whole workeman-ship is abridg'd, where you may see Earth kindled into fire, the fire breath out an exhalation which entring in at the mouth walkes through the Regions of a mans brayne, driues out all ill Vapours but itselfe, drawes downe all bad Humours by the mouth, which in time might breed a Scabbe ouer the whole body if already they haue not; a plant of singular vse, for on the one side, Nature being an Enemie to Vacuitie and emptines, and on the other, there beeing so many empty braynes in the World as there are, how shall Natures course be continued? How shall thiese empty braines be filled, but with ayre, Natures immediate instrument to that purpose? If with ayre, what so proper as your fume: what fume so healthfull as your perfume? what

perfume so soueraigne as Tabacco? Besides the excellent edge
it giues a mans wit, (as they can best iudge that haue been
present at a feast of Tabacco where commonly all good Witts
are consorted) what varietie of discourse it begetts? What
sparkes of wit it yeelds, it is a world to heare: as likewise
to the courage of a man ... To conclude as there is no enemy
to Tabacco but Garlick, so there is no friend to Garlick but a
sheeps head and so I conclude.

George Chapman

Monsieur D'Olive (1606)

AGAINST TOBACCO

AND for the vanities committed in this filthie custome, is it
not both great vanitie and vncleanenesse, that at the table, a
place of respect, of cleanlinesse, of modestie, men should not
be ashamed, to sit tossing of *Tobacco pipes*, and puffing of the
smoke of *Tobacco* one to another, making the filthy smoke
and stinke thereof, to exhale athwart the dishes, and infect
the aire, when very often, men that abhorre it are at their
repast? Surely Smoke becomes a kitchin far better then a
Dining chamber, and yet it makes a kitchin also oftentimes
in the inward parts of men, soiling and infecting them, with
an vnctuous and oily kinde of Soote, as hath bene found in
some great *Tobacco* takers, that after their death were opened.
And not onely meate time, but no other time nor action is
exempted from the publicke vse of this vnciuill tricke: so as
if the wiues of *Diepe* list to contest with this Nation for good
maners their worst maners would in all reason be found at
least not so dishonest (as ours are) in this point. The publike
vse whereof, at all times, and in all places, hath now so farre
preuailed, as diuers men very sound both in iudgement, and
complexion, haue bene at last forced to take it also without

desire, partly because they were ashamed to seeme singular, (like the two Philosophers that were forced to duck themselues in that raine water, and so become fooles aswell as the rest of the people) and partly, to be as one that was content to eate Garlicke (which hee did not loue) that he might not be troubled with the smell of it, in the breath of his fellowes. And is it not a great vanitie, that a man cannot heartily welcome his friend now, but straight they must bee in hand with *Tobacco*? No it is become in place of a cure, a point of good fellowship, and he that will refuse to take a pipe of *Tobacco* among his fellowes, (though by his own election he would rather feele the sauour of a Sinke) is accounted peeuish and no good company, euen as they doe with tippeling in the cold Easterne Countries. Yea the Mistresse cannot in a more manerly kinde, entertaine her seruant, then by giuing him out of her faire hand a pipe of *Tobacco*. But herein is not onely a great vanitie, but a great contempt of Gods good giftes, that the sweetenesse of mans breath, being a good gift of God, should be willfully corrupted by this stinking smoke, wherein I must confesse, it hath too strong a vertue: and so that which is an ornament of nature, and can neither by an artifice be at the first acquired, nor once lost, be recouered againe, shall be filthily corrupted with an incurable stinke, which vile qualitie is as directly contrary to that wrong opinion which is holden of the wholesomnesse thereof, as the venime of putrifaction is contrary to the vertue Preseruatiue.

Moreouer, which is a great iniquitie, and against all humanitie, the husband shall not bee ashamed, to reduce thereby his delicate, wholesome, and cleane complexioned wife, to that extremitie, that either shee must also corrupt her sweete breath therewith, or else resolute to liue in a perpetuall stinking torment.

Haue you not reason then to bee ashamed, and to forbeare this filthie noueltie, so basely grounded, so foolishly receiued and so grossely mistaken in the right vse thereof? In your abuse thereof sinning against God, harming your selues both in persons and goods, and taking also thereby the markes and notes of vanitie vpon you: by the custome thereof making your selues to be wondered at by all forraine ciuil Nations, and by all strangers that come among you, to be scorned and contemned. A custome lothsome to the eye, hatefull to the Nose, harmefull to the braine, dangerous to the Lungs, and in the blacke stinking fume thereof, neerest resembling the horrible Stigian smoke of the pit that is bottomelesse.

James I

A Counterblaste to Tobacco (1604)

TRAJAN

WHERFORE (most noble Traian) thou mayst well be called the patterne of all princely qualities, comely, bountiful, martial, mercifull, a louer of learning, moderate in priuate expences, magnificent in publike, most goodly of stature, amiable, not onely in thy vertues, but euen in thy vices. For to say the worst was euer said of thee, these were all thy faults, ambition, or desyir of glorie in warres, loue of women, and persecuting of religion ... To which thus I aunswer without a fee, but with all my heart: that thy ambition was so honorable, and thy warlicke humour so well tempered, that thou didst truly witnesse of thy selfe, that thou didst neuer enuy any mans honour, for the confidence thou haddest of thine owne worth: and all the world can witnesse, that thou neuer didst make vniust warre, nor refuse anie iust or indifferent peace. For that same sweet sinne of lecherie, I would say as the Frier sayd, a young man and a young woman in a greene arber in a May morning; if God do not forgiue it, I would. For as Sir *Thomas More* saith of *Edward* the fourth: he was subiect to a sin, from which health of bodie in great prosperitie of fortune, without a speciall grace, hardly refrayneth. And to speake vprightly of him, his lusts were not furious, but friendly, able with his goodly person, his sweete behauiour, and his bountifull gifts, to haue won *Lucretia*. Besides, no doubt his sinne was the lesse, in that he euer loued his wife most dearely, and vsed her most respectiuely: for I haue euer maintained this paradox, it is better to loue two too many, then one too few.

Sir John Harington
The Metamorphosis of Ajax (1596)

MONEY-LENDER

THE Vsurer, seeing the minde of his prisoner preciselye bent to doo his commaunde, openeth his heart vnto him thus.

Gentleman, for that I haue an opinion of your honestye, and truste in your secrecye, I will open vnto you my minde, and according as I find your aunswere, I will shape your deliuerance. Such time as you were at libertie, you know you had acquaintaunce with manye Gentlemen, and they not of the meanest: who at sometimes, as well as yourselfe, were destitute of siluer. Such as those be you must finde out for me. I will delyuer you presentlye: apparayle you in print, giue you money in your pursse, and at such an Ordinarye shall you lye, where the greatest resorte is. Your behauiour and vsage towardes all men must be verye honest; especiallye in all causes looke into the natures of men. If you spie out any one Gentleman pensiue, enter into discourse with him: if you maye perceiue that either by parentage or possession hee is worthie credite, laye holde on him, feede him with money if he want, and (as though it proceeded of your own good nature) profer

respectiuely] with respect
Ordinarye] tavern

him to be bound for him : if he accept your offer, come to me, I will furnish him. Nowe you may deuide the commoditie or the money between you, and out of your part (considering me after the bignesse of the summe) take the rest for your owne fee; which if you looke into, in a yeare will growe vnto no small summe. This is the Load-stone must lead you: and by all meanes you must fashion your selfe to feede humours. This is an honest meanes to lyue by: this is a way to libertie: by this you may pleasure your selfe: and to conclude in dooing this, you maye mightelye in short space inrich me. When you haue found out one fit to your vaine, remember this lesson, that what so euer vauntage you get of him, either for me, or for your self, care not how little paper and inke he can shewe of yours, keepe still your owne stake cleere. In these matters you must be verie circumspect, for there be now a daies such vnderminers start vp, that scarce a man can imagine his owne profit, but they preach it a broad, and laye it open. Thus doo you see whereto you must trust: howe saye you nowe? will you be content to doo this?

The young man aunswereth: Good sir, there is nothing that you haue sayde that by mee shall anie wayes be forgotten. I am readie and willing to put in practise what you haue taught, and no doubt you shall finde me so diligent that your selfe shal say, you were happie in putting me in trust. In briefe the conclusion is this: the vsurer, glad of this new Gentleman broker, dischargeth him, sets him afloate. Now who so braue as our late prisoner, or who so frolicke? The olde sorrowes are forgotten, and new inuentions to cousin possesse the receptacle of his reason. His olde acquaintaunce flocke about him, some reioycing at his recouered libertie, some wondering at his sodaine brauerie, yet few suspecting his pretended and hidden knauerie.

Thomas Lodge

An Alarum against Vsurers . . . (1584)

A School for Authors

(Gabriel Harvey quotes a defender of Thomas Nashe)

WELL, my maisters, you may talke your pleasures of Tom Nash; who yet sleepeth secure, not without preiudice to some, that might be more ielous of their name: but assure your selues, if M. Penniles had not bene deepely plunged in a profound exstasie of knauery, M. Pierce had neuer written that famous worke of Supererogation, that now stayneth all the bookes in Paules-churchyard, and setteth both the vniuersties to schoole. Till I see your finest humanitie bestow such a liberall exhibition of conceit, and courage, vpon your neatest wittes; pardon me though I prefer one smart Pamflet of knauery, before ten blundring volumes of the nine Muses. Dreaming, and smoke amount alike: Life is a gaming, a iugling, a scoulding, a lawing, a skirmishing, a warre; a Comedie, a Tragedy: the sturring witt, a quintessence of quicksiluer; and there is noe dead fleshe in affection, or courage. You may discourse of Hermes ascending spirit; of Orpheus enchanting harpe; of Homers diuine furie; of Tyrtæus enraging trumpet; of Pericles bounsinge thunderclaps; of Platos enthusiasticall rauishment; and I wott not what maruelous egges in mooneshine: but a flye for all your flying speculations, when one good fellow with his odd iestes or one madd knaue with his awke hibber-gibber, is able to putt downe twentye of your smuggest artificiall men, that simper it so nicely, and coylie in their curious pointes. Try, when you meane to be disgraced: and neuer giue me credit, if Sanguine witt putt not Melancholy Arte to bedd. I had almost said, all the figures of Rhetorique must abate me an ace of Pierces Supererogation: and Penniles hath a certayne nimble and climbinge reach of Inuention, as good as a long pole, and a hooke, that neuer fayleth at a pinch. It were

awke] strange *pointes*] figures of rhetoric

vnnaturall, as the sweete Emperour, Marcus Antoninus said, that the fig-tree should euer want iuice. You that purpose with great summes of studdy, and candles to purchase the worshipfull names of Dunses, and Dodipoles, may closely sitt, or sokingly ly at your bookes: but you that intende to be fine companionable gentlemen, smirkinge wittes, and whip-sters in the world, betake yee timely to the liuely practis of the minion profession, and enure your Mercuriall fingers to frame semblable workes of Supererogation. Certes other rules are fopperies: and they that will seeke out the Arch-mistery of the busiest Modernistes, shall find it nether more, nor lesse, than a certayne pragmaticall secret, called Villany, the verie science of sciences, and the Familiar Spirit of Pierces Supererogation. Coosen not your selues with the gay-nothings of children, and schollers: no priuitie of learning, or inspiration of witt, or reuelation of misteryes, or Arte Notory, counteruayleable with Pierces Supererogation: which hauing none of them, hath them all, and can make them all Asses at his pleasure. The Book-worme was neuer but a pick-goose: it is the Multiplying spirit, not of the Alchimist, but of the villanist, that knocketh the naile on the head, and spurreth cutt farther in a day, than the quickest Artist in a weeke. Whiles other are reading, wryting, conferring, argu-ing, discoursing, experimenting, platforminge, musing, buzzing, or I know not what: that is the spirrit, that with a woondrous dexterity shapeth exquisite workes, and atchieu-eth puissant exploites of Supererogation. O my good friends, as ye loue the sweete world, or tender your deare selues, be not vnmindfull what is good for the aduauncement of your commendable partes. All is nothing without aduancement. Though my experience be a Cipher in these causes, yet hauing studiously perused the newe Arte-notory, that is, the foresaid Supererogation; and hauing shaken so many learned

Coosen] delude

asses by the eares, as it were by the hands; I could say no lesse, and might think more.

Gabriel Harvey

Pierces Supererogation (1593)

PIERS PENNILESS AND THE DEVIL

I WAS informde of late dayes, that a certaine blind Retayler called the Diuell, vsed to lend money vpon pawnes, or any thing, and would lette one for a neede haue a thousand poundes vppon a Statute Merchant of his soule: or, if a man plide him thoroughly, would trust him vppon a Bill of his hande, without any more circumstance. Besides, he was noted for a priuy Benefactor to Traitors and Parasites, and to aduance fooles and Asses far sooner than any; to be a greedy pursuer of newes, and so famous a Politician in purchasing, that Hel (which at the beginning was but an obscure Village) is now become a huge Cittie, whereunto all Countries are tributary.

These manifest coniectures of Plentie, assembled in one common-place of abilitie, I determined to clawe Auarice by the elbowe, till his full belly gaue mee a full hande, and lette him bloud with my penne (if it might be) in the veyne of liberalitie: and so (in short time) was this Paper-monster, *Pierce Penilesse* begotten.

But written and all, here lies the question; where shal I finde this olde Asse, that I may deliuer it? Masse, thats true: they say the Lawyers haue the Diuell and all; and it is like enough he is playing Ambodexter amongst them. Fie, fie, the Diuell a driuer in Westminster hall, it can neuer be.

Now, I pray, what doe you imagine him to bee? Perhaps you thinke it is not possible he should bee so graue. Oh then you are in an errour, for hee is as formall as the best Scriuener of them all. Marry, he doth not vse to weare a night-cap, for his hornes will not let him; and yet I know a hundred as well headed as he, that will make a iolly shift with a Court-cup on their crownes, if the weather be colde.

To proceede with my tale: toWestminster hall I went, and made a search of Enquiry, from the black gown to the buckram bagge, if there were any such Sergeant, Bencher, Counsellor, Attorney, or Pettfogger, as *Signior Cornuto Diabolo*, with the good face. But they al (*vna voce*) affirmed, that he was not there: marry, whether he were at the Exchaunge or no, amongst the rich Merchantes, that they could not tell: but it was the likelier of the two, that I should meet with him, or heare of him at the least, in those quarters. I faith, and say you so, quoth I? and Ile bestowe a little labour more, but Ile hunt him out.

Without more circumstance thither came I; and thrusting my selfe, as the manner is, amongst the confusion of languages, I asked (as before) whether he were there extant or no? But from one to another, *Non noui Dæmonem*, was all the answer I could get. At length (as Fortune serued) I lighted vpon an old, stradling Vsurer, clad in a damaske cassocke, edged with Fox fur, a paire of trunke slops, sagging down like a Shoomakers wallet, and a shorte thridbare gown on his backe, fac't with moatheaten budge; vpon his head he wore a filthy, course biggin, and next it a garnish of night-caps, which a sage butten-cap, of the forme of a cow-sheard, ouer spread very orderly: a fat chuffe it was, I remember, with a gray beard cut short to the stumps, as though it were grimde, and a huge, woorme-eaten nose, like a cluster of grapes hanging downewardes. Of him I demaunded if hee could tell me any tidings of the partie I sought for.

By my troth, quoth he, stripling, (and then he cought) I

budge] lambskin   *biggin*] cap

saw him not lately, nor know I certainely where he keepes: but thus much I heard by a Broker, a friend of mine, that hath had some dealings with him in his time, that he is at home sicke of the gout, and will not bee spoken withal vnder more than thou art able to giue, some two or three hundred angels at least, if thou hast anie sute to him: & then parhapes, hele straine curtesie, with his legges in childe-bed, and come forth and talke with thee: but, otherwise, *Non est domi*, hee is busy with *Mammon*, and the prince of the North, how to build vp his kingdome, or sending his sprites abroad to vndermine the maligners of his gouernment.

I, hearing of this cold comfort, tooke my leaue of him verie faintly, and like a carelesse malecontent, that knew not which way to turne, retired me to Paules, to seeke my dinner with Duke *Humfrey*;[1] but, when I came there, the olde souldier was not vp. He is long a rising, thought I, but thats all one, for he that hath no mony in his purse, must go dine with sir Iohn Best-betrust,[2] at the signe of the chalk and the Post.

Two hungry turnes had I scarce fetcht in this wast gallery, when I was encountred by a neat pedantical fellow, in the forme of a Cittizen; who thrusting himselfe abruptly into my companie, like an Intelligencer, began very earnestly to question with me about the cause of my discontent, or what made me so sad, that seemed too yoong to be acquainted with sorrow. I nothing nice to vnfold my estate to any whatsoeuer, discourst to him the whole circumstaunce of my care, and what toyle and paines I had tooke in searching for him that would not be heard of. Why sir (quoth he), had I beene priuie to your purpose before, I could haue easd you of this trauell; for if it be the diuell you seeke for, know I am his man. I pray, sir, how might I call you? A knight of the Post, quoth he, for

1. The supposed tomb of Humphrey, Duke of Gloucester, in St Paul's; those who dined there went without.
2. One who tries to live on credit.

so I am tearmed; a fellowe that will sweare you any thing for twelue pence; but indeed, I am a spirite in nature and essence, that take vpon me this humaine shape, onely to set men together by the eares, and send soules by millions to hell.

Now trust me, a substantiall trade; but when doe you thinke you could send next to your maister? why, euery day: for there is not a cormorant that dies, or Cutpurse that is hanged, but I dispatch letters by his soule to him, and to all my friends in the Low-cuntries: wherefore, if you haue any thing that you would haue transported, giue it me, and I will see it deliuered.

Yes, marry haue I (quoth I) a certaine Supplication here vnto your Maister, which you may peruse if it please you.

Thomas Nashe

Pierce Penilesse His Supplication to the Diuell (1592)

ELIOT'S APOLOGY

To the learned professors of the French tongue

Messires, what newes from Fraunce, can you tell? Still warres, warres. A heauie hearing truly: yet if you be in good health, haue many schollers, get good store of Crowns, and drinke good wine, I doubt not but you shall do well, and I desire the good God of heauen to continue it so still. Haue they had a fruitful vintage in France this yere, or no? me thinks our Bourdeaux wines are very deare, and in good faith I am very sorie for it. But they will bee at a more reasonable reckoning, if these same loftie leaguers would once crouch and come to some good composition. A vengeance of the mutinous race of the deuourers, demogorgons, demi-diuels, who eat vp the poore populace of France. I pray the prince of Paradice to

poure downe his peace priuily vpon them, that we may safelie
fetch their deifiyng liquor, which dieth quickly our flegma-
ticke faces into a pure sanguine complexion. Surely, for my
part, Fraunce I loue well, French-men I hate not, and vnto you
I sweare by *S. Siobe cap de Gascongne*, that I loue a cup of new
Gascon, or old *Orleans* wine, as wel as the best French of you
al: Which loue you must know was ingendered in the sweete
soile of Fraunce, where I piaffed like a bon companion, with a
steele at my girdle, till the Friars (a canker of the curssed
Couent) fell to drawing of naked kniues, and kild indeed the
good king *Henrie* of Fraunce, the more was the pittie. Since
which time I retired my selfe among the merrie muses, and
by the worke of my pen and inke, haue dezinkhornistibulated
a fantasticall Rapsody of dialogisme, to the end that I would
not be found an idle drone among so many famous teachers
and professors of noble languages, who are very busie dayly
in deuising and setting forth new bookes, and instructing our
English gentlemen in this honorable cittie of London: but
after the worthie example of the wise Philosopher *Diogenes*,
who among the Syracusians seeing euery man bestir himselfe,
some to repaire walles, others to new furbish their armes,
some sounding drums, others trumpets, some riding horses,
other trayning soldiors, and al in very great expedition of
warre; least hee should seeme only idle amongst so many
busie-bodies, what doth he good folkes? what doth he? marie
I shall tell you by and by, if you will giue me but a little
leisure; In great vehemencie of spirit he tucketh vp his sleeues,
girdeth close his gowne, chargeth on his shoulders his tunne,
the imperiall pallace, and runneth vp to the toppe of a high
mountaine nere the citie, where in all diligence hee begins to
belabour his roling citie, to set it going, to turne it, ouerturne
it, spurne it, bind it, wind it, twind it, throw it, ouerthrow it,
tumble it, rumble it, iumble it, did ring it, swing it, sling it,

<table>
<tr><td>piaffed] strutted</td><td>couent] convent</td></tr>
</table>

ding it, made it leape, skip, hip, trip, thumpe, iumpe, shake, crake, quake, washt it, swasht it, dasht it, slasht it, naild it, traild it, tipt it, tapt it, rapt it, temperd it, tamperd it, hammerd it, hoopt it, knockt it, rockt it, rubd it, tugd it, lugd it, stopt it, vnstopt it, tied it fast, then losed it againe, rusht it, crusht it, brusht it, pusht it, charmd it, armd it, farmd it, set it on end, laid it along, harnest it, varnest it, burnisht it, furnisht it, stickte it full of feathers, caparrassond it, and rold it amaine from the steepe rocke to the low bottome, ouertakes it, takes it on his shoulder, mounts the hill, and turles it downe agayne with violence, staies it, plaies with it, and fetcheth it a mile from him. Whom when the Siracusians espied, what did they, I pray you? what might they imagine? what could they thinke? did they not laugh at the poore philosophers extreme paines? Go looke if you haue the leisure: and do not blame me, if because I would not be found a loyterer in mine own countrie, among so many vertuously occupied, I haue put my pen to paper: if I haue bene busie, labourd, sweat, dropt, studied, deuised, sought, bought, borrowed, turnd, translated, mined, fined, refined, enterlined, glosed, composed, and taken intollerable toile to shew an easie entrance and introduction to my deare countrimen, in your curious and courtesan French tongue: to the end to aduance them as much as may bee, in the knowledge of all vertuous and noble qualities, to the which they are all naturally addicted. But I pray you be readie quickely to cauill at my booke, I beseech you heartily calumniate my doings with speede, I request you humbly controll my method as soone as you may, I earnestly entreat you hisse at mine inuentions, I desire you to peruse my periodicall punctuations, find fault with my pricke, nicks, and tricks, proue them not worth a pin, not a point, not a pish: argue me a fond, foolish, friuolous and phantasticall author, and persuade euery one that you meet, that my booke is a false, fained, slight, confused, absurd, barbarous, lame, vnperfect, single, vncertaine, childish peece of worke, and not able to teach, and why so? Forsooth because it is not your owne, but an Englishmans doing. Faile you not to do so, if you loue me, and would haue me do the like for you another time.

John Eliot
Ortho-Epia Gallica (1593)

NEUROSIS

THIS for the most part is setled in the spleane, and with his vapours anoyeth the harte and passing vp to the brayne, counterfetteth terrible obiectes to the fantasie, and polluting both the substance, and spirits of the brayne, causeth it without external occasion, to forge monstrous fictions, and terrible to the conceite, which the iudgement taking as they are presented by the disordered instrument, deliuer ouer to the hart, which hath no iudgement of discretion in it self, but giuing credite to the mistaken report of the braine, breaketh out into that inordinate passion, against reason. This commeth to passe, because the instrument of discretion is depraued by these melancholick spirites, and a darknes and cloudes of melancholie vapours rising from that pudle of the splene obscure the clearenes, which our spirites are endued with, and is requisite to the due discretion of outward obiectes. This at the first is not so extreame, neither doth it shew so apparauntly, as in processe of time, when the substance of the brayne hath plentifully drunke of that spleneticke fogge, whereby his nature is become of the same quality, and the pure and bright spirites so defiled, and eclipsed, that their indifferency alike to all sensible thinges, is now drawen to a partiality, and inclination, as by melancholy they are inforced. For where that naturall and internall light is darkened, their fansies arise vayne, false, and voide of ground: euen as in the externall sensible darkenes, a false illusion will appeare vnto our imagination, which the light being brought in is discerned to be an abuse of fancie: now the internall darknes affecting more nigh our nature, then the outward, is cause of greater feares, and more molesteth vs with terror, then that which taketh from vs the sight of sensible thinges: especially arising not of absence of light only, but by a presence of a substantiall obscurity, which is possessed with an actual power of operation: this taking hold of the brayne by processe of time giueth it an habite of depraued conceite, whereby it fancieth not according to truth: but as the nature of that humour leadeth it, altogether gastely and fearefull. This causeth not only phantasticall apparitions wrought by apprehension only of common sense, but fantasie, an other parte of internall sense compoundeth, and forgeth disguised shapes, which giue great terror vnto the heart, and cause it with the liuely spirit to hide it selfe as well as it can, by contraction in all partes, from those counterfet goblins, which the brayne dispossessed of right discerning, fayneth vnto the heart. Neither only is common sense, and fantasie thus ouertaken with delusion, but memory also receiueth a wound therewith: which disableth it both to keepe in memory, and to record those thinges, whereof it tooke some custody before this passion, and after, therewith are defaced ... The memory being thus fraight with perills past: and embracing only through the braynes disorder that which is of discomforte, causeth the fantasie out of such recordes, to forge new matters of sadnes and feare, whereof no occasion was at any time before, nor like to be giuen hereafter: to these fancies the hart answering with like melancholicke affection, turneth all hope into feare, assurance into distrust and dispaire, ioye into discomforte: and as the melancholie nature, or bodie any waie corrupt, defileth the pure and holesome nourishment, and conuerteth it into the same kinde of impuritie: and as the fire of all kinde of matter giueth increase of heate whether it be wood, stone, metal, or liquor: so the body thus possessed with the vnchearefull, and discomfortable darknes of melancholie, obscureth the Sonne and Moone, and all the comfortable planetts of our natures, in such sort, that if they appeare, they appeare all darke, and more then half eclipsed of this mist of blackenes, rising from that hidious lake: and in all thinges comfortable, either curiously pryeth out, and snatcheth at whatsouer of mislike may be drawen to the nourishment of it selfe: or else neglecteth altogether that which is of other qualitie, then foode, and pasture of those monsters, which nature neuer bred, nor perfect since conceiued, nor memorie vncorrupt would euer allow entertainement, but are hatched out of this muddie humour, by an vnnaturall temper and bastard spirite, to the disorder of the whole regiment of humane nature, both in iudgement and affection. Thus the hart a while being acquainted, with nothing else, but domestical terror, feareth euery thing, and the brayne simpathetically partaking with the hartes feare, maketh doubt, distrusteth, and suspecteth without cause, alwayes standing in awe of grieuaunce: wherwith in time it becometh so tender, that the least touch, as it were ones naile in an vlcer, giueth discouragement thereto, rubbing it vpon the gale exulcerate with sorow and feare: neither only doubleth it sorow vpon smal occasion, but taketh it where none is offered: euen as the Cholerick man feedeth his passion with ridiculous causes of displeasure.

Timothy Bright

A Treatise of Melancholie (1586)

gale] gall

A Bishop

AND if you woulde haue an ilsample of an excellent pulpit man in deede, go no further then the B. of Glocester nowe liuing: And in him you shall finde a plaine instance of such a one as I meane. On a time he preaching at Worcester before he was B. vpon Sir Johns day: as he trauersed his matter, and discoursed vpon many points, he came at the length vnto the very pithe of his whol sermon, contained in the distinction of the name of Iohn, which he then shewing all his learning at once, full learnedly handled after this manner. Iohn, Iohn, the grace of God, the grace of God, the grace of God: gracious Iohn, not graceless Iohn, but gracious Iohn. Iohn, holy Iohn, not Iohn ful of holes, but holy Iohn. If he shewed not himselfe learned in this sermond, then hath he bene a duns all his life. In the same sermon, two seuerall Iohns, the father and the sonne, that had beene both recusants, being brought publikely to confesse their faults, this worthy doctor, by reason that the yong man hauing bene poysoned beyond the seas with popery, was more obstinate then his father, and by all likelihood, he was the cause of his fathers peruersenesse: with a vehement exclamation, able to pearce a cobweb, called on the father aloud in this patheticall and perswading sort. Old Iohn, olde Iohn, be not led away by the Syren sounds, and intisements of yong Iohn; if yong Iohn will go to the diuell, the diuell go with him. The puritans it may be, will here obiect, that this worthy man was endued with these famous gifts before he was B.; whereas since that time, say they, he is not able to say bo to a goose.

Martin Marprelate

Oh read ouer D. Iohn Bridges, for it is
a worthy worke (1588)

A Tale for Martin

SCRATCH not thy head *Martin*, for be thou *Martin* the bird, or *Martin* the beast; a bird with the longest bill, or a beast with the longest eares, theres a net spread for your necke. *Martin*, Ile tell thee a tale woorth twelue pence, if thy witt bee woorth a pennie.

There came to a Duke in *Italie*, a large lubber and a beggerlie, saying hee had the Philosophers Stone, and that hee could make golde faster, than the Duke could spend it. The Duke askt him, why hee made none to mainteine himself? Because, quoth he, I could neuer get a secret place to worke in; for once I indeuoured, and the Popes holinesse sent for me, whom if he had caught, I should haue been a prentice to mainteine his pride. The Duke minding to make triall of his cunning, and eager of golde, set him to worke closely in a vault, where it was not known to his neerest seruants. This Alcumist, in short time consumed two thousande pound of the Dukes gold, and brought him halfe a Ducket: whie (quoth the Duke) is this all? All quoth he my Lord, that I could make by Art. Wel said the Duke then shalt thou see my cunning: for I will boile thee, straine thee, and then drie thee, so that of a lubber, that weighed three hundred weight, I will at last make a dram of knaues powder. The Duke did it.

Martin, if thou to cousen haue crept into the bosome of some great men, saying thou hast the churches discipline, and that thou canst by thy faction and pollicie, pull down Bishops and set vp Elders, bring the lands of the Clergy, into the cofers of the temporaltie, and repaire Religion, by impairing their liuings, it may bee, thou shalt bee hearkened too, stroakt on the head, greasd in the hand, fed daintelie, kept secretlie, and countenaunst mightilie. But when they perceiue, that all thy deuices bee but *Chymeraes*, monsters of thine owne imaginations, so farre from pulling downe a Cathedrall

Church, that they cannot remooue a corner of a square cap, then will they deale with thee, as the Duke did with the Alcumist, giue thee as many bobs on the eare, as thou hast eaten morsels of their meate, and make thee an example of sedition to be pointed at, that art now so mewde vp, that none can point where thou art. All this tale, with the application, was not of my penning, but found among loose papers; marie he that did it, dares stand to it.

John Lyly (?)
Pappe with an Hatchet (1589)

SEDITION

WHAT malecontent is this that followes him; Looking suspitiouslie, as fearing to bee apprehended; scattering Libels in Court, Westminster, and London? By his apparell hee should be a Frenchman, but his language showes him to bee English. Oh I know him now, it is *Sedition* the Trouble world; This Deuil detected for some notable villanie in his countrie, or after the lewd and prodigall expence of his liuing, flying vnder colour of Religion beyond the seas, is lately come ouer with seditious bookes, false intelligences, and defamatorie Libels, to disgrace his Prince, detract her honourable counsell, and seduce the common sort: This fellow in Poules takes vp all the malecontents, telling them wonders of the entertainement of good wits in other countries, and cals them fooles for liuing so long heare, where men of good wits are most neglected. In the countrie, hee stormes, and railes, against inclosures, telling the husbandmen that the pleasure of their Lords, eates away the fat from their fingers; and these rackt rents (which in good sooth authoritie might wiselie look into) are the vtter ruine of the yeomanrie of England: the conclusion of his talke alwaies is insurrection, and commotion; for saith hee the world will neuer bee mended with the poore whilest these cormorants bee hanged higher. This is hee that saith that warre is a good tree, and bringeth forth good fruit, namelie store of good crownes: and it is a paradox of his, That it is better liue a Rebell then die a begger. If anie mislike his talke, and threaten to bring him in question, My friend (quoth hee) I doe but trie the natures of men how they are inclined, that they may bee lookt into by the better sort, whose intelligencer I am. This is a pestilent fiend, and the more secret hee lurketh, the more harme hee worketh, the whole scope of his discourse is the cause of much inconuenience, for therethrough on euerie side groweth hate, and of hate saith *Machiauell* come deuisions, and of deuisions sects, and of sects ruin. Another method of *Sedition* is this, to innouate in religion, to detract the pollicie of the Cleargie, to disgrace the reuerend fathers and eies of religion, our Bishops, obiecting against them those corruptions, which as they neuer thought, so they neuer practised.

Thomas Lodge

Wits Miserie, and the Worlds Madnesse (1596)

ANGLICAN MOUNTEBANK

THESE Mountebanks, are a free kind of wanderers, Pedlars, Surgeans, Physitians, Historiographers, Poetes, or what so euer name besides you wil geue vnto them, men altogether for the penie, which is the cause that they professe so many thinges. They take vp their standing in Market places, or void roomes meete for the concourse of people, there they set a stoole to stand vpon, or make a litle scaffold for the purpose, from which they play their part. Their Greatest Grace is in the Countenance and Tongue, through which, they looke so saddely, and speake so eloquently, that a man would sweare vpon a booke for them, that they thinke as they speake, and speak no more, than they wil do ...

But what speake I of other? Is M. Iewel[1] him selfe any better than a Mountebanke? Consider by that only which I haue proued against him, how faire spoken he is, how much corrupt stuffe he hath, how highly he setteth by it, how loudely he craketh of it, how singularly he auanceth him self by it. For when he prouoketh *al the learned men that be aliue*, And asketh for no more than *One sufficient sentence*, And requireth to haue that brought out of *any Olde Catholique Doctour or Father, or any Olde General Councel &c.* What other thing is this, but a Mountebankes Preface, to commend his wares vnto the Audience? As if he should say in plainer woordes vnto them:

Deerely beloued in the Lorde, you may take me perchaunce for a Benchwhistler, or a man of litle knowledge and practise, and altogeather vnhable to reproue the General and Catholique Doctrine of the whole world, and to draw you from those Maisters and Teachers which alwaies hitherto, ye haue ben ruled by. But I shal tel you (deere brethren) I haue seene and readen as much as any man, yea – as *all the learned men aliue*: I haue trauailed vnto the very *Primitiue Church* it selfe: I haue bene conuersant with *Old Catholique Doctors, and Fathers, and old General Councels.* As for these Priests, Cardinals and Popes, whom you folowe, they bring nothing, but Conclusions of Scholemen, and deuises of Later Doctours, and Ceremonies of their owne making, &c.

John Rastell

The Third Book ... It is time to Beware of M. Iewel (1566)

CHURCH OF ENGLAND

THE comparison which ye make between your selues and Sophocles, gladly we admitte. Yet we acknowledge that as in many respectes ye are like, so in some vnlike. Sophocles was

1. John Jewel (1522–71), Anglican apologist.

a poet, that is to saye, a fainer, and deuiser of thinges that be not true, but fabulous. Ye also are fainers, and deuisers of nouelties, and folowers of newe deuises, that be false. Sophocles was a tragicall poet, ye are tragicall diuines. A tragedie setteth forth th'ouerthrowes of kingdomes, murder of noble personages, and other great troubles, and endeth in wofull lamentations. Your gospel inuadeth Christes heauenly kingdome the church, it murdereth soules bought with a most dere price, it causeth a hellish garboile in mens consciences, in the end it bringeth to euerlasting weping and gnashing of teeth. Sophocles was accused of his vnkinde sonnes, ye are accused of your fathers, of your brethren, of your mother, who loue you most tenderly and with vnspeakeable griefe of hart bemone your case. Sophocles in his olde dayes, ye in your young dayes. For your English church hath not yet fulfilled the age, or number of those yeres, which we call the yeres of discretion.

Thomas Harding

A Confutation of a Booke intituled An Apologie
of the Church of England (1565)

CAMPION'S CHALLENGE

I DO ask, to the glory of God, with all humility, and under your correction, three sortes of indifferent and quiet audiences: the *first* before your Honours, wherein I will discourse of religion, so far as it toucheth the common weale and your nobilities; the *second*, whereof I make more account, before the Doctors and Masters and chosen men of both Universities, wherein I undertake to avow the faith of our Catholike Church by proofs innumerable, Scriptures, Councils, Fathers, History, natural and moral reasons; the *third* before the lawyers, spiritual and temporal, wherein I will justify the said faith by the common wisdom of the laws standing yet in force and practice.

I would be loth to speak anything that might sound of any insolent brag or challenge, especially being now as a dead man to this world, and willing to put my head under every man's foot, and to kiss the ground they tread upon. Yet have I such a courage in avouching the Majesty of Jhesus my King, and such affiance in His gracious favour, and such assurance in my quarrel, and my evidence so impregnable, and because I know perfectly that no one Protestant, nor all the Protestants living, nor any sect of our adversaries (howsoever they face men down in pulpits and overrule us in their kingdom of grammarians and unlearned ears) can maintain their doctrine in disputation, I am to sue most humbly and instantly for the combat with all and every of them, and the most principal that may be found: protesting that in this trial the better furnished they come, the better welcome they shall be ...

And touching our Societie, be it known to you that we have made a league – all the Jesuits in the world, whose succession and multitude must overreach all the practices of England – cheerfully to carry the cross you shall lay upon us, and never to despair your recovery, while we have a man left to enjoy your Tyburn, or to be racked with your torments, or consumed with your prisons. The expense is reckoned, the enterprise is begun; it is of God, it cannot be withstood. So the faith was planted, so it must be restored.

If these my offers be refused, and my endeavours can take no place, and I, having run thousands of miles to do you good, shall be rewarded with rigour, I have no more to say but to recommend your case and mine to Almightie God, the Searcher of Hearts, who send us His grace, and set us at accord before the day of payment, to the end we may at last be friends in heaven, when all injuries shall be forgotten.

Edmund Campion

Letter to the Council (1580). Text from A. C. Southern's
Elizabethan Recusant Prose (1950)

SUPERSTITION

HOW were our children, old women, and maides afraid to crosse a Churchyeard, or a three-way leet, or to goe for spoones into the Kitchin without a candle? and no marueile. First, because the deuil comes from a smoakie blacke house, he, or a lewd frier was still at hand, with ougly hornes on his head, fire in his mouth, a cowes tayle in his breech, eyes like a bason, fangs like a dogge, clawes like a Beare, a skinne like a Neger, and a voyce rearing like a Lyon; then *boh*, or *oh*, in the dark was enough to make their haire stand vpright. And if that the bowle of curds, and creame were not duly set out for *Robin good-fellow* the Frier, and *Sisse* the dairy-maide, to meete at *hinch pinch, and laugh not*, when the good wife was a bed, why then, either the pottage was burnt to next day in the pot, or the cheese would not curdle, or the butter would not come, or the ale in the fat would neuer haue good head. But if a *Peeter-penny*, or an houzle-egge were behind, or a patch of tyth vnpaid to the Church (*Iesu Maria*) then ware where you walke for feare of *bull-beggers, spirits, witches, vrchins, Elues, hags, fairies, Satyrs, Pans, Faunes, Syluans, Kit with the candle-sticke, Tritons, Centaurs, Dwarffs, Giants, impes, Calcars, con-iurers, Nymphs, changlings, scritchowles, Incubus, the spurne, the mare, the man in the oake, helwayne, the fire-drake, the puckle, Tom thumbe, hobgoblin, Tom-tumbler, Boneles, and the rest*: and what girle, boy, or old wisard would be so hardy to step ouer the threshold in the night for an half-penny worth of mustard amongst this frightfull crue, without a dosen *auemaries*, two dosen crosses surely signed, and halfe a dosen *Pater nosters*, and the commending himselfe to the tuition of S. *Vncumber*, or els our blessed Lady?

These be the Popes, and his holy Legats, and those of his holy mission, and commission from hell, their frightful crue, theyr black-guard, with which they work wonders, amongst a faithlesse, sencelesse generation: these shoute about them, attend them, and are of theyr guard, and trayne, wheresoeuer they goe, or walke, as *Styx*, *Phlegeton*, and the *Eumenides* doe guard *Æacus* in hell: with these they worke their wonders, making Images to speake, vautes to sound, trunks to carry tales, Churchyeards to swarme, houses to rush, rumble, and clatter with chaynes, high-waies, old graues, pittes, and woods ends to be haunted with lights, owles, and poakers; and with these they adrad, and gaster sencelesse old women, witlesse children, and melancholike dottrels, out of their wits.

These Monster-swarmes his *Holiness* and his helly crue haue scraped, and raked together out of old doating heathen Historiographers, wisardizing Augurs, imposturizing South-sayers, dreaming Poets, Chimerial conceiters, and coyners of fables, such as puffe vp our young gallants with bigge lookes, and bombast phrases, as the booke of *Lancelot du Lake*, *Guy of Warwicke*, *The Mirrour of Knighthoode*, *Amadis de Gaule*, and such like their Legends; out of these they conceit their monstrous shapes, vgly bug-beares, hydeous apparitions of ghosts: out of these they conforme their charmes, enchaunt-ments, periapts, amulets, characters, wast coates, and smockes of proofe, against hayle, thunder, lightning, biting of mad dogges, gnawing of Rats, against botches, biles, crosbiting, sparrow-blasting, Owle-hunting, and the like.

Out of these is shaped vs the true *Idæa* of a Witch, an olde weather-beaten Croane, hauing her chinne, and her knees meeting for age, walking like a bow leaning on a shaft, hollow eyed, vntoothed, furrowed on her face, hauing her lips trembling with the palsie, going mumbling in the streets, one that hath forgotten her *pater noster*, and hath yet a shrewd tongue in her head, to call a drab, a drab. If shee haue learned of an olde wife in a chimnies end: *Pax*, *max*, *fax*, for a spel: or can say Sir *Iohn of Grantams* curse, for the Millers Eeles, that were stolne: *All you that haue stolne the Millers Eeles*, Laudate dominum de cælis: *And all they that haue consented thereto*, benedicamus domino: Why then ho, beware, looke about you my neighbours; if any of you haue a sheepe sicke of the giddies, or an hogge of the mumps, or an horse of the staggers, or a knauish boy of the schoole, or an idle girle of the wheele, or a young drab of the sullens, and hath not fat enough for her porredge, nor her father, and mother, butter enough for their bread; and she haue a little helpe of the *Mother*, *Epilepsie*, or *Cramp*, to teach her role her eyes, wrie her mouth, gnash her teeth, startle with her body, hold her armes and hands stiffe, make anticke faces, girne, mow, and mop like an Ape, tumble like a Hedgehogge, and can mutter out two or three words of gibridg, as *obus*, *bobus*: and then with-all old mother *Nobs* hath called her by chaunce, idle young huswife, or bid the deuil scratch her, then no doubt but mother *Nobs* is the Witch: the young girle is Owle-blasted, and possessed: and it goes hard, but ye shal haue some idle, adle, giddie, lymphaticall, illuminate dotrel, who being out of credite, learning, sobriety, honesty, and wit, wil take this holy aduantage, to raise the ruines of his desperate decayed name, and for his better glory wil be-pray the iugling drab, and cast out *Mopp* the deuil.

They that haue their braines baited, and their fancies distempered with the imaginations, and apprehensions of Witches, Coniurers, and Fayries, and all that Lymphatical *Chimæra*: I finde to be marshalled in one of these fiue rankes, children, fooles, women, cowards, sick, or blacke, melancholicke, discomposed wits. The Scythians being a warlike Nation (as *Plutarch* reports) neuer saw any visions.

Samuel Harsnet

A Declaration of Egregious Popishe Impostures (1603)

ORDER

I AM not ignorant that by Law eternall the learned for the most part doe vnderstand the order, not which God hath eternally purposed himselfe in al his workes to obserue, but rather that which with himselfe he hath set downe as expedient to be kept by al his creatures, according to the seueral condition wherewith he hath indued them. They who thus are accustomed to speake, apply the name of *Law* vnto that onely rule of working which Superior Authoritie imposeth: whereas wee somewhat more enlarging the sense thereof, terme any kind of rule or Canon whereby actions are framed, a Law. Now that Law which as it is laid vp in the bosome of God, they call *eternall*, receiueth according vnto the different kind of things which are subiect vnto it, different and sundry kindes of names. That part of it which ordreth naturall Agents, we call vsually *Nature's* Law: that which Angels doe clearly behold, and without swaruing obserue, is a Law *celestiall* and heauenly: the Law of *Reason*, that which bindeth creatures reasonable in this World, and with which by reason they may most plainely perceiue themselues bound; that which bindeth them, and is not knowne but by special reuelation from God, *diuine* Law; *humane* Law, that which out of the Law either of reason or of God, men probably gathering to be expedient, they make it a Law. Al things therefore, which are as they ought to be are conformed vnto this *second Law eternal*; and euen those things which to this *eternal* Law are not conformable are notwithstanding in some sort ordered by the *first eternall Law*. For what good or euill is there vnder the Sunne, what action correspondent or repugnant vnto the Law which God hath imposed vpon his creatures, but in or vpon it God doth worke according to the Law which himselfe hath eternally purposed to keepe, that is to say, the *first Law eternall*? So that a two-fold Law eternall being thus made, it is not hard to conceiue how they both take place in all things. Wherefore to come to the Law of nature, albeit thereby we sometimes meane that manner of working which God hath set for each created thing to keepe: yet for as much as those things are termed most properly naturall Agents, which keepe the Law of their kind vnwittingly, as the Heauens and Elements of the World, which can doe no otherwise then they doe; and for as much as wee giue vnto intellectuall natures the name of *voluntary* Agents, that so wee may distinguish them from the other, expedient it wil be that we seuer the Law of Nature obserued by the one, from that which the other is tyed vnto. Touching the former, their strict keeping of one Tenure, Statute and Law is spoken of by all, but hath in it more then men haue as yet attained to know, or perhaps euer shall attaine, seeing the trauel of wading herein is giuen of God to the sonnes of Men, that perceiuing how much the least thing in the World hath in it more then the wisest are able to reach vnto, they may by this meanes learne humilitie. *Moses*, in describing the worke of Creation, attributeth speech vnto God: *God said, Let there be light: Let there be a firmament: Let the waters vnder the Heauen be gathered together into one Place: let the Earth bring forth; Let there be Lights in the Firmament of Heauen.* Was this onely the intent of *Moses* to signifie the infinite greatnesse of Gods power by the easinesse of his accomplishing such effects, without trauel, paine, or labour? Surely it seemeth that *Moses* had herein, besides this, a further purpose, namely, first, to teach that God did not worke as a necessary, but a voluntary Agent, intending beforehand and decreeing with himselfe that which did outwardly proceed from him; Secondly, to shew that God did then institute a Law general to be obserued by creatures, and therfore according to the manner of Lawes, the Institution therof is described as being established by solemne injunction. His commanding those things to be which are, and to be in such sort as they are, to keepe that tenure and course which they doe, importeth the establishment of Natures Law. This Worlds first Creation, and the preseruation since of things created, what is it, but only so far forth a manifestation by execution, what the Eternal Law of God is concerning things naturall? And as it commeth to passe in a kingdome rightly ordered, that after a Law is once published it presently takes effect far and wide, all States framing themselves thereunto; euen so let vs thinke it fareth in the naturall course of the World: since the time that God did first proclaime the Edicts of his Law vpon it, Heauen and earth haue harkned vnto his voyce, and their labour hath bin to do his will: *He made a Law for the Raine*, He gaue his *Decree vnto the Sea that the Waters should not passe his commandment*. Now if nature should intermit her course, and leaue altogether, though it were but for a while, the obseruation of her own Lawes; if those principall and Mother Elements of the World wherof al things in this lower World are made, should lose the qualities which now they haue; if the frame of that Heauenly Arch erected ouer our heads should loosen and dissolue it selfe; if Celestiall Spheres should forget their wonted Motions and by irregular volubilitie turne themselues any way as it might happen; if the Prince of the Lights of Heauen, which now as a Giant doth run his vnwearied course, should as it were through a languishing faintnesse begin to stand and rest himselfe; if the Moone should wander from her beaten way, the times and seasons of the yeere blend themselves by disordered and confused mixture, the Winds breathe out their last gaspe, the Clouds yeeld no Raine, the Earth be defeated of heauenly Influence, the Fruits of the Earth pine away as Children at the withered brests of their Mother, no longer able to yeeld them reliefe; what would become of Man himselfe whom these things now doe all serue? See wee not

plainly that obedience of Creatures vnto the Law of Nature
is the stay of the whole World?

Richard Hooker

Of the Lawes of Ecclesiasticall Politie (1593)
Text from 1632 edition

THE CONDITIONS OF HAPPINESS

ALL men desire to leade in this world an happy life. That life
is led most happily wherin all vertue is exercised without
impediment or let. The Apostle, in exhorting men to contentment, although they haue in this world no more than very
bare food and raiment, giueth vs thereby to vnderstand, that
those are euen the lowest of things necessary, that if we should
be stripped of all those things without which we might
possibly be, yet these must be left; that destitution in these is
such an impediment, as, til it be remoued, suffereth not the
mind of man to admit any other care. For this cause first God
assigned *Adam* maintenance of life, and then appointed him a
law to obserue. For this cause, after men began to grow to a
number, the first thing we reade they gaue themselues vnto,
was the tilling of the earth, and the feeding of cattle. Hauing
by this meane whereon to liue, the principall actions of their
life afterward are noted by the exercise of their religion. True
it is, that the Kingdom of God must be the first thing in our
purposes and desires. But in as much as righteous life pre-
supposeth life, in as much as to liue virtuously it is impossible
except we liue; therefore the first impediment, which
naturally we endeuour to remoue, is penury and want of
things without which we cannot liue. Vnto life many imple-
ments are necessary; moe, if we seek (as all men naturally do)
such a life as hath in it ioy, comfort, delight, and pleasure. To
this end we see how quickly sundry Arts mechanical were
found out in the verie prime of the World. As things of

greatest necessitie are alwayes first prouided for, so things of greatest dignitie are most accounted of by all such as iudge rightly. Although therefore Riches be a thing which euery man wisheth, yet no man of iudgement can esteeme it better to bee rich, than wise, vertuous, and religious. If wee bee both, or eyther of these, it is not because we are so borne. For into the world we come as empty of the one as of the other, as naked in mind as wee are in body. Both which necessities of man had at the first no other helpes and supplies, than onely domesticall; such as that which the Prophet implieth, saying, *Can a mother forget her child?* Such as that which the Apostle mentioneth, saying, *He that careth not for his owne is worse than an Infidell*; such as that concerning ABRAHAM. *Abraham will command his sonnes and his houshold after him, that they keepe the way of the Lord.* But Neyther that which we learne of our-selues, nor that which others teach vs can preuayle, where wickednesse and malice haue taken deepe roote. If, therefore, when there was but as yet one onely Family in the World, no meanes of instruction, humane or diuine, could preuent effusion of blood: how could it bee chosen but that when Families were multiplied and increased vpon earth, after separation, each prouiding for it selfe, enuy, strife, contention, and violence must grow amongst them? For hath not nature furnisht man with wit and valour, and as it were with armour, which may bee vsed as well vnto extreame euill as good? Yea, were they not vsed by the rest of the world vnto euill; vnto the contrarie onely by *Seth, Enoch,* and those few the rest in that line? We all make complaint of the iniquitie of our times; not vniustly, for the dayes are euill. But compare them with those times wherein there were no ciuill societies, with those times wherein there was as yet no manner of publique regiment established, with those times wherein there were not aboue eight righteous persons liuing vpon the face of the earth; and wee haue surely good cause to thinke that God hath blessed vs exceedingly, and hath made vs behold most happy daies. To take away all such mutuall greeuance, iniuries and wrongs, there was no way but onely by growing vpon composition and agreement amongst themselues; by ordaining some kinde of gouernement publique, and by yeelding themselues subiect thereunto; that vnto whom they graunted authority to rule and gouerne, by them the peace, tranquility, and happy estate of the rest might be procured.

Richard Hooker

Of the Lawes of Ecclesiasticall Politie (1593)
Text from 1632 edition

NIGHT FEARES

NOW consider farther yet, that the Prophete in the forerememberd vearses, sayeth not that in the night walks onely the Lions whelpes, but also *omnes bestiæ siluarum*, all the beastes of the wood. Nowe wote you well, that if a man walke thorowe the wood in the nighte, many thynges may make hym afrayde, of which, in the daye he woulde not be afrayde a whit: for in the nyghte euery bushe (to hym that waxeth once afrayde) semeth a thefe.

I remember that when I was a younge man, I was once in the warre wyth the king, then my master (God assoile hys soule) and we wer camped within the Turkes ground many a myle beyonde Belgrade, whiche woulde God wer oures now as well as it was then: but so happed it, that in oure campe aboute midnight, there sodaynlye rose a rumoure and a skrye, that the Turkes whole armye was secretely stealyng vpon vs, wherewith oure whole host was warned to arme them in haste, and sette themselfe in aray to fighte, and then wer scurars of ours that brought these sodayne tidinges, examyned more laisorly by the counsayle, what suretye or what likelyhode they had perceyued therein: of whom one shewed that by the glimuring of the moone, he had espyed and perceiued and sene them hymselfe, comming on softely and soberly in a longe raunge all in good ordre, not one farther foorth then the other in the forefrunte, but as euen as the threde, and in bredth farther than he coulde see in length. Hys fellowes beyng examined, saied that he was somewhat pricked foorth beefore them, and came so fast backe to tel it them, that they thought it rather time to make haste and geue warninge to the campe, than to goe nerer vnto them for they were not so farre of, but that they had yet themselfe somewhat an vnperfecte syghte of them too. Thus stoode we watching al the remnaunte of the nyghte, euermore harkenyng when we shoulde heare them come with hushte, stande styll, me thynke I heare a tramplyng, so that at laste many of vs thoughte we heard them oure selfe also. But when the daye was sprongen, and that we sawe no manne, oute was oure scurer sente againe, and some of oure capitaines with him to shewe them where aboute the place was, in whiche he perceiued them: and when they came thyther, they found that the great fearefull armye of the Turkes, so soberlye commyng on, turned (God be thanked) into a fayre long hedge standyng euen stone styll.

And thus fareth it in the nyghtes feare of tribulacyon, in whiche the deuill to beare downe and ouerwhelme with dreade, the faythfull hope that we shoulde haue in GOD, casteth in oure imaginacion muche more feare then cause. For whyle there walke in the nighte, not onely the Lyons whelpes, but ouer that all the beastes of the wood beside, the beastes that we heare roaring in the darke nighte of tribulacion, and feare it for a Lyon, we sometyme fynde well afterwarde in the daye that it was no Lyon at all, but a sely rude roaring asse: and the thyng that on the sea semeth sumtime a rocke, is in dede nothing els but a mist.

Sir Thomas More

A Dialoge of Comfort against Tribulacion (1553)

DEVILISH PLOUGHING

OH that our prelates woulde be as diligente to sowe the corne of good doctrine as Sathan is, to sowe cockel and darnel. And this is the deuilyshe ploughinge, the which worcketh to haue thinges in latine, and letteth the fruteful edification. But here some man will saie to me, what sir are ye so priuie of the deuils counsell that ye know al this to be true? Truli I know him to wel, and haue obeyed him a little to much in condescentinge to some follies. And I knowe him as other men do, yea, that he is euer occupied and euer busie in folowinge his plough. I know bi saint Peter which saieth of him. *Sicut leo rugiens circuit querens quem deuoret.* He goeth aboute lyke a roaringe lyon seekynge whome he maye deuoure. I woulde haue thys texte wel vewed and examined euerye worde of it. *Circuit,* he goeth aboute in euerye corner of his dioces. He goeth on visitacion daylye. He leaueth no place of hys cure vnuisited. He walketh round aboute from place to place and ceaseth not, *Sicut leo,* as a Lyon that is strongly, boldly, and proudlye, straytelye and fiercelye with haute lookes, wyth hys proude countenaunces, wyth hys stately braggynges. *Rugiens,* roaringe, for he letteth not slippe any occasion to speake or to roare out when he seeth his tyme. *Querens,* he goeth about seekyng and not sleepyng, as oure bishoppes do, but he seketh diligently, he searcheth diligently al corners, wheras he may haue his pray. He roueth abrode in eueri place of his dioces, he standeth not styl, he is neuer at reste, but euer in hande wyth his plough that it may go forwarde. But there was neuer suche a preacher in England as he is. Who is able to tel his diligente preachyng? whiche euery daye and euery houre laboreth to sowe cockel and darnel, that he may bryng oute of forme and out of estimation and roume, th' institution of the Lordes supper and Christes crosse, for there

letteth] prevents

he lost his righte, for Christe saied. *Nunc iudicium est mundi, princeps seculi hujus eiicietur foras, et sicut exaltauit Moises serpentem in deserto, ita exaltari oportet filium hominis, et cum exaltatus fuero, a terra, omnia traham ad meipsum.* Nowe is the iudgemente of thys worlde and the Prynce of thys worlde shall be caste oute. And as Moyses dyd lyfte vp the serpente in the wyldernesse, so muste the sonne of manne be lyfte vp. And when I shall be lyfte vp from the earthe, I wyl drawe all thinges vnto my selfe. For the Deuyll was dysapoynted of hys purpose, for he thoughte all to be hys owne.

And when he had once broughte Christe to the crosse, he thought all cocke sure. But there loste he all his reygning, for Christ saied *Omnia traham ad meipsum.* I wyll drawe all thynges to my selfe. He meaneth drawynge of mans soule to saluacion. And that he sayde he woulde do *per semetipsum,* by his owne selfe, not by any other bodyes sacrifice. He ment by his own sacrifice on the crosse wheare he offred him selfe for the redemption of mankynd, and not the sacrifice of the masse to be offered by an other. For who can offer him but him selfe? He was bothe the offerer and the offeryng. And thys is the pricke, thys is the marke at the whyche the Deuyll shooteth, to euacuate the crosse of Chryste and to mingle the institucion of the Lordes supper, the whiche although he canne not brynge to passe: yet he goeth aboute bi his sleyghtes and subtyle meanes, to frustrate the same, and these fyftene hundred yeres he hath bene a dooer, onelye purposinge to euacuate Christes death, and to make it of smal efficacitie and vertue.

For where as Christe accordyng as the serpent was lyfte vp in wyldernes: so woulde he hym self to be exalted, that therby as manye as trusted in hym, shoulde haue saluation. But the deuyl would none of that. They would haue vs saued by a daily oblation propitiatorie, by a sacrifice expiatorie, or remissorie.

Hugh Latimer

A Notable Sermon . . . in the Shroudes (1548)

Many are Called

If wee come to reason, wee may rather wonder that any shall bee saued, then so fewe shall be saued. For, we haue all the lets and hinderances that may be, both within vs and without vs. Wee haue (as they say) the Sunne, Moone, and seuen Starres against vs. We haue al the diuels in hell against vs, with all their hornes, heads, maruellous strength, infinite wiles, cunning deuices, deepe sleights, and methodicall temptations. Here runnes a sore streame, against vs. Then haue we this present euill world against vs, with her innumerable baits, snares, nets, gins, and grins to catch vs, fetter vs, and entangle vs. Here haue we profits and pleasures, riches and honor, wealth and preferment, ambition and couetousnes. Here comes in a camp royall of spirituall and inuisible enemies. Lastly, we haue our flesh, that is, our corrupted nature against vs: we haue our selues against our selues. For we our selues are as great enemies to our saluation, as either the world or the diuel. For, our vnderstanding reason, will and affections, are altogether against vs. Our natural wisdome is an enemy vnto vs. Our concupisences and lusts do minister strength to Satans temptations. They are al in league with Satan against vs. They take part with him, in euery thing, against vs and our saluation. They fight al vnder his standard, and receiue their pay of him. This then goeth hard on our side, that the diuell hath an inward party against vs: and we carrie alwaies within vs our greatest enemie, which is euer ready, night and day, to betray vs into the hands of Satan; yea, to vnbolt the doore, and let him in, to cut our throats. Here then we see an huge army of dreadfull enemies, and a very Legion of diuels, lying in ambush, against our soules. Are not we therfore, poore wretches, in a most pittifull case, which are thus betraied and besieged on euery side? Al things then considered, may we not iustly maruel, that any shall be saued? For who seeth not

who knoweth not, that thousand thousands are carried head-
long to destruction? either with the temptations of the world,
he flesh, or the diuell. But yet further. I will shew, by another
very manifest apparant reason, that the number of Gods elect,
vpon the face of the earth, are very few in comparison: which
may thus be considered. First let there be taken away, from
amongst vs, all Papists, Atheists, and Heretickes. Secondly,
let there be shoaled out al vicious and notorious euill liuers: as
wearers, drunkeards, whoremongers, worldlings, deceiuers,
coseners, proud men, riotors, gamesters, and all the prophane
multitude. Thirdly, let there be refused and sorted out al
hypocrites, carnall Protestants, vaine professors, backsliders,
decliners, and cold Christians. Let al these, I say, be separated:
and then tell me, how many sound, sincere, faithful, and
zealous worshippers of God will be found among vs. I suppose, we should not need the art of Arithmetike, to number
them. For I thinke, there would be very fewe, in euery village,
towne, and citie. I doubt, they would walk very thinly in the
streetes: so as a man might easily tell them, as they goe. Our
Lord Jesus asketh a question, in the Gospel of S. Luke, saying;
*Do you thinke, when the sonne of man commeth, that he shall find
faith on the earth?* To the which we may answere; surely very
little.

Arthur Dent

The Plaine-Mans Path-way to Heauen (1601)

MARTYRDOM

MARTYRDOME is the bridge ouer which wee passe to our
contentment. *Sardanapulus* lay not with more delight on his
bed stopped with Millan downe, than Saint *Laurence* lay on
he cradle he was broiled on. Perfumed *Helen* was not so sweet
in all hir odoriferous balmes as was Saint *Cycily* in the smoake

of her martyrdome. But why do I glean in so plentifull a haruest? Collect the coles, the wheeles, the ropes, the rakes, and all the torments that tyrants haue inuented or martyrs suffered, and you shall see the Crosse of Christ and meditation of the passion, to haue made those torments delightfull to martyrs, that haue seemed vnsupportable to the executioners themselues. A strange kinde of triumph, where the conqueror is haled on the hirdle, with his hands manacled; his triumphant arche, the disgracefull gallowes; his spoiles and prizes, his vnbodied bowels; his pompe, punishment; his maiestie, miserie.

The Silkworme first eateth hir selfe out of a very little seed, and groweth to bee a small worme: afterward when by feeding a certain time vpon fresh and greene leaues it is waxed of greater sise, eateth it self againe out of the other coate, and worketh it selfe into a case of silke; which when it hath once finished, in the end casting the seed for many yoong to breed of, and leauing the silke for mans ornament, dieth all white and winged, in shape of a flying thing:

Euen so the martyrs of the Catholicke Church, first breake out of the dead seed of originall sinne by Baptisme: then, when by feeding on the Sacraments and leaues of Gods word, they are growne to more ripenesse, casting the coate of worldly vanities, they cloath themselues with the silke of vertue and perfection of life, in which worke perseuering to the end, euen when the persecution is greatest, they finally as need requireth, shed their blood, as seed for new offspring to arise of, and leaue moreouer the silke of their vertues as an ornament to the Church; and thus depart white for their good works, and winged with innocencie of hands, and cleannesse of heart, they presently flie to their heauenly repose, agreeably to *Dauids* saying, *Quis ascendet in montem domini? Innocens manibus et mundus corde.* Who shall ascend to the mount of God? The innocent of hands, and cleane of heart. So that though he ripe fruit of the Church bee gathered, yet their blood engendreth new supply, and it increaseth the more, when the disincrease therof is violently procured. It is like the bush that burned and was not consumed. Of the own ruines it riseth, and of the owne ashes it reuiueth, and by that increaseth, by which the world decayeth.

Elizabeth Grymestone

Miscelanea . . . (1604)

JOURNEY OF THE MAGI

IT is not commended, to stand *gazing up into heaven* too long, Not *on* CHRIST *Himself ascending*: much lesse on His *star*. For, hey sate not still gazing on the *star*. Their *Vidimus* begat *Venimus*; their *seeing* made them *come*; come a great journey. *Venimus* is soone *sayd*; but a *short Word*: But, many a wide and weary step they made, before they could come to say *Venimus*, Lo, here *we are come*; *Come* and at our journeys end. To looke a little on it. In this their *Comming*, we consider 1. First, the *distance* of the Place, they came from, It was not hard by, as he *shepherds* (but a step to *Bethlehem*, over the fields:) This was riding many a hundred miles, and cost them many a days journey. 2. Secondly, we consider the *Way*, that they came: f it be *pleasant*, or plaine and *easy*: For, if it be, it is so much he better. This was nothing *pleasant*; for, through *desarts*: all he way waste and desolate. Nor (secondly) *easy* neither: For, over the rocks and crags of both *Arabies* (specially *Petræa*) their journy lay. 3. Yet if *safe*: But it was not; but exceeding dangerous, a lying through the middest of the *Blacke Tents* of *Kedar*, a Nation of *Theeves* and Cut-throats; to passe over the hills of *Robbers*: Infamous then, and infamous to this day. No passing, without great troop, or convoy. 4. Last we consider he *time* of their *comming*, the season of the yeare. It was no

summer progresse. A cold comming they had of it, at this time
of the yeare; just the worst time of the yeare, to take a journey
and specially a long journey, in. The waies deep, the weathe
sharp, the daies short, the sun farthest off *in solstitio brumali*, the
very dead of *winter*. *Venimus*, wee are come, if that be one
Venimus, Wee are (now) come, come at this time, that (sure) i
another.

Lancelot Andrewes

XCVI. Sermons (1629)

THE PRODIGAL SON

(*Luke XV*)

A CERTAINE man had two sonnes. And the yonger of them
said to his father, Father, giue me the portion of the good
that falleth to me. So he diuided vnto them his substance. So
many dayes after, when the yonger sonne had gathered al
together, he tooke his iourney into a farre countrey, and there
he wasted his goods with riotous liuing. Now when he had
spent all, there arose a great dearth throughout that land, and
he began to be in necessitie. Then he went and claue to a
citizen of that countrey, and he sent him to his farme, to
feede swine. And he would faine haue filled his belly with the
husks, that the swine ate: but no man gaue them him. Then
hee came to himselfe, and said, How many hired seruants a
my fathers haue bread inough, and I die for hunger? I wil
rise and goe to my father, and say vnto him, Father, I haue
sinned against heauen and before thee, And am no more
worthy to bee called thy sonne: make me as one of thy hired
seruants. So he arose and came to his father, and when he was
yet a great way off, his father saw him, and had compassion
and ranne and fell on his necke, and kissed him, And the sonne
said vnto him, Father, I haue sinned against heauen, and

before thee, and am no more worthy to be called thy sonne. Then the father saide to his seruants, bring forth the best robe, and put it on him, and put a ring on his hand, and shooes on his feete, And bring the fat calfe, and kill him, and let vs eate, and be merrie. For this my sonne was dead, and is aliue againe: and he was lost, but he is found. And they began to be merrie.

Now the elder brother was in the field, and when he came and drew neere to the house, he heard melodie and dancing, And called one of his seruants, and asked what those things meant. And hee sayd vnto him, Thy brother is come, and thy father hath killed the fatte Calfe because hee hath receiued him safe and sound. Then he was angry, and would not goe in: therefore came his father out and intreated him. But hee answered and sayd to his father, Loe, these many yeeres haue I done thee seruice, neither brake I at any time thy commande-ment, and yet thou neuer gauest me a Kidde, that I might make merrie with my friends. But when this thy sonne was come, which hath deuoured thy goods with harlots, thou hast for his sake killed the fat Calfe. And he said vnto him, Sonne, thou art euer with me, and all that I haue, is thine. It was meet that we should make merrie, and be glad: for this thy brother was dead, and is aliue againe: and he was lost, but he is found.

The New Testament (Geneva Version, 1560)

THE MESSIAH

(*Isaiah LIII*)

BUT who hath geuen credence vnto our preaching? or to whom is the arme of the Lorde knowen? For he dyd growe before the Lorde like as a braunche, and as a roote in a drye grounde, he hath neither beautie nor fauour: when we loke vpon hym, there shalbe no fairenesse, we shall haue no lust vnto hym. He is dispised and abhorred of men, he is such a man as hath good experience of sorowes and infirmities: We haue reckened hym so vile, that we hyd our faces from hym. Howbeit, he only hath taken on hym our infirmitie, and borne our paynes: Yet we dyd iudge hym as though he were plagued, and cast downe of God. Whereas he (notwithstandyng) was wounded for our offences, and smitten for our wickednesse: for the payne of our punishment was layde vpon hym, and with his stripes are we healed. As for vs we are all gone astray lyke sheepe, euery one hath turned his owne way: but the Lord hath throwen vpon hym all our sinnes. He suffered violence, and was euyll intreated, and dyd not open his mouth: He shalbe led as a sheepe to be slayne, yet shall he be as styll as a lambe before the shearer, and not open his mouth. From the prison and iugement was he taken, and from his generation who can declare? for he was cut of from the grounde of the lyuing, which punishment dyd go vpon hym for the transgression of my people. His graue was geuen hym with the condempned, and with the riche man at his death, whereas he dyd neuer violence nor vnright, neither hath there ben any disceiptfulnesse in his mouth. Yet hath it pleased the Lord to smite hym with infirmitie, that when he had made his soule an offeryng for sinne, he might see long lastyng seede: and this deuice of the Lorde shall prosper in his hande. Of the trauayle and labour of his soule, shall he see the fruite & be satisfied: My righteous seruaunt shall with his knowledge iustifie the multitude, for he shall beare their sinnes. Therfore wyll I geue hym among the great ones his part, and he shal deuide the spoyle with the mightie, because he geueth ouer his soule to death, and is reckened among the transgressours which neuerthelesse hath taken away the sinnes of the multitude, and made intercession for the misdoers.

Bishops' Bible (1568)

Divine Benefits

How farre better is that way whereby the hope of friendship is reserued to him, and the opinion of our friendship likewise, if he be thankefull and entertaine a better thought? Incessant goodnesse conquereth euill men; neyther is there any man of so hard and hatefull a minde against those things that are to be beloued, that loueth not those, who euen in their greatest wrongs continue good men, to whom he beginneth to owe this also, that he sustaineth no displeasure at their hands for not requiting. Reflect thy thoughts therefore vpon these: there is no correspondencie held with me: what shall I doe? euen that which the gods the best authors of all things do, who begin to bestow their benefites on those, that know not whence they come, and perseuer also to do good to those that are vngratefull. One chargeth them with little regard of vs, another that they haue vniustly dispensed their graces, another thrusteth them out of his world, and leaueth them there alone in sloth and heauinesse, without light or doing anything; another saith that Sun (to whom we owe this, that we haue distinguished the time betweene labour and rest, that being deliuered from darkness we have escaped the confusion of a perpetuall night; for that by his course he tempereth the year, and nourisheth our bodies, and hasteneth our haruest, and ripeneth our fruit) is som stone or globe of casuall fires, and call him anything rather than god. All this notwithstanding, the gods like good parents that smile at the iniuries of their little children, cease not to heape benefites vpon those who suspect that they are not the authors of all benefites, but with an equall hand distribute their blessings amongst al nations, reseruing only to themselues the power to do good. They water the earth with timely showers, they moue the Seas with fitting windes, they distinguish times by the course of the starres, they weaken both winters and sommers by the gratious intercourse of gentler winds; they pardon and mildely winke at, and suffer the errours and sinnes of our sinfull soules. Let vs imitate them; let vs giue although many things haue beene giuen in vaine, yet let vs giue vnto others, let vs giue euen vnto those by whom we haue sustained the losse: no man forbeareth to build a house for feare it should be ruinated, and whenas fire hath consumed the place of our aboad, we suddenly lay a new foundation againe ere the floore be halfe colde, and ofttimes we build cities in that very place where they were destroyed and sunke: so constant and confirmed is the mind to good hopes; mens labors would cease both by land and sea, if they had not a will to re-edifie and re-attempt the ruines that were past.

Thomas Lodge

The Workes both Morrall and Naturall of . . . Seneca (1614)

HUMAN LIFE

Now for the rest: If wee truly examine the difference of both conditions; to wit of the rich and mighty, whome wee call fortunate; and of the poore and oppressed, whome we account wretched: wee shall find the happinesse of the one and the miserable estate of the other, so tied by GOD to the very instant, and both so subiect to interchange (witnesse the suddaine downefall of the greatest Princes, and the speedy vprising of the meanest persons) as the one hath nothing so certaine, whereof to boast; nor the other so vncertaine whereof to bewaile it self. For there is no man so assured of his honour, of his riches, health, or life; but that hee may be depriued of either or all, the very next houre or day to come *Quid vesper vehat, incertum est, What the euening will bring with it, it is vncertaine. And yet yee cannot tell* (saith Saint James *what shalbe to morrow. To day he is set up, and to morrow he shall not be found: for hee is turned into dust, and his purpose perisheth.* And although the aire which compasseth aduersitie, be very obscure: yet therin wee better discerne G O D, than in that shining light which enuironeth worldly glorie; through which, for the clearnesse thereof, there is no vanitie which escapeth our sight. And let aduersitie seeme what it will; to happie men, ridiculous, who make them-selues merrie at other mens misfortunes; and to those vnder the *crosse*, greiuous: yet this is true, That for all that is past, to the very instant, the portions remaining are equall to either. For bee it that wee haue liued many yeares, *and* (according to *Salomon*) *in them all wee haue reioyced*; or bee it that we haue measured the same length of daies, and therein haue euer-more sorrowed: yet looking backe from our present being, we find both the one and the other, to wit, the ioy and the woe, sayled out of sight; and death, which doth pursue vs and hold vs in chace, from our infancie, hath gathered it. *Quicquid ætatis retro est, mors tenet: What-so-euer of our age is past, death holds it.* So as who-so-ever hee bee, to whome Fortune hath beene a seruant, and the Time a friend: let him but take the accompt of his memory (for wee haue no other keeper of our pleasures past) and truelie examine what it hath reserued, either of beauty and youth, or foregone delights; what it hath saued, that it might last, of his dearest affections, or of what euer else the amorous Spring-time gaue his thoughts of contentment, then vnualuable; and hee shall finde that all the art which his elder yeares haue, can draw no other vapour out of these dissolutions, than heauie, secret, and sad sighes. Hee shall finde nothing remaining, but those sorrowes, which grow vp after our fast-springing youth; ouer-take it, when it is at a stand; and ouer-top it vtterly, when it beginnes to wither: in so much as looking backe from the very instant time, and from our now being; the poore, diseased, and captiue creature, hath as little sence of all his former miseries and paines; as hee,

that is most blest in common opinion, hath of his fore-passed
pleasures and delights. For what-so-euer is cast behind vs, i
iust nothing: and what is to come, deceiptfull hope hath it
Omnia quæ euentura sunt, in incerto iacent. Onely those few
blacke Swannes I must except: who hauing had the grace to
value worldly vanities at no more than their owne price; doe
by retayning the comfortable memorie of a well acted life
behold death without dread, and the graue without feare; and
embrace both, as necessary guides to endlesse glorie.

Sir Walter Ralegh

The History of the World (1614)

III

THE WORLD OF IMAGINATION, FEELING AND COMIC INVENTION: FICTION, HISTORICAL AND OCCASIONAL WRITING

A DOLPHIN

IN the daies of *Augustus Caesar* the Emperour, there was a Dolphin entred the gulfe or poole Lucrinus, which loved wonderous well a certain boy, a poore mans son; who using to go every day to schoole from Baianum to Puteoli, was woont also about noone-tide to stay at the water side, and to call unto the Dolphin, *Simo*, *Simo*, and many times would give him fragments of bread, which of purpose hee ever brought with him, and by this meane allured the Dolphin to come ordinarily unto him at his call. (I would make scruple and bash to insert this tale in my storie and to tell it out, but that *Mecænas Fabianus*, *Flauius Alfius*, and many others have set it downe for a truth in their Chronicles.) Well, in processe of time, at what houre soever of the day this boy lured for him and called *Simo*, were the Dolphin never so close hidden in any secret or blind corner, out he would and come abroad, yea and skud amaine to this lad; and taking bread and other victuals at his hand, would gently offer him his backe to mount upon, and then downe went the sharp pointed prickes of his finnes, which he would put up as it were within a sheath for fear of hurting the boy. Thus when he had him once on his back,

bash] hesitate

he would carrie him ouer the broad arme of the sea as farre as
Puteoli to schoole; and in like manner convey him backe
againe home: and thus he continued for many yeeres together,
so long as the child lived. But when the boy was falne sicke
and dead, yet the Dolphin gave not over his haunt, but
usually came to the woonted place, and missing the lad, seemed
to be heavie and mourne again, untill for verie griefe and
sorrow (as is doubtles to be presumed) he also was found dead
upon the shore.

Philemon Holland (translator)

Pliny's *Historie of the World* (1601)

NERO AND HIS MOTHER

HIS owne mother, for looking narrowly into him, and
examining his words and deedes somewhat streightly; for
seeming also to correct and reforme the same, thus farre forth
onely at the first he was grieved and offended with, as that
eftsoones he made her odious to the world, pretending that
he was about to resigne vp the Empire and depart to Rhodes
Soone after, he deprived her of all honour, dignity, and
authority: and removing from about her the guard of Ger-
maine Souldiours that attended upon her person, hee banished
her out of the same house with him, and so forth out of the
precincts of the Palace: neither cared he what he did, so he
might molest and trouble her: suborning some of purpose
both to disquiet her whiles shee abode in *Rome* with suites and
actions; and also when shee was desirous of repose and ease
in a retiring place out of the way, to course her with reproach-
full taunts and flouting scoffes as they passed that way either
by land or sea. But beeing terrified with her threats and violen
shrewdnesse, hee determined to kill and dispatch her at once
Having attempted it with poison thrice, and perceiving tha

shee was defended with Antidotes and preservatiues, he provided a bed-chamber for her, with so ticklish an arched roufe
ouer her head, as beeing easily vnioincted, the frame thereof
might fall in peeces in the night, and light vpon her as she lay
a sleepe. When this dessigne could not be kept close, but was
revealed by some of the complices privie thereto, hee deuised
a ship, so made as that quickly it should cleave a sunder: that
either by the wrack, or fall of the fore-deck aloft, she might
come to a mischiefe and perish. And so, making a semblance
of a Love-day and reconciliation, hee sent for her by most
sweet and kinde Letters, training her unto *Baiæ*, there to
celebrate with him the solemnity of the *Quinquatrian*. And
hauing giuen order before hand to certaine Maisters of
Gallies for to split the Foist wherein she was embarqued, as
if by chaunce they were run full upon her; he made it late ere
he went to the feast and sat long at it. Now when she was to
returne back againe unto *Bauli*, in lieu of that vessell thus
shaken and crackt, he put unto her the other abouesaid made
with joints and vices, easie to fall in pieces: and so, with a
cheerefull countenance accompanied her (to the water side)
and at the parting also kissed her paps. All the time after, he
lay awake in great trouble and feare, waiting for the issue of
these enterprises. But when he vnderstood that all went crosse,
and that she was escaped to land by swimming; being altogether to seeke what course to take, as L. *Agerinus*, her freed-
man brought word with great ioy, *How she was escaped aliue
and safe*, he conueied privily a dagger close by him; and as if
he had been suborned and hired secretly (by her) to kill him,
caused the said *Agerinus* to be apprehended and bound with
chaines: and withall, his mother aforesaid, to be murdred:
pretending, as if by voluntary death she had avoided the
odious crime thus detected, and so make her selfe away.
Worse matter yet than all this and more horrible, is reported

Foist] galley

beside, and that by Authors of good credit and who wil
stand to it: namely, *That he ran in all hast to view the dead body
of his mother when she was killed*: that he handled every par
and member of it: found fault with some, commended
others: and being thirsty in the meane time, tooke a draugh
of drink. Howbeit, notwithstanding hee was hartned by the
ioyous gratulation of Souldiours, Senate, and People, yet
could he not either for the present or euer after, endure the
worme and sting of conscience for his foule fact, but confesse
many a time, that haunted and harried he was with the appari-
tion of his mothers ghost: tormented also with the scourges
and burning torches of the Furies. Moreover, with a sacrifice
made by direction of magicians, he assaied to raise up her
soule and spirite, and to intreate the same to forgiue him.
Verily as hee travailed through *Greece*, at the sacred Eleusine
ceremonies (from the institution and professing wherein al
impious, godlesse, and wicked persons are by the voyce of
a cryer debarred) he durst not be present.

Philemon Holland (translator)
Suetonius' *The Historie of Twelve Cæsars* (1606)

A FATHER'S SACRIFICE

IT chaunced that this young Prince *Antiochus* (as loue ouer-
commeth all men) became in loue with his mother in law
Stratonice, who alreadie had a sonne by *Seleucus* his father. She
being young, and passing fayer, he was so rauished with her,
that though he proued all the wayes possible to maister his
furie and passion that way: yet he was still the weaker. So that
in the end, condemning him selfe to death bicause he found
his desire abhominable, his passion incurable, and his reason
vtterly ouercome: he resolued to kill him selfe by litle and

litle, with abstinence from meate and drinke, and made no other reckoning to remedie his griefe, faining to haue some secret inward disease in his body. Yet could he not so finely cloke it, but that *Erasistratus* the Phisitian easely found his griefe, that loue, not sicknes, was his infirmitie: howbeit it was hard for him to imagine with whom he was in loue. *Erasistratus* being earnestly bent to finde out the partie he loued, he sate by this young Prince all day long in his chamber, and when any fayer young boy or wife came to see him, he earnestly looked *Antiochus* in the face, and carefully obserued all the partes of the bodie, and outward mouings, which do commonly bewray the secret passions and affections of the mind. So hauing marked him diuers times, that when others came to see him, whatsoeuer they were, he still remeined in one selfe state, and that when *Stratonice* his mother in lawe came alone or in companie of her husband *Seleucus* to visite him, he commonly perceiued those signes in him, which *Sappho* wryteth to be in louers (to wit, that his words and speech did faile him, his colour became red, his eyes still rowled to and fro, and then a sodaine swet would take him, his pulse would beate fast and rise high, and in the end, that after the force and power of his hart had failed him, and shewed all these signes, he became like a man in an extasie and traunse, and white as a kearcher) he then gathering a true coniecture by these so manifest signes and declaracions, that it was only *Stratonice* whom this young Prince fansied, and the which he forced him selfe to keepe secret to the death: thought that to bewray it to the king it would offend him muche, but yet trusting to his great affection and fatherly loue he bare to his sonne, he ventred one day to tell him, that his sonnes sicknesse was no other but loue, and withall, that his loue was impossible to be enioyed, and therefore that he must of necessitie dye, for it was incurable. *Seleucus* was cold at the harte to heare these

kearcher] kerchief

newes: so he asked him, What, is he incurable? Yea, Sir, aunswered the Phisitian, bicause he is in loue with my wife. Then replied *Seleucus* againe, Alas *Erasistratus*, I haue alwayes loued thee as one of my dearest frendes, and wouldest thou not now doe me this pleasure, to lette my sonne marry thy wife, sith thou knowest it well that I haue no moe sonnes but he, and that I see he is but cast away, if thou helpe me not? But your grace would not doe it your selfe, sayd *Erasistratus*: if he were in loue with *Stratonice*. O, sayd *Seleucus* to him againe, that it were the wil of the gods, some god or man could turne his loue that way: for mine owne parte, I would not only leaue him the thing he loued, but I would geue my kingdom also to saue his life. Then *Erasistratus* seeing that the king spake these words from his hart, and with abundance of teares: he tooke him by the right hand, and told him plainly, Your grace needeth not *Erasistratus* helpe in this. For being father, husbande, and king, your selfe also may onely be the Phisitian, to cure your sonnes disease. When *Seleucus* heard that, he called an assemblie of the people, and declared before them all that he was determined to crown his sonne *Antiochus* king of the high prouinces of *Asia*, and *Stratonice* Queene, to marry them together: and that he was perswaded that his sonne, (who had alwayes shewed him selfe obedient to his fathers will) would not disobey him in this mariage. And as for *Stratonice*, if she misliked this mariage, and would not consent vnto it bicause it was no common matter: then he prayed that his frendes would perswade her she should thinke all good and comely that should please the king, and withall that concerned the general benefit of the realme and common wealth. Hereuppon *Antiochus* and *Stratonice* were married together.

Sir Thomas North (translator)

Plutarch's *The Liues of the noble Grecians and Romanes* (1579)

Cato's Death

WHEN he had sayd thus, his sonne went out of his chamber weeping, and all his frends also, no man remayning with Cato, but *Demetrius* and *Appollonides*, vnto whom he spake more gently, and reasoned in this sorte. What, doe you thinke to keepe an old man as I am, aliue by force? And haue you taried behinde but to sit staring apon me, and say nothing vnto me? If otherwise else, by reason you come to perswade me, that it shall be no shame for *Cato*, dispairing of the safetie of his life, to seeke it by the grace and mercy of his enemy: why then doe you not now tell me your reasons to perswade me, that forsaking all other fancies and determinations which hetherunto we haue holden for good, being on a sodaine become wiser by *Cæsars* meanes, we should be bound the more therefore to geue him thankes? I do not tell you this that I haue determined any thing of my life, but that it is in my power (if I list) to put the thing in execution I haue determined: but yet I will consult with you, when I am so determined, to heare the reasons and opinion of your bookes, which your selues doe vse in discourse and argument together. Goe your way therefore hardily vnto my sonne, and tell him, that he must not thinke to compell his father vnto that, which he can not proue good vnto him by reason. After this talke, *Demetrius* and *Appollonides* being nothing comforted, weeping, departed out of his chamber. Then his sword was brought him by a litle boy. When he had it, he drew it out, and looked whether the point and edge of his sword was sharpe and woulde cut: when he saw it was well, O, sayd he, now I am where I would be, and so laying downe the sword naked by him, he tooke his booke againe in his hand, and red it ouer (as they say) twise together. Then he slept so soundly after it, that his men which were without his chamber heard him snort againe. About midnight, he called for two of his freemen, *Cleanthes* his Phisitian, and *Butas*, whom he chiefly employed in his weightiest affaires of the common wealth. So he sent him vnto the hauen to see, if all his men that were imbarked were vnder saile: and gaue his hand vnto the Phisitian to be bound up, bicause it was swollen with the blow he gaue one of his slaues when he hit him on the face. All his seruaunts were glad to heare of that, hoping then that he desired to liue. Soone after came *Butas* backe againe from the hauen, and brought him word that all were gone but *Crassus*, who stayed about some busines he had, and yet that he was going to take shippe: howbeit that the sea was very roughe, and winde exceeding great. *Cato* hearing this, sighed, being sory for them that were apon the sea; and sent *Butas* backe againe to the hauen, to see if any man came backe for any matter they had to say vnto him. The litle birdes began to chirpe, and *Cato* fel againe in a litle slumber. But thereuppon *Butas* returned, and brought him word that all was quiet in the hauen, and there was no sturre. Then *Cato* bad him goe his way, and shut to the dore after him, and layed him downe in his bed, as though he had ment to haue slept out all the rest of the night. *Butas* backe was no sooner turned, but *Cato* taking his naked sword in his hand, thrust it into his breast: howbeit the swelling of his hand made the blowe so weake, that it killed him not presently, but drawing on to his latter ende, he fell downe vpon his bedde, and made such a noyse with his fall (ouer-throwing a litle table of geometry hard by his bedde) that his seruaunts hearing the noyse, gaue a great shreeke for feare. Thereuppon his sonne and his friendes ranne into the chamber, and found him all of a gore bloud, and the most part of his bowells comming out of his bodye, him selfe being yet aliue, and seeing them. They were all striken with such sorow to behold it, that at the first they were so amased, as they could not tel what to say to it. His Phisitian comming to him, he went about to put in his bowels againe which were not perished, and to sow vp his wound. But *Cato* comming to him selfe, thrust backe the Phisitian, and tare his bowells with his owne handes, and made his wound very great, and immediatly gaue vp the ghost. Whereuppon the three hundred *Romanes* (in lesse time then a man would haue thought *Catoes* owne houshold seruaunts could haue knowen of his death) were at his dores, and immediatly after, all the people of *Vtica* also came thither, and with one voyce called *Cato* their benefactor and sauior, and sayd he onely was a free man, and had an inuincible minde: and this was done, when they heard say that *Cæsar* was not farre from *Vtica*. Furthermore, nether feare of the present daunger, nor the desire to flatter the Conqueror, nether any priuate quarrell amongest them selues, could keepe them from honoring *Catoes* funeralls. For, sumptuously setting out his body, and honorably accompanying his funeralls as might be, they buryed him by the sea side, where at this present time is to be seene his image, holding a sworde in his hande. After that, they made their best way to saue them selues and their citie. Nowe *Cæsar* beeing aduertised by them that came vnto him, howe *Cato* sturred not from *Vtica*, nor fled not, but sent all others away, sauing him selfe, and his sonne, and a few of his friends that remained there, being afraid of nothing: he could not deuise what he ment by it. Therefore esteeming *Cato* much, he made haste with all the speede he could with his armie, to come thether. But when he vnderstoode that *Cato* had slaine him selfe, writers doe reporte he sayd thus: O *Cato*, I enuy thy death, sithe thou hast enuied mine honor to saue thy life. For in deede, had Cato beene contented *Cæsar* should haue saued his life, he had not so much impaired his owne honor, as he had augmented *Cæsars* glory.

Sir Thomas North (translator)

Plutarch's *The Liues of the noble Grecians and Romanes* (1579)

GYGES' DILEMMA

THIS *Candaules* was passing well affectioned to his wyfe, in so much that for the singuler loue he bare her, he thought her to excell al women in the comly feature of the body. And hereof beyng himselfe fully perswaded, hee fortuned to fall in talke with *Gyges* sonne of *Bascylus*, one of the chiefe and principall of his garde (whom also he especially fauoured, and not seldome employed him in matters of greate weight) aduancing vnto him the seemly shape of his wife aboue measure. In short space after (for the euill hap haunted hym) meetinge with the aforesayde *Gyges*, hee beganne thus:

My faythfull seruant *Gyges*, wheras thou seemest not to credite the large vauntes and often bragges which I make of my Ladyes beauty and comlynesse (the eares of men beyng much more incredulous then their eyes) behold I wil so bring to passe, that thou shalt see her naked. Wherat the pore Gentleman greatlye abashed, and in no wyse willyng to assent therto, made answere as followeth. My Lord (quoth he) what manner of speech is this which vnaduisedly you vse in perswading me to beholde my ladyes secrets. For a woman you know, the more in sight the lesse in shame, who togeather with her garmentes layth assyde her modestye. Honest preceptes haue bene deuised by our elders which wee ought to remember, Whereof this is one, that euery man ought to beholde his owne. For myne own part I easily beleeue you, that of all women in the world, there is none comparable vnto her in beauty.

Wherfore I beseech your grace, to haue me excused, if in a case so heynous and vnlawfull, I somewhat refuse to obay your wil. *Gyges* hauing in this sort acquited himselfe, fearing the daunger that might ensue, the King began a fresh to replye, saying, My good *Gyges*, take hart at grace, and feare not, least eyther my selfe do goe about to examine and feele thy

meaning by the coloured glose of fayned speach, or that the
Queene my Ladye take occasion to worke thy displeasure
hereby. Pull vpp thy spirites, and leaue al to mee: it is I that
wil worke the meanes, whereby shee shall neuer know any
part of her selfe to haue bene seene by anye creature liuing.
Listen then awhyle and geue eare to my counsayle.

When night is come the dore of the chaumber wherein wee
lye beyng wyde set open, I will couertly place thee behynde
the same: strayght at my entraunce thereinto, her custome is
not to be long after mee; directly at her comming in, there
standeth a bench, wherat vnclothing herselfe, shee accus-
tometh to lay her garmentes vppon it, propoundinge her
deuine and angelicall body, to bee seene and viewed for
a long space; this done, as she turnes from the bench to bed-
warde, her backe beyng toward thee, haue care to slip priuily
out of the dores least happily she espye thee.

The gentleman seynge hymselfe taken in a trap, that in no
wyse he could escape without perfourmance of his Lords
folly, gaue his assent, and at an howre appoynted stood in a
readines, whom *Candaules* closely brought into his chaumber:
and immediatly after came the Queene: whom *Gyges* hauyng
beheld at his pleasure, when her back was turned crept out of
the dore, yet not so secretly, but that the Queene had a
glympse of hym, and perceyued, who hee was.

The Lady seyng the fond and vndiscrete treacherye of her
husband made little adoe, and seemed as though shee had
seene nothing, Albeit fully myndinge to bee reuenged of the
shameless foolish facte of her espoused Lord.

For with the *Lydians*, and welnygh also with the rest of the
Barbarians, it is a greate reproach euen for a man to be seene
vnclothed. Howbeit for the present tyme she kept silence,
makyng no semblaunce of any displeasure.

The day following, hauing assembled certayne of her
household seruauntes, in whom shee hadde especiall affyaunce,

Gyges was sent for, who suspecting nothing lesse then that hys deceipt was knowen: spedely and with all diligence, adressed hym to come: beyng wont also at other tymes to come to the Queene as oft as yt pleased hyr to sende for him. Beyng entred the chaumber she began to assayle him in these wordes: Now, *Gyges* of two present wayes I geue thee free choyce which of them both thou wilt take: eyther to slay the King *Candaules* and enioy mee with the Kingedome of *Lydia*: or thy selfe presently to leese thy lyfe. Lest in obayng thy Lord in that thou oughtest not, thou be henseforth priuye to that which thou shouldest not.

There is nor remedy but that one of you both must to the pot, ether the mayster or the man, ether hee which led thee hereunto, or thy selfe that sawest mee naked, and diddest those thinges that wer vnlawful to be done. *Gyges* herewith amazed beganne first to beseech her humbly, entreating her not to bynd him to so harde a condition. Neuerthelesse being not hable to perswade her, and seinge it necessarye eyther to murther his Lord, or to be murthered by other, he deemed it the better choyse to lyue hymselfe, addressing his speech to the Queene in this wyse. My Soueraynge Lady (quoth he) synce of necessity you compell mee to become guylty of the bloude of my Kinge, let mee heare by what meanes wee shall set vppon him. Of a truth (sayd shee) our treason shall proproceede from the same place from whence he bewrayed my shame. The assault shall be geuen when hee is a sleepe. The wretched Gentleman dryuen to so harde a strayght, that eyther hee must slaye or be slayne, made no delay but followed the Queene into her bed chaumber, whom with a naked dagger in hys hand, she priuely placed behynd the same dore, from whence *Gyges* afterwardes arysing bereaued *Candaules* of his life, and obtayned both hys wyfe and his kingdome.

B.R. (translator)

The Famous Hystory of Herodotus (1584)

FOTIS

WHEN I was within the house I found my deere and sweete loue Fotis minsing of meate, and making pottage for her Master and Mistris, the cupborde was all set with wines, and I thought I smelled the sauor of some deintie meates: she had about her middle a white and clean apron, and she was girded about her bodie vnder her pappes with a swathell of redde silke, and she stirred the potte and turned the meate with her fayre and white handes, in such sort that with stirringe and turninge the same her loines and hippes did likewise moue and shake, which was in my mind a comely sight to see.

These things when I sawe I was halfe amased, and stoode musinge with my selfe, and my courage came then vpon me, whiche before was skant. And I spake vnto Fotis merely and said: O Fotis, how trimly you can stirre the potte, and how finelie, (with shakinge your buttockes) you can make potage. O happy and twice happy is he to whom you give leaue and licence but to touch you there: Then she beeing likewise merely disposed, gan answeare, Depart I say, miser from me, departe from my fire, for if the flame thereof doo neuer so little blase foorth it will burne thee extremely, and none can extinguishe the heate thereof but I alone who in stirring the potte, and making the bedde can so finely shake my selfe: when she had saied these woordes she cast her eies vpon mee and laughed, but I did not departe from thence vntill such time as I had viewed her in every point: but what should I speake of others? When as I doo accustome abroade to marke and viewe the face and heare of euery dame, and afterwards delight my selfe therwith priuately at home, and thereby iudge the residew of their shape, because the face is the principall parte of all the bodie, and is firste open to our eies: And whatsoeuer flourishyng and gorgeous apparell

merely] merrily   *heare*] hair

doth worke and set foorth in the corporal partes of a woman, the same doth the naturall and comely beautie set out in the face. Moreouer there be diuers that (to the intent to showe their grace and feauture) wil cast of their partlettes, collars, habilimentes, frontes, cornettes and krippins, and doo more delight to showe the fairenes of their skinne, than to decke themselues vp in gold and pretious stones. But because it is a crime vnto me to say so, and to give no example thereof, know ye: that if you spoile and cut of the heare of any woman or depriue her of the colour of her face, though she were neuer so excellent in beautie, though she weare throwen downe from heauen, spronge of the seas, nourished of the floudes, though she weare Venus her selfe, though she weare accompanied with the Graces, though she weare wayted vpon of all the Court of Cupide, though she weare girded with her beautifull skarfe of love, and though she smelled of perfumes and musks, yet if she appered balde: shee could in no wise please, no not her owne Vulcanus.

O how well doth a fayre colour, and a shininge face agree with glittering heare! Behold it encountereth with the beames of the sunne, and pleaseth the eie meruelously. Sometimes the beautie of the heare resembleth the colour of Golde and honie, sometimes the blewe plumes and azured feathers about the neckes of dooues, especially when it is either anointed with the gumme of Arabia, or trimely tufte out with the teeth of a fine combe, whiche if it be tied up in the pole of the necke, it seemeth to the louer (that beholdeth the same) as a glasse that yeldeth foorth a more pleasant and gratious comelines than if it shoulde be sparsed abroade on the shoulders of the woman, or hange down scatteringe behinde. Finally, there is suche a dignitie in the heare, that what so euer she be, though she be neuer so brauely attired with gold, silkes, pretious

partlettes] neckerchiefs *cornettes*] head-dresses
krippins] hair-nets

stones, and other riche and gorgeous ornamentes, yet if her heare be not curiously set foorth, she cannot seeme faire. But in my Fotis, her garmentes vnbraste and vnlaste did encrease her beautie, her heare hanged about her shoulders, and was disparsed abroade vpon her partlette, and in euery parte of her necke, howbeit the greater parte was trussed vp in her pole with a lace. Then I vnable to sustaine the broylinge heate that I was in, ran vpon her and kissed the place where she had thus layd her heare, whereat she turned her face, and cast her rolling eies vpon me, saying, O schollar, thou hast tasted now both hony and galle, take heede that thy pleasure doo not turne into repentance: Tushe (quoth I) my sweete harte, I am contented for such another kisse to be broyled here vpon this fier, wherewithal I embrased and kissed her more often, and she embrased and kissed me likewise, and moreouer her breath smelled like sinnamome, and the licour of her tongue was like vnto sweete Nectar, wherewith when my minde was greatly delighted. I saide, Beholde Fotis I am yours, and shall presently die vnlesse you take pittie vpon me. Which when I had said, she eftsoones kissed me, and bidde me be of good courage, and I will (quoth she) satisfie your whole desire, and it shall be no lenger delaied than vntill night, when as (assure your selfe) I will come and lie with you; wherefore go your waies and prepare your selfe, for I entende valiantly and couragiously to encounter with you this night: Thus when we had louingly talked and reasoned together, we departed for that time.

William Adlington (translator)
Apuleius' The XI Bookes of the Golden Asse (1566)

BLIND BEGGAR

BUT to retourne to my blynde master, and to shew his nature
I assure you that sith the beginning of the worlde God neuer
made man more deceitfull and craftie: for in his art and trade
of liuing he far passed all other: he could recite by hart a
hundred long prayers and moe, yea, and the life of all the holy
saincts: at his deuotion time he vsed such a loude tunable
voyce, that it might be heard throughout the Churche where
hee praied, and besides all that, he could counterfet a good
deuoute countenance in praying, without any strange gesture,
either with mouth or eye, as other blinde men are accustomed
to vse. I am not able to recite a thousand other manner of
wayes which hee had to get money: hee would make many
beleeue that he had praiers for diuers good purposes, as for to
make women bring foorth children, yea, and to make men
to loue their wiues, although they had hated them neuer so
much. He would prognosticate to women that were with
childe, whether they should bring foorth a Sonne or a
daughter: in matters of Physicke, hee woulde affirme that
Galen neuer knew halfe so much as hee: also for any griefe,
the tooth ach, or anye other disease, there was neuer one complained, but that immediatly he would say, do this, doe that,
seeth such an herbe, take such a roote: So that by this his continuall practise, he had daily great resorte made vnto him
(especially of women) which did faithfully beleeue all that
euer he said: by them hee had great gaine, for he wan more in
a moneth, then twenty of his occupation did in a whole yeere.
Yet for all his daily gaines, you must vnderstand that there was
neuer man so wretched a niggarde. For hee caused mee not
onely to die for hunger, but also to wante what so euer I
needed. And therefore to confesse the troth, if I had not
founde out meanes to helpe my selfe, I had bene buried long
sithence. Wherfore oftentimes I would so preuent him of all

his crafte, that my portion shoulde proue as good as his: and to bring my matter so to passe I vsed wonderfull deceits (whereof I will recite vnto you some) although somtimes my practising of them did cost mee bitter paines. This blind man caried alwayes his bread and his vittell in a little bag of cloth, which was shutte at the mouthe with an Iron buckle, vnder a miserable locke and keye: at the time of putting his meate in, and taking it out, he would keepe such straight account, that all the world was not able to deceiue him of one crumme, and therefore there was no helpe, but that I must needes bee content with that small allowance that hee gaue mee, which alwayes I was sure to dispatch at two morsels: and as sone as euer he had shut his little lock, he wold thinke then that all were sure, imagining that I had other matters in hand: then would I boldly vnrip and sowe vp againe the syde of his couetous sacke, vsing daily to launce one of the sides, there to take out not onely bread at mine owne pleasure, but also slices of flesh, and sweete carbonados: So that by such meanes I found conuenient time to ease the raging hunger which he was cause of. Moreouer all the money that euer I could conuey and steale from him, I changed alwayes into halfe blanks, and when any man demanded any praier, he had always of ordinarie a blanke giuen him for his hire, and because he could not see, it should be deliuered mee: but he could neuer so soone put foorth his hand to receiue it, but I was readie to throwe it into my mouth, and by quicke exchaunge to giue him the iust value of halfe of it, whereat he would much murmure, knowing by the onely feeling of it what it was, and would say: How in the diuels name chanceth it that sithence thy comming to me, I receiue but halfe blankes, and before I had alwayes a whole blanke and sometimes two? I thinke surely that thy vnluckinesse be cause thereof. From that time forwarde hee thought good to shorten

blanke] small French coin

his prayers, cutting them off in the middest: wherefore he
commanded me, that as soone as the almes giuer had turned
his back, I shold plucke him by the cloake. Then streight
wayes changing tune, he would begin to crie with loude
voice (as blindmen vse to do) who will heare such a deuout
prayer, or else the life of some holie Sainct? At dinner or
supper time, he had alwayes before him a little potfull of
wine, which oftentimes I woulde laye hande on, and after
two or three kisses sende it him secretely home againe: But
that happie time continued for but a while, for I was wont to
leaue so little behinde mee, that he might soone espie the
faulte, as in deede immediatly hee did mistrust the whole
matter, wherefore hee began a newe order, not to leaue his
wine anie more at random, but to auoyde daunger, had
always his little pot fast by the eare, so to be sure of his drinke.
Yet notwithstanding for all this, the Adamant stone had neuer
such vertue to drawe Iron to it, as I had to sucke vp his wine
with a long reede which I had prepared for the purpose: for
as soone as the ende of my reede had bene once in, I might
well desire him to fill the pot againe. Yet at the last the craftie
blinde man chaunced to feele mee, and being angrie, determined to take an other way, to place his pot betweene his
legges, couering it still with his hande, so to auoyde all former
daungers: when hee had so done, I being accustomed to
drinke wyne, did long to taste of it, and perceiuing that my
reede coulde then no more preuaile at all, I deuised an other
kinde of fetche, howe to make a hole in the bottome of his
wine pot, and to stoppe the same with a little softe waxe, so
that at dynner time making a shewe as I were readie to dye
for colde, I would creepe betweene the blynd mans legges, to
warme myselfe at his small fire, by the heate whereof, the
wax being little in quantitie, woulde so melte away, that the
wyne would issue down into my mouth freshely and trime,
I being sure to gape vpward so iust, that one droppe should

neuer fall beside. So that when my blinde master would taste of his wine, hee shoulde neuer finde drop to quench his thurst, whereat he would much maruell, cursing and swering all maner of othes, yea wishing the pot and all that was within it at the diuell, musing still how his wine should bee so consumed away. Then straightwayes to excuse my selfe, I would say, I trust you will not mistrust mee gentle uncle, seeing that the pot came neuer out of your owne hands.

David Rowland (translator)
The Pleasaunt Historie of Lazarillo de Tormes (1586)

EGYPTIAN THIEF

FOR by this time was the battell begonne, and a man might see those that dwelled a farre, euen in outer coaste of the Fenne, come into theire enimies handes, for they, who came vppon them, burned vp the Boates, and Cotages of suche as either were slaine, or else fledde out of the Battaile, whose eyes also were daseled with the greate and intollerable brightnesse of the fire, that burned vp the Reedes, whereof there was great plentie, and theire eares filled with the great noyse, and tumulte, so that now a man might both see, and heare the whole manner of the skirmishe, those who dwelled there mainteininge the Battaile with all theire power, and strength, and theire enimies beinge more in number, and takinge them at a suddaine, killed somme of them on the earthe, other somme they drowned in the Poole with Boates, and houses too. Of all whiche, as well of those that fought by lande, and lake, did kill and were killed, as also of those, who were besette with Fiere and Water, arose a marueilous sounde in the Ayre. Which when *Thyamis* sawe, he remembred his

153

dreame, wherein he sawe *Isis*, and her Churche filled with
fiere, and deade menne, and supposinge thereby to be meante
that whiche he nowe had seene, geathered thereof a contrarie
interpretation to that he made before, that hauinge, thou shal
not haue *Cariclia*, as taken awaie by Warre, and that he
shoulde kill, and not wound her, that is, with his sworde, and
not with Carnall copulation. At lengthe railinge on the Goddes, as though shee had beguiled him, and thinkinge it not
meete that any other shoulde enioye *Cariclia*, commaundinge
his men to keepe their places, and mainteine the Battaile as
longe as thei might: him selfe fighting in euery part of the
Ilande, and diuers times making priuy erruptions out of euery
quarter vppon his enimies, thinkinge it also to be good, if
that waie he could preuaile againste them, him selfe, as though
he wente to seeke for *Thermutis*, and doo certaine Sacrifices to
his priuie Goddes, sufferinge no man to goe with him, in
haste wente to the Caue. Surely a barbarous nature cannot
easily be withdrawen, or turned from that, that he hathe
once determined. And if the Barbarous people be once in
dispaire of their owne safetie, they haue a custome to kill all
those, by whome they sette muche, and whose companie they
desire after deathe, or els would keepe them from the violence and wronge of theire enimies. For that same cause also
Thyamis, forgettinge all that hee had to doo, beinge incloased
with his enimies armie, as if he had been caughte in a Nette,
almoste enraged with loue, gelousie, and anger, after he came
in haste to the Caue, goinge into the same, crieng with a
loude voyce, and speaking many thinges in the *Egyptian*
tongue, as soone as hee hearde one speake *Greeke* to him
aboute the entrie of the Caue, and was conducted to her by
her voyce, hee laied his left hande vpon her heade, and with
his sworde thrust her through the body, a little beneath the
pappes. And after this sorrowfull sorte, that woman geuinge
vp her laste, and ghastly grone, was slaine. But he, after he

:ame out, and had shut the doore, and cast a little grauell
hereon, with teares, said, These espousalles hast thou at my
iande.

Thomas Underdowne (translator)

An Æthiopian Historie of Heliodorus (1569)

DAPHNIS AND CHLOE

HEREWITH *Daphnis* hauing taken his flute sounded thereupon
diuers excellent ditties. And for so much as it grewe towards
the middest of the daie, the melodiousnesse of the sound together with the heate of the season, brought *Chloe* a sleepe,
their flockes by this time beeing couched all together vnder
the shadie toppes; which *Daphnis* perceiuing, stayed quickly
his musique, withdrawing his flute, gaue him selfe thereupon
to gaze at full vpon her most exquisite perfections. And seeing
that there was none about him to countermaund his de-
meanors, hee began secretly thus to deliuer in him selfe. Oh
howe sweetlie these eie liddes of my fayre and blissefull *Chloe*
are couched together, howe delicate is the sent and sauour of
her breath, the sweetnesse whereof neither these albpine
buddes, nor flowres them selues, doe in any sort imitate; yet
dare I not for this, to kisse at all, these sweete sauours for that
the very touch is more peercing than the swords point, and
the force thereof cutteth the verie heart on sonder, and as the
receipt of the newe made honie, so swelleth in those that
touche it the harmefull poyson hereof: Neither would I yet
inforce that iniurie to my *Chloe*, as by too rude pressing her
lippes, to yeeld disturbance to her quiet. Alas these gras-
hoppers I feare me with their piping tunes, will wake my
deerling. Yee cruell beastes, why hurt yee so rudely with your
hornes, vnpacient as it seemeth to giue vnto my derling any
rest. O yee wolfes, at this instant more crauinlike then the
foxes them selues, why rush yee not into these heardes to

albpine] alpine

scatter them on sonder: Whylest, *Daphnis* continued in these
and such like complaintes, a seelie grashopper egerly pursued
by a swallowe, cast her selfe by chance, for her sauegarde
into the bosome of *Chloe*, by meanes whereof, the Swallowe
neither was able to catche her, nor lenger could vse vnto her
the force of her wing, notwithstanding the birde came so
neere that with fluttering vp and downe about her face, shee
awakened *Chloe* out of her sleepe, the feare whereof, made
the *Nymphe*, (for that shee knewe not what it was) to skritche
alowde, but when shee sawe the Swallowe yet fluttering too
and fro about her, and *Daphnis* laughing by her at the harmelesse feare and sporte thereof, shee deemed the lesse of the
matter, and rubbing her eies, yet greedie of sleepe, shee made
her selfe readie to arise.

The grashopper was yet betweene her brestes, and as one
deliuered as it seemed from danger, and in the kinde it bare,
willing to shewe it selfe thankefull, began to chante where
shee sate, remunerating thereby the good turne at her handes
receiued, by reason of which, *Chloe* not yet experienced of
the accident, cried outright, and *Daphnis* againe laughed a
pace at the sport, and loathing to grieue her ouermuch, conueied thereupon his hande betweene her breastes, and tooke
out the grassehopper, which yet thankefull of hir sauegarde
continued chaunting betweene his handes, whereupon the
faire Shepheards knowing what it was, tooke it againe & returned it forthwith into her bosome.

Angel Day (translator)
Longus' *Daphnis and Chloe* . . . (1587)

EUROPA AND THE BULL

WHEN I had sufficiently gazed on their offerings to their gods
hung at their tabernacles, I by chance espied a faire large
picture, wherin was drawen the sea and land, and the whole

history of *Europe*: the sea was called the *Phænician* sea, but the land was called the *Sydonian*: on the land was a groue full of yong damsels: in the sea was a bull swimming, carying on his back a most beautiful virgin, directing his course towards *Creet*: the groue was garnished with variety of many flowers, and planted with many faire trees, and pleasant shrubs, whose boughs and leaues did so naturally (as it were) imbrace and tie one another, as that they did serue for vse of a house. More-ouer, the painter had with such cunning workmanship drawn a thin shadow vnder the leaues, that in some places the beams of the sun pearcing throgh, did somwhat shine: this groue was compassed round with reeds, and set throughout with sweete and odoriferous plants, as myrrhe, roses, spike, daffa-dill, whereunder were made pleasant seats to rest vpon: but in the bottom of this groue there was a most bright fountaine, which winding it self through the midst of it did water these flowers and plants: neither were they wanting who had the ouersight of it: for one was weeding and picking the beds, another pruning the trees, another standing ouer the riuer with a spade in his hand, did open the course of the water: but on that part of the groue which bordered on the sea, the painter had so artificially drawne the maides, as that they did shew both mirth and sorrow by their countenances, hauing garlands on their heads, their haire about their shoulders, their feet without shooes, their legs bare, their clothes tuckt vp to the knee, their faces pale, their cheekes wrinckled and wan, their eies beholding the sea, their lips, as it were for feare about to speake somewhat, a little gaping, their hands were stretched forth toward the bull, and they went so far into the sea, that the water came vp to the vpper part of theyr legs: their cariage and gesture of their bodie did appeare to be such, as that they seemed they would go to the bull, yet feared to commit themselues to the violence of the water. The sea had two colours, that part which was next to the land was somewhat red, but the deeper and further off, of his natural colour: there out of the midst of the water did appeare certaine rocks, as it were cast vp out of the earth, which seemed to be all white with the fome of the swelling and raging waues beating on the side. In the midle of the sea was painted a bull, which was caried by the waues, casting vp the water before him like vnto a mountain. The virgin sitting vpon his back, not after the manner of horsmen, but both her legs being fitly laid downe on his right side, with her left hand held his horne, as wagoners accustome to hold their reines, whose direction the bull did follow: her breast to her priuy parts was attired with a vaile of lawne, the rest of hir body was couered with a purple mantle, all the other parts were to be seene, saue there where her garments couered, for she had a deepe nauill, a plaine smooth belly, narrow flanke, round buttocks: her tender brests seemed to swel, throgh the midle of which went down a faire narrow way most pleasant and delightfull to the beholders: with one hand she did holde his horne, with the other his taile, but yet so that the attire of her head couered with a scarf cast ouer her shoulders, was held on fast against the force of the wind, which did so beat on her bosom, that euery where it seemed to swell. She thus sitting on the bull, was caried like a shippe, her scarfe seruing in stead of a sayle. Round about the bull Dolphins floted about, and sported at their loues in such sort, as that you would thinke, you saw their verie motions drawne. There was a litle boy, which led the bull, displaying his wings abroade, holding in his hand a Torch, and turning to *Iupiter* did smile, as though he mocked him, that he for his cause was thus transformed into a Bull.

William Burton (translator)

*The Most Delectable and Plesant History of
Clitophon and Leucippe* (1597)

Spanish Pastoral

Now the day being come wherin the feast was celebrated, I with other sheppardesses, leving off our working day and baser apparell, and arraying our selues in the best wee had, wee went the day before the feast to watch in the Temple that euen as formerly we had done, and being as I say in the company of my frends, wee saw enter in at the dore, a crewe of beautifull sheppardesses whom certen sheppardes did accompanie, who leauing them within and hauing ended theire deuotions went out into the pleasant valleys; for it was the fashon of that contrie that noe sheppard might enter into the Temple to doe more than his obeysance, but shold presentlie turne backe againe vntill the daie following, when they might all enter and participate of those ceremonies and sacrafices, which there were done. And the cause hereof was, that the Nimphes and sheppardesses might remaine alone without any occasion to entend any other matter then to celebrate the feast one with an other, a thing that manie more yeares they had vsed to doe; and the sheppards taryed without in a greene Meadow at hand by the light of the Moone. Now the sheppards that I tell yow of being entred this sumptious Temple, after they had done theire devotion and offered theire Offeringes vppon the Alter they sate them downe hard by vs, and as my fortune wold haue it there sate one downe next mee, by whose meanes I shold become miserable, soe long as the memory of her remained.

The sheppardesses came in masked, theire faces couered with whyte vayles, with chapplets of straw most finely wrought, with devises in garnishing of the same so well wrought and framed that the Goulde it self cold not haue made it ashamed. I standing beholding her that was sett by mee, I saw her eyes were neuer off mee, and when I looked vppon her she abased her eyes fayneing as if she wold fayne

behold mee but wold not that I shold perceiue it. I desired
extreamly to know whome shee was, that if shee spake vnto
mee I might not fall into anie errour by reason of my not
knowing her, and yet alwaies when I did not regard it the
sheppardesse neuer lett her eyes goe off mee, in soe much that
a thousand tymes I was about to speake vnto her being enamored of those faire eyes which only shee had discouered
but I standing so with all possible attention, shee putt forth
the most beautifull and delicate hand that since then I euer
sawe and taking mee by myne, shee stoode looking vppon
me a whyle. I that was more enamored of her then can
bee told said vnto her, Faire and gratious sheppardesse, it is
not only this hand that is ready to serue yow, but the verry
hart and soule of her whose hand it is. *Ismenia* (for soe was
shee called that was the cause of all my thoughts disquiet)
hauing purposed before to floute mee (as hereafter yow shall
heare) answeared verry softlie that noe body cold heare,
Gratious sheppardesse quoth shee, so much I am your owne,
that it hath made me doe that which I haue done. I beseech
yow bee not offended that seeing your beautifull countenance,
I retaine noe more anie powre ouer my self.

Sir Thomas Wilson (translator)

Diana de Montemayor (1596). Text from
the *Revue Hispanique* (1920)

ARCADIA

THERE were hilles which garnished their proud heights with
stately trees: humble valleis, whose base estate semed comforted with refreshing of siluer riuers: medows, enameld with
al sorts of ey-pleasing floures: thickets, which being lined with
most pleasant shade, were witnessed so to by the chereful
deposition of many wel-tuned birds: each pasture stored with

sheep feeding with sober security, while the prety lambs with bleting oratory craued the dams comfort: here a shepheards boy piping, as though he should neuer be old: there a yong shepherdesse knitting, and withall singing, and it seemed that her voice comforted her hands to work, and her hands kept time to her voices musick. As for the houses of the country (for many houses came vnder their eye) they were all scattered, no two being one by th'other, and yet not so far off as that it barred mutual succour: a shew, as it were, of an accompanable solitarines, and of a ciuil wildnes.

Sir Philip Sidney

The Countesse of Pembrokes Arcadia (1590)

CECROPIA TEMPTS PHILOCLEA

Philoclea looked vpon her, and caste downe her eie again. Aunt (said she) I would I could be so much a mistres of my owne mind, as to yeelde to my cousins vertuous request: for so I construe of it. But my hart is already set (and staying a while on that word, she brought foorth afterwards) to lead a virgins life to my death: for such a vow I haue in my selfe deuoutly made. The heauens preuent such a mischiefe (said *Cecropia*). A Vowe, quoth you? no, no, my deere neece, Nature, when you were first borne, vowed you a woman, and as she made you child of a mother, so to do your best to be mother of a child: she gaue you beautie to moue loue; she gaue you wit to know loue; she gaue you an excellent body to reward loue: which kind of liberall rewarding is crowned with vnspeakable felicitie. For this, as it bindeth the receiuer, so it makes happy the bestower: this doth not impouerish, but enrich the giuer. O the sweet name of a mother: O the comfort of comforts, to see your children grow vp, in whom you are (as it were) eternized: if you could conceiue what a hart-tickling ioy it is to see your own litle ones, with awfull loue come running to your lap, and like litle models of your selfe, still cary you about them, you would thinke vnkindnes in your own thoughts, that euer they did rebell against the mean vnto it. But perchance I set this blessednes before your eies, as Captains do victorie before their souldiers, to which they might come through many paines, grieues and dangers, No, I am content you shrinke from this my counsel, if the way to come vnto it, be not most of all pleasant. I know not (answered the sweet *Philoclea*, fearing least silence would offend for sullennes) what contentment you speake of: but I am sure the best you can make of it, (which is mariage) is a burdenous yoke. Ah, deer neece (said *Cecropia*) how much you are deceiued? A yoke indeed we all beare, laid vpon vs in our creation, which by mariage is not increased, but thus farre eased, that you haue a yoke-fellow to help to draw through the cloddy cumbers of this world. O widow-nights, beare witnes with me of the difference. How often alas do I embrace the orfan-side of my bed, which was wont to be imprinted by the body of my deare husband, and with teares acknowledge, that I now enioy such a liberty as the banished man hath; who may, if he list, wander ouer the world, but is euer restrained from his most delightful home? that I haue now such a liberty as the seeled doue hath, which being first depriued of eies, is then by the falconer cast off? For beleue me, neece, beleue me, mans experience is womans best eie-sight. Haue you euer seene a pure Rosewater kept in a christal glas; how fine it lokes, how sweet it smels, while that beautifull glasse imprisons it? Breake the prison, and let the water take his owne course, doth it not imbrace dust, and loose all his former sweetneesse, and fairenesse? Truly so are we, if we haue not the stay, rather then the restraint of Cristalline mariage. My hart meltes to thinke of the sweete comfortes, I in that happie time receiued, when I had neuer cause to care, but the care

was doubled: when I neuer reioiced, but that I saw my ioy
shine in anothers eies. What shall I say of the free delight,
which the hart might embrace, without the accusing of the
inward conscience, or feare of outward shame? and is a
solitary life as good as this? then can one string make as good
musicke as a consort: then can one colour set forth a beautie.

Sir Philip Sidney

The Countesse of Pembrokes Arcadia (1590)

PASTORAL

As soone as the sunne appeared the shepheard got him vp, and
fed fat with this hope, went merely with his men to the foldes,
and there letting foorth his sheepe, after that hee had appointed where they should graze, returned home, and looking
when his guests should rise, hauing supt il the last night went
roundly to his breakfast: by that time he had ended his *desiune*,
Lamedon was gotten vp, and so was *Samela*. Against their
rising *Carmela* had showen her cookerie, and *Menaphon* tired
in his russet iacket, his redde sleeues of chamlet, his blew bon-
net, and his round slop of countrey cloth, bestirred him, as
euerie ioynt had been set to a sundrie office. *Samela* no sooner
came out of her chamber, but *Menaphon* as one that claimed
pitie for his passions, bad her good morrow with a firme louers
looke: *Samela* knowing the fowle by the feather, was able to
cast his disease without his water, perceiued that *Cupide* had
caught the poore shepheard in his net, and vnles he sought
quickly to break out of the snare would make him a tame
foole: faire lookes she gaue him, and with a smiling sorow
discouered how she grieued at his misfortune, and yet
fauoured him. Well, to breakfast they went: *Lamedon* and
Samela fed hard, but *Menaphon* like the *Argiue* in the Date
gardens of *Arabia*, liued with the contemplation of his Mistres

desiune] breakfast

beautie: the Salamander liueth not without the fire, the Herring from the water, the Mole from the earth, nor the Cameleon from the aire, nor coulde *Menaphon* liue from the sight of his *Samela*; whose breath was perfumed aire, whose eyes were fire wherein he delighted to dallie, whose heart the earthlie Paradice wherein hee desired to ingraffe the essence of his loue and affection: thus did the poore shepheard bathe in a kinde of blisse, whiles his eye feeding on his mistres face, did surfet with the excellencie of her perfection. So long he gazde, that at length breakfast was ended, and he desirous to doo her anie seruice first put her childe to nurse, and then led her forth to see his folds; thinking with the sight of his flockes to inueigle her, whose minde had rather haue chosen anie misfortune, than haue deined her eyes on the face and feature of so lowe a peasant. Well, abroad they went, *Menaphon* with his sheephooke fringed with cruell, to signifie he was chiefe of the swaynes, *Lamedon* and *Samela* after: plodding thus ouer the greene fields, at last they came to the mountaines where *Menaphons* flockes grazed, and there he discoursed vnto *Samela* thus; I tell thee faire Nymph, these Plaines that thou seest stretching Southward, are pastures belonging to *Menaphon*: there growes the cintfoyle, and the hyacinth, the cowsloppe, the primrose, and the violet, which my flockes shall spare for flowers to make thee garlands, the milke of my ewes shall be meate for thy pretie wanton, the wool of the fat weathers that seemes as fine as the fleece that *Iason* fet from *Colchos*, shall serue to make *Samela* webbes withall; the mountaine tops shall be thy mornings walke, and the shadie valleies thy euenings arbour: as much as *Menaphon* owes shall be at *Samelas* command, if she like to liue with *Menaphon*. This was spoken with such deepe effects, that *Samela* could scarce keepe her from smiling, yet she couered her conceipt with a sorrowful countenance, which *Menaphon* espying, to make her merrie, and rather for his own aduantage, seeing

Lamedon was a sleepe, tooke her by the hand and sate downe, and pulling foorth his pipe, began after some melodie to carroll out this roundelay.

Robert Greene

Menaphon (1589)

MARPISSA

WHAT reason hast thou (*Marpissa*) to contend with loue, that is both restlesse and vnreasonable, adding so to fire fuell? or what standest thou vpon these ouer-curious points, thy fathers displeasure, *Crisippus* his Pettigree, or thine own Modestie: when the first may be pacified, or else by meanes auoided, for from whom we are deriued by birth, to them what can we more returne than reuerent mindes: but to whom we are driuen by loue, from them what may we lesse with-hold than our own parsons? yea *Marpissa* thou maist also reuerence as a daughter, and loue as a wife, and yet the later not preiudicial to the first. Secondly, and as concerning *Crisippus* his Pettigree, or Pouertie, what is that to be respected: seeing thou doest delight in his parsonage, not descant of his parentage, whose vertue doth counteruaile the want of Nobilitie: for better the man lacking wealth, then wealth lacking the man. Thirdly, what shouldest thou bee more nise than wise: That art therefore to be pardoned because in loue, and who is ignorant that loue respecteth no persons? for howsoeuer in all other things hapneth a superioritie, yet Nature that hath giuen to vs al one Byrth, one Breath, and one Death, in this one only thing remaineth vncorrupt, and is to all alike indifferent, making *Phœbus* a Shepheard, and *Hercules* a Cot-queane: but admit the Discord, yet marriage maketh the Concord.

parsons] persons   *Cot-queane*] man who plays the housewife

Mariage (qd. I) yea but all the craft in catching, and cunning in keeping: I marie, *Marpissa*, this was sweetly spoken if faire wordes might win him, but *Crisippus* is no Pigeon to bee taken with a beane, nor a child to be intised with a Ball, he may be perhaps a Louer, but not loue for losse, and will more esteeme a dowrie that is bountifull, than a Kings Daughter though beautifull. Alas, *Marpissa*, what dowrye canst thou bring him: Ah, Death, if he be taken: Banishment, if he escape: and Pouertie, howsoeuer he speedeth? Wherfore if thou wilt loue him, then leaue to loue him, but that (alas) will neuer be, except thou also leaue to liue. Nay, rather moue the question, and afterwards dispose of thy selfe according to his answere: they are more than miserable, that secke a sword to perishe on the point, before a salue to applie to their paine: the vexed parson that in most anguish, cryeth out to be deliuered of griefe, the same woulde not with the least violence, be then dispatched of life: speake *Marpissa* nowe, or else neuer speede, sue to him for loue, that perhaps woulde, but feares to attempt thee in the like: thou shalt, no doubt, obtaine, he is neither discurteous, nor timerous, and so constant a Partner shall the rather make him venterous of the perill.

William Warner

Pan his Syrinx, or Pipe, compact of seven Reedes (1584)

MARGARITE'S CHAMBER

THUS sumptuous was the lodging of *Protomachus*, but far more glorious the chamber of *Margarita* which seemed from the first day to be fashioned to her affections, for ouer the entrance of the doores was drawen and carued out of curious white marble, the faire goddesse of chastitie blushing at the sodaine interception of *Acteon*, and her naked nymphes, who with the one hand, couering their owne secret pleasures with blushes, with the other cast a beautifull vaile ouer their mistresse daintie nakednes: the two pillers of the doore were beautified with the two *Cupids* of *Anacreon*, which well shaped modestie often seemed to whip lest they should growe ouer wanton: no sooner was the inward beauties of the chamber discouered, but the worke wrought his wonder, and the wonder it selfe was equalled by the worke, for al the chaste Ladies of the world, inchased out of siluer, looking through faire mirrours of chrisolites, carbuncles, saphires and greene Emeraults, fixed their eies on the picture of eternitie, which fixed on the toppes of a testerne, seemed with a golden trumpet to applaud to them al: in the tapistrie (beautified with gold, and pearle) were the nine Muses curiously wrought, who from a thicket beheld amorous *Orpheus* making the trees leape through his laments, and as he warbled his songs the flouds of *Hebrus* staied their sources; and the birds that beheld their comfort, began likewise to carrol. It was strange to thinke, and more strange to behold, in what order Art matched with nature, and how the lymning painter had almost exceeded nature in life, sauing that the beauteous faces wanted breath, to make them aliue, not cunning to proue them liuely

Thomas Lodge

A Margarite of America (1596)

ROSALYNDE

AT this *Rosalynd* began to comfort her, and after shee had wept a fewe kinde teares in the bosome of her *Alinda*, she gaue her heartie thankes, and then they sat them downe to consult how they should trauell. *Alinda* grieued at nothing but that they might haue no man in their companie: saying

it would be their greatest preiudice in that two women wen
wandring without either guide or attendant. Tush (quoth
Rosalynd) art thou a woman, and hast not a sodaine shift to
preuent a misfortune? I (thou seest) am of a tall stature, and
would very well become the person and apparell of a page
thou shalt bee my Mistris, and I will play the man so properly
that (trust me) in what company so euer I come I will not bee
discouered. I will buy mee a suite, and haue my rapier very
handsomely at my side, and if any knaue offer wrong, your
page wil shew him the poynt of his weapon. At this *Alinda*
smiled, and vpon this they agreed, and presentlie gathered vp
all their Iewels, which they trussed vp in a Casket, and
Rosalynd in all hast prouided her of roabes, and *Alinda* (from
her royall weedes) put her selfe in more homelie attire. Thus
fitted to the purpose, away goe these two friends, hauing now
changed their names, *Alinda* being called *Aliena*, and *Rosalynd*
Ganimede: they trauailed along the Vineyards, and by many
by-waies; at last got to the Forrest side, where they trauailed
by the space of two or three daies without seeing anie creature
being often in danger of wild beasts, and payned with many
passionate sorrowes. Now the black Oxe began to tread on
their feete, and *Alinda* thought of her wonted royaltie: but
when she cast her eyes on her *Rosalynd*, she thought euerie
daunger a step to honour. Passing thus on along, about
midday they came to a Fountaine, compast with a groue of
Cipresse trees, so cunninglie and curiouslie planted, as if some
Goddesse had intreated Nature in that place to make her an
Arbour. By this Fountaine sat *Aliena* and her *Ganimede*, and
foorth they pulled such victualls as they had, and fedde as
merilie as if they had been in *Paris* with all the Kings delicates:
Aliena onely grieuing that they could not so much as meete
with a shepheard to discourse them the way to some place
where they might make their aboade. At last *Ganimede* casting vp his eye espied where on a tree was ingrauen certaine

verses: which assoone as he espied, he cried out, bee of good cheere, Mistrisse: I spie the figures of men; for heere in these trees bee ingrauen certaine verses of shepheards, or some other swaines that inhabite here about.

Thomas Lodge
Rosalynde . . . (1590)

THE COUNTRYMAN'S LETTER

TRUELY Sweet-heart, I am so out of order with my self with the extremitie of loue that I beare you, that my heart is euen at my mouth to say Sweet-heart, when I thinke on you: and if I heare but your name it makes me start, as though I should see you, and when I looke on my Handkercheiffe, that you wrought me, I thanke you, with Couentrie-bleue: O how I lift vp my eies to heauen, and say to my selfe. Oh, there is a Wench in the World, wel, goe too: but when I see my ieat Ring that you sent me by your Brother *Will*, I do so kisse it, as if thou wert euen within it. Oh *Nell*, it is not to be spoken that affection that I beare to thee. Why, I ferretted all night for the Rabbet I sent thee, and haue beene in the Wood all day to seeke a Birds nest for thee: my Mother is making of a Cheese-cake, and she hath promised it me for thee: wel, be-leeue me I loue thee; and my high shooes come home on Saturday, Ile see thee on Sunday, and wee will drinke to-gether, that is once, for indeed I doe loue thee. Why, my heart is neuer from thee: for ouer and besides that I thinke on thee all day, I do so dreame on thee al night, that our folkes say in my sleepe I call thee Sweet-heart, and when I am awake and remember my dreame, I sigh and say nothing, but I would I wot what: but it is no matter, it shal be, and that sooner than some thinke: for though the old Crust my Father, and old Cramme my Mother will not come out with their Crownes, I care not, I am al their sons, and therefore I shall haue al the Lands: and hauing a good Farme, wee shal make shift for money: and therefore Sweet-heart, for so I well dare call thee, I pray thee be of good cheere, wash thy face, and put on the gloues that I gaue thee, for we are ful askt next Sunday, and the Sunday after you know what, for I haue your Fathers good will, and you haue my Mothers: if Buckle and Thong hold, we will load our packs together: I would haue said somewhat else to you, but it was out of my head, and our Schoolmaster was so busie with his Boies, that he would scarce write thus much for me. But farewell, and remember Sunday.

Thine owne, from all the world, T.P.

Nicholas Breton
A Poste with a Mad Packet of Letters (1602)

HERO AND LEANDER

LET me see, hath any bodie in Yarmouth heard of Leander and Hero, of whome diuine *Musæus* sung, and a diuiner Muse than him, *Kit Marlow*? Twoo faithfull louers they were, as euerie apprentise in Paules churchyard will tell you for your loue, and sel you for your mony: the one dwelt at Abidos in Asia, which was Leander; the other, which was Hero, his Mistris or Delia, at Sestos in Europe, and she was a pretty pinckany and Venus priest; and but an arme of the sea diuided them; it diuided them and it diuided them not, for ouer that arme of the sea could be made a long arme. In their parents the most diuision rested, and their townes that like Yarmouth and Leystoffe were stil at wrig wrag, and suckt from their mothers teates serpentine hatred one against each other. Which droue Leander when he durst not deale aboue boord, or be seene aboorde any ship, to saile to his Lady deare, to play the didopper and ducking water spaniel to swim to her, nor that in the day, but by owle-light.

What will not blinde night doe for blinde Cupid? And what will not blinde Cupid doe in the night, which is his blindmans holiday? By the sea side on the other side stoode Heroes tower, such an other tower as one of our Irish castles, that is not so wide as a belfree, and a cobler cannot iert out his elbowes in; a cage or pigeonhouse, romthsome enough to comprehend her and the toothlesse trotte, her nurse, who was her onely chatmate and chambermaide; consultiuely by her parents being so encloistred from resort, that she might liue chast vestall Priest to Venus, the queene of vnchastitie. Shee would none of that, she thanked them, for shee was better prouided, and that which they thought serued their turn best of sequestring her from company, serued her turne best to embrace the company she desired. Fate is a spaniel that you cannot beate from you; the more you thinke to crosse it, the more you blesse it and further it.

Neither her father nor mother vowed chastitie when she was begote, therefore she thought they begat her not to liue chaste, and either she must proue her selfe a bastard, or shew herselfe like them. Of Leander you may write vpon, and it is written vpon, she likte well, and for all he was a naked man, and cleane dispoyled to the skinne, when hee sprawled through the brackish suddes to scale her tower, all the strength of it could not hold him out. O, ware a naked man; Cithereaes Nunnes haue no power to resiste him: and some such qualitie is ascribed to the lion. Were hee neuer so naked when he came to her, bicause he shuld not skare her, she found a meanes to couer him in her bed, and, for he might not take cold after his swimming, she lay close by him, to keepe him warme. This scuffling or bopeepe in the darke they had a while without weame or bracke, and the olde nurse (as there

weame] break   *bracke*] flaw, break

bee three things seldome in their right kinde till they bee old
a bawd, a witch, and a midwife) executed the huckstring
office of her yeres very charily and circumspectly til thei
sliding starres reuolted from them; and then, for seauen daye
togither, the winde and the Hellespont contended which
shuld howle lowder; the waues dashed vp to the cloudes, and
the clouds on the other side spit and driueld vpon them as fast

Hero wept as trickling as the heauens, to thinke that heauen
should so diuorce them. Leander stormed worse than the
stormes, that by them hee should be so restrained from hi
Cinthya. At Sestos was his soule, and hee coulde not abide to
tarry in Abidos. Rayne, snowe, haile, or blowe it howe i
could, into the pitchie Helespont he leapt, when the moone
and all her torch-bearers were afraide to peepe out thei
heads; but he was peppered for it, hee hadde as good haue
tooke meate, drinke, and leisure, for the churlish frampold
waues gaue him his belly full of fish-broath, ere out of thei
laundry or washe-house they woulde graunt him his coquet
or *transire*, and not onely that, but they sealde him his *quietu.
est* for curuetting any more to the mayden tower, and tossed
his dead carcasse, well bathed or parboyled, to the sandy
threshold of his leman or orenge, for a disiune or morning
breakfast.

Thomas Nashe

Nashes Lenten Stuffe . . . (1599)

STRANGE EXPERIENCE OF AN ELDERLY GENTLEMAN

IT was my chance in Februarie last to be in the Countrey
some threescore myle off from London; where a Gentleman
of good worship and credit falling sicke, the verie second day
of his lying downe, hee pretended to haue miraculous waking

frampold] disagreeable *coquet*] certificate of clearance issued by
Customs officers

visions: which before I enter to describe, thus much I will informe ye by the way, that at the reporting of them he was in perfect memorie; nor had sicknes yet so tirannizd ouer him to make his tongue grow idle. A wise graue sensible man he was euer reputed, and so approou'd himselfe in all his actions in his life time. This which I deliuer, (with manie preparatiue protestations) to a great Man of this Land hee confidently auouched: beleeue it or condemn it, as you shal see cause, for I leaue it to be censured indifferently.

The first day of his distemprature, he visibly saw (as he affirmed) al his chamber hung with silken nets and siluer hookes, the diuell (as it should seeme) comming thether a fishing; whereupon, euery Pater noster while, he lookt whether in the nets he should be entangled, or with the hookes ensnared; with the nets he feard to be strangled or smothred, & with the hooks to haue his throat scractcht out, and his flesh rent and mangled: at length, he knew not how, they sodainly vanished, and the whole chamber was clered. Next a companie of lusty sailers (euerie one a sharker or a swaggerer at the least) hauing made a braue voyage, came carousing and quaffing in large siluer kans to his helth. Fellowes they were that had good big pop mouths to crie Port a helme Saint George, and knew as well as the best what belongs to haling of bolings yare, and falling on the star-boord buttocke.

But to the issue of my tale: their drunken proffers he vtterly put by, and sayd hee highly scorned and detested both them and their hellish disguisings: which notwithstanding, they tost their cups to the skies, and reeled and staggered vp and downe the roome like a ship shaking in the winde.

After all they danst Lustie gallant, & a drunken Danish Laualto or two, and so departed. For the third course, rusht in a number of stately diuels, bringing in boystrous chests of

bolings] bowlines

173

massie tresure betwixt them. As braue they were as Turkish Ianissaries, hauing their apparel all powdred with gold and pearle, and their armes as it were bemayled with rich chaynes and bracelets; but faces far blacker than anie ball of Tobacco, great glaring eyes that had whole shelues of Kentish oysters in them, and terrible wyde mouthes, whereof not one of them but would well haue made a case for *Molenax*[1] great Gloabe of the world.

These louely youths and full of fauour, hauing stalkt vp and downe the iust measures of a sinkapace, opened one of the principall chests they brought, and out of it pluckt a Princely royall Tent, whose empearled shining canopie they quickly aduanced on hie, and with all artificiall magnificence adorned like a state: which performed, pompous *Lucifer* entred, imitating in goodly stature the huge picture of *Laocoon* at *Rome*: who sent vnto him a gallant Embassadour, signifying thus much, that if hee would serue him, hee should haue all the rich treasure that he saw there, or anie farther wealth hee would desire.

The Gentleman returned this milde aunswere, that he knew not what he was, whether an Angell or a wicked feend: and if an Angell, he was but his fellow seruant, and no otherwise to be serued or regarded; if a fiend or a diuell, hee had nothing to doo with him, for God had exalted and redeemed him aboue his desperate out-cast condition, and a strong faith he had to defie & with-stand all his iugling temptations. Hauing vttered these words, all the whole traine of them inuisibly auoyded, and hee neuer set eye on them after.

Then did there, for the third pageant, present themselues vnto him, an inueigling troupe of naked Virgins, thrice more amiable and beautifull than the bright Vestals, that brought in *Augustus* Testament to the Senate, after hys decease: but no Vestall-like Ornament had they about them; for from top to

1. Emerie Molyneux completed his great globe in 1592.

toe bare despoyled they were, except some one or two of them that ware maskes before their faces, and had transparent azur'd lawne veyles before the chiefe iewell houses of their honors.

Such goodly lustfull Bonaroebaes they were (by his report) as if anie sharpe eyd Painter had beene there to peruse them, he might haue learned to exceed diuine *Michel Angelo* in the true boske of a naked, or curious *Tuns* in quicke life, whom the great masters of that Art do terme the sprightly old man.

Their haire they ware loose vnrowled about their shoulders, whose dangling amber trammells reaching downe beneath their knees, seemed to drop baulme on their delicious bodies; and euer as they moou'd too and fro, with their light windye wauings, wantonly to correct their exquisite mistresses.

Their daintie feete in their tender birdlike trippings, enameld (as it were) the dustie ground; and their odoriferous breath more perfumed the aire, than Ordinance would, that is charged with Amomum, Muske, Cyuet, and Amber-greece.

But to leaue amplifications and proceed: those sweet bewitching naked maides, hauing maiestically paced about the chamber to the end their naturall vnshelled shining mother pearle proportions might be more imprintingly apprehended, close to his bed-side modestly blushing they approched, & made impudent profer vnto him of theyr lasciuious embraces. He, obstinatly bent to withstand these their sinfull allurements no lesse than the former, bad them goe seek entertainment of hotter bloods, for he had not to satisfie them. A cold comfort was this to poore wenches no better cloathed, yet they hearing what to trust too, verie sorrowfully retyred, and shrunk away.

Lo, in the fourth Act, there sallied out a graue assembly of sober attyred Matrones, much like the Virgines of *Marie Magdalens* order in *Rome*, which vowe neuer to see man; or the chast daughters of Saint *Philip*.

boske] bosh, sketch   *Tuns*] Wilhelm Tons (?)

With no incontinent curtesie they did greete him, but tolde him, if hee thought good they would praye for him.

Thereupon, from the beginning to the ending he vnfolded vnto them, how he had been mightely hanted with wicked illusions of late: but neuertheles, if he could be perswaded that they were Angels or Saintes, their inuocations could not hurt him; yea, he would adde his desire to their requestes, to make their prayers more penetrably enforcing.

Without further parley, vppon their knees they fell most deuoutly, and for halfe an hower neuer ceased extensiuely to intercessionate God for his speedie recouerie.

Rising vp agayne on the right hand of his bed, there appeared a cleare light, and with that he might perceiue a naked slender foote offring to steale betwixt the sheets in to him.

At which instant, entred a messenger from a Knight of great honour thereabouts, who sent him a most precious extract quintessence to drinke: which no sooner he tasted, but he thought hee saw all the fore-named Enterluders at once hand ouer leap, & drowne themselues in puddles and ditches hard by, and hee felt perfect ease.

But long it lasted not with him, for within foure howers after, hauing not fully settled his estate in order, hee grewe to trifling dotage, and rauing dyde within two daies following.

Thomas Nashe
The Terrors of the Night Or, A Discourse of Apparitions (1594)

MIDNIGHT ASSIGNATION

SUPPER time came and passed ouer, and not long after came the handmayd of the Lady *Elynor* into the great chamber, desiring *F.J.* to repayre vnto their Mistresse, the which hee willingly accomplished: and being now entred into hir chamber, he might perceyue his Mistresse in hir nightes

attyre, preparinge hir selfe towardes bed, to whom *F.J.*
sayed: Why howe now Mistresse? I had thought this night to
haue sene you daunce (at least or at last) amongst vs? By my
troth good seruaunt (qd. she) I aduentured so soone vnto the
great chamber yesternight, that I find my selfe somewhat
sickly disposed, and therfore do streyne curtesie (as you see)
to go the soner to my bed this night: but before I slepe (quod
she) I am to charge you with a matter of waight, and taking
him apart from the rest, declared that (as that present night)
she would talke with him more at large in the gallery neere
ajoyning to hir chamber. Here vppon *F.J.* discretely dis-
simuling his ioye, toke his leaue and returned into the great
chamber, where he had not long continued before the Lord
of the Castell commaunded a torch to light him vnto his
lodging, whereas he prepared himselfe and went to bed, com-
maunding his seruant also to go to his rest. And when he
thought aswell his seruant, as the rest of the houshold to be
safe, he arose again, and taking his night gowne, did vnder
the same conuey his naked sword, and so walked to the
gallerie, where he found his good Mistresse walking in hir
night gowne and attending his comming. The Moone was
now at the full, the skies cleare, and the weather temperate,
by reason wherof he might the more playnely and with the
greater contentation behold his long desired ioyes, and spred-
ing his armes abrode to embrace his louing Mistresse, he
sayd: oh my deare Lady when shall I be able with any desert
to counteruayle the least parte of this your bountifull goodnesse? The dame (whether it were of feare in deede, or that the
wylynes of womanhode had taught hir to couer hir conceites
with some fyne dissimulation) stert backe from the Knight,
and shriching (but softly) sayd vnto him. Alas seruaunt what
haue I deserued, that you come against me with naked sword
as against an open enimie. *F.J.* perceyuing hir entent excused
himselfe, declaring that he brought the same for their defence,

and not to offend hir in any wise. The Ladie being therwith somwhat apeased, they began with more comfortable gesture to expell the dread of the said late affright, and sithens to become bolder of behauiour, more familier in speech, and most kind in accomplishing of comon comfort. But why hold I so long discourse in discribing the ioyes which (for lacke of like experience) I cannot set out to the ful? Were it not that I knowe to whom I write, I would the more beware what I write. *F.J.* was a man, and neither of vs are sencelesse, and therfore I shold slaunder him, (ouer and besides a greater obloquie to the whole genealogie of *Enaeas*) if I should imagine that of tender hart he would forbeare to expresse hir more tender limbes against the hard floore. Suffised that of hir curteouse nature she was content to accept bords for a bed of downe, mattes for Camerike sheetes, and the night gowne of *F.J.* for a counterpoynt to couer them, and thus with calme content, in steede of quiet sleepe, they beguiled the night, vntill the proudest sterre began to abandon the fyrmament, when *F.J.* and his Mistresse, were constrayned also to abandon their delightes, and with ten thousand sweet kisses and straight embracings, did frame themselues to play loth to depart. Wel, remedie was there none, but dame *Elynor* must returne vnto hir chamber, and *F.J.* must also conuey himselfe (as closely as might be) into his chamber, the which was hard to do, the day being so farre sprong, and hee hauing a large base court to passe ouer before he could recouer his staire foote doore. And though he were not much perceyued, yet the Ladie *Fraunces* being no lesse desirous to see an issue of these enterprises, than *F.J.* was willing to couer them in secresy, did watch, and euen at the entring of his chamber doore, perceyued the poynt of his naked sworde glistring vnder the skyrt of his night gowne: wherat she smyled and said to hir selfe, this geare goeth well about. Well, *F.J.* hauing now recouered his chamber, he went to bedde, and there let him

sleepe, as his Mistresse did on that otherside. Although the
Lady *Fraunces* being throughly tickled now in all the vaynes,
could not enioye such quiet rest, but rising, toke another
gentlewoman of the house with hir, and walked into the
parke to take the fresh ayre of the morning.

George Gascoigne
A Hundreth Sundrie Flowres (1573)

NURSEMAID

NOWE forsooth, I must attend vppon my young Mistresse,
the olde Womans Daughter, the most ilfauoured and vn-
towarde vrchin that euer was borne: This baggage must I go
teach her Booke, and forsooth touch her I must not, but
Good Mistresse looke on your Booke: Yea, that is a fayre
Gentlewoman, when shee saide neuer a word, but I was faine
to speake for her: If I complained of her, then, Oh you thinke
much of your paynes, would you haue her reade as well as
you the first daye: go, come not to mee with such twittle
twattle, then go to the Gyrle, Ha! Mouse, doth she say thou
wilt not learne? Marrie she lyes. Holde heere, wilt thou haue
a Plum or an Apple? yea marrie, it is a good Gyrle: then was
I glad to get Apples and Peares, and such geere to bring her
to the Booke. And then the apish elfe, for my heart, would not
say a word, so that I could not for my life, but giue her a
little slap on the shoulders: and if I did but euen touch her,
the Monkie would set out the throate, and crie so vengeouslie,
that to it must the mother come: and then, How now gyrle?
tell me, doth shee beate thee? Minion, you were best not
touch her, see you? the Wench would learne well inough, and
you were willing to teach her, well, you were best vse her
gently, least yee fare the worse for it, and so away shee goes.
   Nowe would I sit weeping for greefe, that the squall would

learne no faster: and if the hilding had got out of my sight, and by chaunce spotted any of her cloathes, or taken a fall, (and yet it was olde inough) beeing betwixt seuen and eight yeeres of age, to go alone. Yet as I say, if ought were amisse with her, I was checkt, snibd, called proude minks, rated like a Dogge, and nowe and then beaten so extreamely, if the old crone were in an angrie moode, as shee was seldome little better.

Nicholas Breton
The Will of Wit, Wits Wil, or Wils Wit (1599)

MURDER STORY

THOMAS of *Reading* hauing many occasions to come to London, as well about his own affaires, as also the Kings businesse, being in a great office vnder his Maiestie, it chanced on a time, that his Host and Hostesse of *Colebrooke*, who through couetousnes had murdered many of the guests, and hauing euery time he came thither great store of his mony to lay vp, appointed him to be the next fat pig that should be killed: For it is to be vnderstood, that when they plotted the murder of any man, this was alwaies their terme, the man to his wife, and the woman to her husband: wife, there is now a fat pig to be had, if you want one.

Whereupon she would answer thus, I pray you put him in the hogstie till to-morrow. ...

Well, to his Inne he came, and so heauy was his heart that he could eate no meat: his host and hostesse hearing he was so melancholy, came vp to cheare him, saying, Iesus Master *Cole*, what ayles you to night? neuer did we see you thus sad before: will it please you to haue a quart of burnt sacke?

With a good will (quoth he) and would to God *Tom Doue* were here, hee would surely make me merry, and we should lacke no musicke: but I am sorry for the man with all my heart, that he is come so farre behind hand: but alasse, so much can euery man say, but what good doth it him? No no, it is not words can helpe a man in this case, the man had need of other reliefe then so. Let me see: I haue but one child in the world, and that is my daughter, and halfe that I haue is hers, the other halfe my wifes. What then? shall I be good to no body but them? In conscience, my wealth is too much for a cupple to possesse, and what is our Religion without charity? And to whom is charity more to be shewen, then to decayed housholders?

Good my hoast lend me a pen and inke, and some paper, for I will write a letter vnto the poore man straight; and something I will giue him: That almes which a man bestowes with his owne hands, he shal be sure to haue deliuered, and God knowes how long I shall liue.

With that, his hostesse dissemblingly answered, saying: Doubt not, Master *Cole*, you are like enough by the course of nature to liue many yeares.

God knowes (quoth he) I neuer found my heart so heauy before.

By this time pen, inke, and paper was brought, setting himselfe in writing as followeth.

In the name of God, Amen, I bequeath my soule to God, and my body to the ground, my goods equally betweene my wife Elenor, *and* Isabel, *my daughter. Item I giue to* Thomas Doue *of* Exeter *one hundred pounds,* nay that is too little, *I giue to* Thomas Doue *two hundred pounds in money, to be paid vnto him presently vpon his demand thereof by my said wife and daughter.*

Ha, how say you hoast (qd he) is not this well? I pray you reade it.

His hoast looking thereon, said, why Master *Cole*, what haue you written here? you said you would write a letter, but me thinks you haue made a Will, what neede haue you to doe thus? thanks be to God, you may liue many faire yeares.

Tis true (quoth *Cole*) if it please God, and I trust this writing cannot shorten my daies, but let me see, haue I made a Will? Now, I promise you, I did verily purpose to write a letter: norwithstanding, I haue written that that God put into my mind: but looke once againe my host, is it not written there, that *Doue* shall haue two hundred pounds, to be paid when he comes to demand it?

Yes indeed (said his hoste).

Well then, all is well (said *Cole*) and it shall go as it is for me. I will not bestow the new writing thereof any more.

Then folding it vp, he sealed it, desiring that his host would send it to *Exeter*: he promised that he would, notwithstanding *Cole* was not satisfied: but after some pause, he would needs hire one to carry it. And so sitting downe sadly in his chaire againe, vpon a sudden he burst forth a weeping; they demanding the cause thereof, he spake as followeth:

No cause of these feares I know; but it comes now into my minde (said *Cole*) when I set toward this my last iourney to *London*, how my daughter tooke on, what a coyle she kept to haue me stay: and I could not be rid of the little baggage a long time, she did so hang about me, when her mother by violence tooke her away, she cryed out most mainly, O my father, my father, I shall neuer see him againe.

Alas, pretty soule (said his hoastesse) this was but meer kindnesse in the girle, and it seemeth she is very fond of you. But alasse, why should you grieue at this? you must consider that it was but childishnes.

I, it is indeed (said Cole) and with that he began to nod.

Then they asked him if he would go to bed.

No (said he) although I am heauy, I haue no mind to go to bed at all.

With that certaine musitians of the towne came to the

chamber, and knowing Master *Cole* was there, drue out their
nstruments, and very solemnly began to play.

This musicke comes very well (said *Cole*) and when he had
istned a while thereunto, he said, Methinks these instruments
sound like the ring of *S. Mary Oueries* belles, but the base
drownes all the rest: and in my eare it goes like a bell that
rings a forenoones knell, for Gods sake let them leaue off, and
geare them this simple reward.

The musitians being gone, his hoste asked if now it would
please him to go to bed; for (quoth he) it is welneare eleuen
of the clocke.

With that *Cole* beholding his host and hostesse earnestly,
began to start backe, saying, what aile you to looke so like
pale death? good Lord, what haue you done, that your hands
are thus bloody?

What my hands (said his host)? Why, you may see they are
neither bloudy nor foule: either your eies doe greatly dazell,
or else fancies of a troubled minde do delude you.

Alas my hoste, you may see (said he) how weake my wits
are, I neuer had my head so idle before. Come, let me drinke
once more, and then I will to bed, and trouble you no
longer.

With that he made himselfe vnready, and his hostesse was
very diligent to warme a kerchiffe, and put it about his head.

Good Lord (said he) I am not sicke, I praise God, but such
an alteration I find in my selfe as I neuer did before.

With that the scritch owle cried piteously, and anone after
the night rauen sate croking hard by his window.

Iesu haue mercy vpon me (quoth hee) what an ill fauoured
cry doe yonder carrion birds make, and therewithall he laid
him downe in his bed, from whence he neuer rose againe.

His host and hostesse, that all this while noted his troubled
mind, began to commune betwixt themselues thereof. And
the man said, he knew not what were best to be done. By my

consent (quoth he) the matter should passe, for I thinke it i
not best to meddle on him.

What man (quoth she) faint you now? haue you done s
many and doe you shrinke at this? Then shewing him a grea
deale of gold which *Cole* had left with her, she said, would i
not grieue a bodies heart to lose this? hang the old churle
what should he doe liuing any longer? he hath too much, anc
we haue too little: tut husband, let the thing be done, anc
then this is our owne.

Her wicked counsell was followed, and when they hac
listned at his chamber doore, they heard the man souni
asleepe: All is safe (quoth they) and downe into the kitchii
they goe, their seruants being all in bedde, and pulling out th
yron pins, downe fell the bed, and the man dropt out into th
boyling caldron.

Thomas Deloney

*The Pleasant History of Thomas of
Reading* (? 1602). Text of 1623

ADVICE TO ALEXANDER

I CAN not tel, *Alexander*, whether the reporte be more shame-
full to be heard, or the cause sorrowfull to be beleeued!
What! is the sonne of *Phillip*, king of Macedon, become the
subiect of *Campaspe*, the captiue of Thebes? Is that minde,
whose greatnes the world could not containe, drawn within
the compasse of an idle alluring eie? Wil you handle the
spindle with *Hercules*, when you should shake the speare with
Achilles? Is the warlike sound of drumme and trumpe turned
to the soft noyse of lire and lute? the neighing of barbed steeds,
whose loudnes filled the ayre with terrour, and whose breathes
dimmed the sunne with smoak, conuerted to dilicate tunes
and amorous glaunces? O *Alexander*, that soft and yeelding
minde should not bee in him, whose hard and vnconquered

heart hath made so many yeelde. But you loue, ah griefe! but whom? *Campaspe*, ah shame! a maide forsooth vnknowne, vnnoble, and who can tell whether immodest? whose eies are framed by arte to inamour, and whose heart was made by nature to inchaunt. I, but she is bewtiful; yea, but not therefore chast: I, but she is comly in al parts of the body: yea, but she may be crooked in some part of the mind: I, but she is wise, yea, but she is a woman! Bewty is like the blackberry, which seemeth red, when it is not ripe, resembling pretious stones that are polished with honny, which the smother they look, the sooner they breake. It is thought wonderful among the seamen, that Mugil, of all fishes the swiftest, is found in the belly of the Bret, of al the slowest: And shall it not seeme monstrous to wisemen, that the hearte of the greatest con-querour of the worlde, should be found in the handes of the weakest creature of nature? of a woman? of a captiue? Hermyns haue faire skinnes, but fowle liuers; Sepulchres fresh colours, but rotten bones; women faire faces, but false heartes. Remember *Alexander* thou hast a campe to gouerne, not a chamber; fall not from the armour of *Mars* to the armes of *Venus*, from the fiery assaults of war, to the maidenly skirmishes of loue, from displaying the Eagle in thine ensigne, to set downe the sparow. I sighe *Alexander* that where fortune could not conquer, folly shuld ouercome.

John Lyly

Campaspe (1584)

FAUSTUS' FAREWELL

Enter Faustus with the Schollers

Fau. Ah Gentlemen!

1 *Sch.* What ailes Faustus?

Fau. Ah my sweete chamber-fellow! had I liued with thee, then had I liued stil, but now I die eternally: looke, comes he not? comes he not?

2 *Sch.* What meanes Faustus?

3 *Sch.* Belike he is growne into some sickenesse by being ouer solitary.

1 *Sch.* If it be so, weele haue Physitians to cure him: tis but a surffet, neuer feare man.

Fau. A surffet of deadly sinne that hath damnd both body and soule.

2 *Sch.* Yet Faustus, looke vp to heauen, remember gods mercies are infinite.

Fau. But Faustus offence can nere be pardoned. The Serpent that tempted *Eue* may be sau'd, but not Faustus: Ah Gentlemen, heare me with patience, and tremble not at my speeches. Though my heart pants and quiuers to remember that I haue beene a student here these thirty yeeres, O would I had neuer seene *Wertenberge*, neuer read booke: and what wonders I haue done, al *Germany* can witnes, yea all the world, for which Faustus hath lost both *Germany*, and the world, yea heauen it selfe, heauen the seate of God, the throne of the blessed, the kingdome of ioy, and must remaine in hel for euer, hel, ah hel for euer, sweete friends, what shall become of Faustus, being in hel for euer?

3 *Sch.* Yet Faustus call on God.

Fau. On God whome Faustus hath abiurde, on God, whome Faustus hath blasphemed: ah my God, I woulde weepe, but the diuel drawes in my teares. Gush foorth bloud, insteade of teares, yea life and soule. Oh he stayes my tong, I would lift vp my hands, but see, they hold them, they hold them.

All. Who Faustus?

Fau. Lucifer and *Mephastophilis.*

Ah Gentlemen! I gaue them my soule for my cunning.

All. God forbid.

Fau. God forbade it indeede, but Faustus hath done it: for vaine pleasure of 24 yeares hath Faustus lost eternall ioy

and felicitie. I writ them a bill with mine owne bloud, the
date is expired, the time wil come, and he wil fetch mee.

Sch. Why did not Faustus tel vs of this before, that Diuines
might haue prayed for thee?

Fau. Oft haue I thought to haue done so, but the diuell
threatned to teare mee in peeces, if I namde God, to fetch
both body and soule, if I once gaue eare to diuinitie: and
now tis too late: Gentlemen away, lest you perish with me.

2 Sch. O what shall we do to saue Faustus?

Fau. Talke not of me, but saue your selues, and depart.

3 Sch. God wil strengthen me, I wil stay with Faustus.

Sch. Tempt not God, sweete friend, but let vs into the next
roome, and there pray for him.

Fau. I, Pray for me, pray for me, and what noyse soeuer yee
heare, come not vnto me, for nothing can rescue me.

2 Sch. Pray thou, and we wil pray that God may haue mercy
vpon thee.

Fau. Gentlemen farewel, if I liue til morning, Ile visite you: if
not, Faustus is gone to hel.

All. Faustus, farewel.

Christopher Marlowe

The Tragicall History of Doctor Faustus (1604).
Acted 1592

UNWILLING COURTSHIP

Candius, Silena

Can. Hee must needs goe that the deuill driues! a father? a
fiend! that seekes to place affection by appointment, and
to force loue by compulsion; I haue sworne to woo *Silena*,
but it shall be so coldly, that she shall take as small delight in
my words, as I doe contentment in his commandment. Ile
teach him one schoole-tricke in loue. But behold, who is

that that commeth out of *Stellios* house? it should seeme to be *Silena* by her attire.

Enter *Silena*.

By her face I am sure it is she, oh faire face! oh louely countenance! How now, *Candius*, if thou begin to slip a beautie on a sodaine, thou wilt surfet with carowsing it at the last. Remember that *Liuia* is faithfull, I, and let thine eye witnesse *Silena* is amiable! Heere shall I please my father and my selfe, I will learne to be obedient, and come what will, Ile make a way; if she seeme coy, Ile practice all the art of loue, if I finde her coming, all the pleasures of loue.

Sil. My name is *Silena*, I care not who knowe it, so I doo not my father keepes me close, so hee does; and now I haue stolne out, so I haue; to goe to old *Mother Bombie* to know my fortune, so I will; for I haue as faire a face as euer trod on shoo sole, and as free a foot as euer lookt with two eyes.

Can. What? I thinke shee is lunaticke or foolish! Thou art a foole, *Candius*, so faire a face cannot bee the scabbard of a foolish minde; mad she may bee, for commonly in beautie so rare, there fals passions extreme. Loue and beautie disdaine a meane, not therefore because beautie is no vertue, but because it is happinesse; and we schollers know that vertue is not to be praysed, but honoured. I will put on my best grace. Sweete wench, thy face is louely, thy bodie comely, and all that the eyes can see inchanting! you see how vnacquainted I am bold to boord you.

Sil. My father boordes me alreadie, therefore I care not if your name were *Geoffrey*.

Can. Shee raues, or ouer-reaches. I am one, sweete soule, that loues you, brought hither by report of your beautie, and here languisheth with your rarenesse.

Sil. I thanke you that you would call.

Can. I will alwayes call on such a saint that hath power to release my sorrowes; yeeld, faire creature, to loue.

Sil. I am none of that sect.

Can. Thy louing sect is an ancient sect, and an honourable, and therefore loue should be in a person so perfect.

Sil. Much!

Can. I loue thee much, giue me one word of comfort.

Sil. I' faith, sir, no! and so tell your master.

Can. I haue no master, but come to make choice of a mistres.

Sil. A ha, are you there with your beares!

Can. Doubtlesse she is an idiot of the newest cut! Ile once more try her. I haue loued thee long, *Silena.*

Sil. In your t'other hose.

Can. Too simple to be naturall: too senselesse to bee arteficiall. You sayd you went to know your fortune, I am a scholler, and am cunning in palmistry.

Sil. The better for you, sir; here's my hand, what's a clocke?

Can. The line of life is good, *Venus'* mount very perfect, you shall haue a scholler to your first husband.

Sil. You are well seene in cranes dirt, your father was a poulter. Ha, ha, ha!

Can. Why laugh you?

Sil. Because you should see my teeth.

Can. Alas, poore wretch, I see now also thy folly; a fayre foole is lyke a fresh weed, pleasing leaues and soure iuyce; I will not yet leaue her, shee may dissemble. I cannot chuse but loue thee.

Sil. I had thought to aske you.

Can. Nay then farewell, either too proude to accept, or too simple to vnderstand.

Sil. You need not bee crustie, you are not so hard bakt.

Can. Now I perceiue thy folly, who hath rackt together all the odde blinde phrases, that helpe them that know not how to discourse; but when they cannot aunswere wisely, either with gybing couer their rudenesse, or by some new coyned

arteficiall] artful

by-word bewray their peeuishnesse; I am glad of this, now shall I haue colour to refuse the match, and my father reason to accept of *Liuia*: I will home, and repeat to my father our wise incounter, and hee shall perceiue there is nothing so fulsome as a shee foole.

Sil. Good God, I thinke gentlemen had neuer lesse wit in a yeare. Wee maids are mad wenches, wee gird them and flout them out of all scotch and notch, and they cannot see it; I will know of the old woman whether I be a maide or no, and then, if I bee not, I must needes be a man.

John Lyly

Mother Bombie (1594)

PROPOSAL

Benedick and Beatrice

Bene. Lady *Beatrice*, haue you wept all this while?

Beat. Yea, and I will weepe a while longer.

Bene. I will not desire that.

Beat. You haue no reason, I doe it freely.

Bene. Surelie I do beleeue your fair cosin is wrong'd.

Beat. Ah, how much might the man deserue of mee that would right her!

Bene. Is there any way to shew such friendship?

Beat. A verie euen way, but no such friend.

Bene. May a man doe it?

Beat. It is a mans office, but not yours.

Bene. I doe loue nothing in the world so well as you, is not that strange?

Beat. As strange as the thing I know not, it were as possible for me to say, I loued nothing so well as you, but beleeue me not, and yet I lie not, I confesse nothing, nor I deny nothing, I am sorry for my cousin.

Bene. By my sword *Beatrice* thou lou'st me.

Beat. Doe not sweare by it and eat it.

Bene. I will sweare by it that you loue mee, and I will make him eat it that sayes I loue not you.

Beat. Will you not eat your word?

Bene. With no sawce that can be deuised to it, I protest I loue thee.

Beat. Why then God forgiue me.

Bene. What offence sweet *Beatrice*?

Beat. You haue stayed me in a happy howre, I was about to protest I loued you.

Bene. And doe it with all thy heart.

Beat. I loue you with so much of my heart, that none is left to protest.

Bene. Come, bid me doe any thing for thee.

Beat. Kill *Claudio.*

Bene. Ha, not for the wide world.

Beat. You kill me to denie it, farewell.

Bene. Tarrie sweet *Beatrice.*

Beat. I am gone, though I am heere, there is no loue in you, nay I pray you let me goe.

Bene. Beatrice.

Beat. In faith I will goe.

Bene. Wee'll be friends first.

Beat. You dare easier be friends with mee, than fight with mine enemy.

Bene. Is *Claudio* thine enemie?

Beat. Is a not approued in the height a villaine, that hath slandered, scorned, dishonoured my kinswoman? O that I were a man! what, beare her in hand vntill they come to take hands, and then with publike accusation vncouered slander, vnmittigated rancour? O God that I were a man! I would eat his heart in the market-place.

Bene. Heare me *Beatrice.*

Beat. Talke with a man out at a window, a proper saying.

Bene. Nay but *Beatrice*.

Beat. Sweet *Hero*, she is wrong'd, shee is slandered, she is vndone.

Bene. Beat — ?

Beat. Princes and Counties! surelie a Princely testimonie, a goodly Count, Comfect, a sweet Gallant surelie, O that I were a man for his sake! or that I had any friend would be a man for my sake! But manhood is melted into cursies, valour into complement, and men are onelie turned into tongue, and trim ones too: he is now as valiant as *Hercules,* that only tells a lie, and sweares it: I cannot be a man with wishing, therfore I will die a woman with grieuing.

Bene. Tarry good *Beatrice*, by this hand I loue thee.

Beat. Vse it for my loue some other way then swearing by it.

Bene. Thinke you in your soule the Count *Claudio* hath wrong'd *Hero*?

Beat. Yea, as sure as I haue a thought, or a soule.

Bene. Enough, I am engagde, I will challenge him, I will kisse your hand, and so leaue you: by this hand *Claudio* shall render me a deere account: as you heare of me, so thinke of me: goe comfort your coosin, I must say she is dead, and so farewell.

William Shakespeare

Much Adoe about Nothing (1600). Text from First Folio (1623)

ORLANDO AND ROSALIND

The Forest of Arden: Rosalind disguised as Ganymede, Celia as Aliena, Orlando

Ros. Why how now *Orlando*, where haue you bin all this while? you a louer? and you serue me such another tricke, neuer come in my sight more.

Orl. My faire *Rosalind*, I come within an houre of my promise.

Ros. Breake an houres promise in loue? hee that will diuide a
minute into a thousand parts, and breake but a part of the
thousand part of a minute in the affaires of loue, it may be
said of him that *Cupid* hath clapt him oth'shoulder, but Ile
warrant him heart hole.

Orl. Pardon me deere *Rosalind*.

Ros. Nay, and you be so tardie, come no more in my sight,
I had as liefe be woo'd of a Snaile.

Orl. Of a Snaile?

Ros. I, of a Snaile: for though he comes slowly, hee carries
his house on his head; a better ioyncture I thinke then
you make a woman: besides, he brings his destinie with
him.

Orl. What's that?

Ros. Why hornes: which such as you are faine to be beholding
to your wiues for: but he comes armed in his fortune, and
preuents the slander of his wife.

Orl. Vertue is no horne-maker: and my *Rosalind* is vertuous.

Ros. And I am your Rosalind.

Cel. It pleases him to call you so: but he hath a *Rosalind* of a
better leere then you.

Ros. Come, wooe me, wooe mee,: for now I am in a holyday
humor, and like enough to consent: What would you say
to me now, and I were your veric, verie *Rosalind*?

Orl. I would kisse before I spoke.

Ros. Nay, you were better speake first, and when you were
grauel'd, for lacke of matter, you might take occasion to
kisse: verie good Orators when they are out, they will spit,
and for louers, lacking (God warne vs) matter, the clean-
liest shift is to kisse.

Orl. How if the kisse be denide?

Ros. Then she puts you to entreatie, and there begins new
matter.

Orl. Who could be out, being before his beloued Mistris?

Ros. Marrie that should you if I were your Mistris, or I should thinke my honestie ranker then my wit.

Orl. What, of my suite?

Ros. Not out of your apparrell, and yet out of your suite: Am not I your *Rosalind*?

Orl. I take some ioy to say you are, because I would be talking of her.

Ros. Well, in her person, I say I will not haue you.

Orl. Then in mine owne person, I die.

Ros. No faith, die by Attorney: the poore world is almost six thousand yeeres old, and in all this time there was not anie man died in his owne person (*videlicet*) in a loue cause: *Troilous* had his braines dash'd out with a Grecian club, yet he did what hee could to die before, and he is one of the patternes of loue. *Leander*, he would haue liu'd manie a faire yeere though *Hero* had turn'd Nun; if it had not bin for a hot Midsomer-night, for (good youth) he went but forth to wash him in the Hellespont, and being taken with the crampe, was droun'd, and the foolish Chronoclers[1] of that age, found it was *Hero* of Cestos. But these are all lies, men haue died from time to time, and wormes haue eaten them, but not for loue.

Orl. I would not haue my right *Rosalind* of this mind, for I protest her frowne might kill me.

Ros. By this hand, it will not kill a flie: but come, now I will be your *Rosalind* in a more comming-on disposition: and aske me what you will, I will grant it.

Orl. Then loue me *Rosalind*.

Ros. Yes faith will I, fridaies and saterdaies, and all.

Orl. And wilt thou haue me?

Ros. I, and twentie such.

Orl. What saiest thou?

Ros. Are you not good?

1. Usually emended to 'coroners'.

Orl. I hope so.

Ros. Why then, can one desire too much of a good thing: Come sister, you shall be the Priest, and marrie vs: giue me your hand *Orlando*: What doe you say sister?

Orl. Pray thee marrie vs.

Cel. I cannot say the words.

Ros. You must begin, will you *Orlando*.

Cel. Goe too: wil you *Orlando*, haue to wife this *Rosalind*?

Orl. I will.

Ros. I, but when?

Orl. Why now, as fast as she can marrie vs.

Ros. Then you must say, I take thee *Rosalind* for wife.

Orl. I take thee *Rosalind* for wife.

Ros. I might aske you for your Commission, But I doe take thee *Orlando* for my husband: there's a girle goes before the Priest, and certainely a Womans thought runs before her actions.

Orl. So do all thoughts, they are wing'd.

Ros. Now tell me how long you would haue her, after you haue possest her?

Orl. For euer, and a day.

Ros. Say a day, without the euer: No, no *Orlando*, men are Aprill when they woe, December when they wed: Maides are May when they are maides, but the sky changes when they are wiues: I will bee more iealous of thee, then a Barbary cocke-pidgeon ouer his hen, more clamorous then a Parrat against raine, more new-fangled then an ape, more giddy in my desires, then a monkey; I will weepe for nothing, like *Diana* in the Fountaine, and I wil do that when you are dispos'd to be merry: I will laugh like a Hyen, and that when thou art inclin'd to sleepe.

Orl. But will my *Rosalind* doe so?

Ros. By my life, she will doe as I doe.

Orl. O but she is wise.

Ros. Or else shee could not haue the wit to doe this : the wiser, the waywarder : make the doores vpon a womans wit, and it will out at the casement : shut that, and 'twill out at the key-hole : stop that, 'twill flie with the smoake out at the chimney.

Orl. A man that had a wife with such a wit, he might say, wit, whether wil't?

Ros. Nay, you might keepe that checke for it, till you met your wiues wit going to your neighbours bed.

Orl. And what wit could wit haue, to excuse that?

Rosa. Marry to say, she came to seeke you there : you shall neuer take her without her answer, vnlesse you take her without her tongue : O that woman that cannot make her fault her husbands occasion, let her neuer nurse her childe her selfe, for she will breed it like a foole.

Orl. For these two houres *Rosalinde*, I wil leaue thee.

Ros. Alas, deere loue, I cannot lacke thee two houres.

Orl. I must attend the Duke at dinner, by two a clock I will be with thee againe.

Ros. I, goe your waies, goe your waies : I knew what you would proue, my friends told mee as much, and I thought no lesse : that flattering tongue of yours wonne me : 'tis but one cast away, and so come death : two o'clocke is your howre.

Orl. I, sweet *Rosalind*.

Ros. By my troth, and in good earnest, and so God mend mee, and by all pretty oathes that are not dangerous, if you breake one iot of your promise, or come one minute behinde your houre, I will thinke you the most patheticall breake-promise, and the most hollow louer, and the most vnworthy of her you call *Rosalinde*, that may be chosen out of the grosse band of the vnfaithfull : therefore beware my censure, and keep your promise.

Orl. With no lesse religion, then if thou wert indeed my *Rosalind* : so adieu.

Ros. Well, Time is the olde Iustice that examines all such offenders, and let time try: adieu.

William Shakespeare

As You Like It (1623). Acted 1599

RECRUITING

Shallow, Silence, Bardolph and villagers

Enter *Falstaffe*

Shal. It is very iust: Looke, heere comes good Sir *Iohn*. Giue me your hand, giue me your Worships good hand: Trust me, you looke well: and beare your yeares very well. Welcome, good Sir *Iohn*.

Fal. I am glad to see you well, good M. *Robert Shallow*: Master *Sure-card* as I thinke?

Shal. No sir *Iohn*, it is my Cosin *Silence*: in Commission with mee.

Fal. Good M. *Silence*, it well befits you should be of the peace.

Sil. Your good Worship is welcome.

Fal. Fye, this is hot weather (Gentlemen) haue you prouided me heere halfe a dozen of sufficient men?

Shal. Marry haue we sir: Will you sit?

Fal. Let me see them, I beseech you.

Shal. Where's the Roll? Where's the Roll? Where's the Roll? Let me see, let me see, let me see: so, so, so, so: yea marry Sir. *Raphe Mouldie*: Let them appeare as I call: let them do so, let them do so: Let mee see, Where is *Mouldie*?

Moul. Heere, if it please you.

Shal. What thinke you (Sir *Iohn*) a good limb'd fellow: yong, strong, and of good friends.

Fal. Is thy name *Mouldie*?

Moul. Yea, if it please you.

Fal. 'Tis the more time thou wert vs'd.

Shal. Ha, ha, ha, most excellent. Things that are mouldie, lacke vse: very singular good. Well saide Sir *Iohn*, very well said.

Fal. Pricke him.

Moul. I was prickt well enough before, if you could haue let me alone: my old Dame will be vndone now, for one to doe her Husbandry, and her Drudgery; you need not to haue prickt me, there are other men fitter to goe out, then I.

Fal. Go too: peace *Mouldie*, you shall goe. *Mouldie*, it is time you were spent.

Moul. Spent?

Shal. Peace, fellow, peace; stand aside: Know you where you are? for the other sir *Iohn*: Let me see: *Simon Shadow.*

Fal. I marry, let me haue him to sit vnder: He's like to be a cold souldier.

Shal. Where's *Shadow*?

Shad. Heere sir.

Fal. *Shadow*, whose sonne art thou?

Shad. My Mothers sonne; Sir.

Falst. Thy Mothers sonne: like enough, and thy Fathers shadow: so the sonne of the Female, is the shadow of the Male: it is often so indeede, but much of the Fathers substance.

Shal. Do you like him, sir *Iohn*?

Falst. *Shadow* will serue for Summer: pricke him: For wee haue a number of shadowes to fill vppe the Muster-Booke.

Shal. *Thomas Wart*?

Falst. Where's he?

Wart. Heere sir.

Falst. Is thy name *Wart*?

Wart. Yea sir.

Fal. Thou art a very ragged Wart.

Shal. Shall I pricke him downe, Sir *Iohn*?

Falst. It were superfluous: for his apparrel is built vp on his backe, and the whole frame stands vpon pins: pricke him no more.

Shal. Ha, ha, ha, you can do it sir: you can doe it: I commend you well. *Francis Feeble.*

Feeble. Heere sir.

Shal. What Trade art thou *Feeble*?

Feeble. A Womans Taylor sir.

Shal. Shall I pricke him, sir?

Fal. You may: But if he had beene a mans Taylor, he would haue prick'd you. Wilt thou make as many holes in an enemies Battaile, as thou hast done in a Womans petticote?

Feeble. I will doe my good will sir, you can haue no more.

Falst. Well said, good Womans Tailour: Well sayde Couragious *Feeble*: thou wilt bee as valiant as the wrathfull Doue, or most magnanimous Mouse. Pricke the womans Taylour well, Master *Shallow*, deepe Maister *Shallow*.

Feeble. I would *Wart* might haue gone sir.

Fal. I would thou wert a mans Tailor, that thou might'st mend him, and make him fit to goe. I cannot put him to a priuate souldier, that is the Leader of so many thousands. Let that suffice, most Forcible *Feeble*.

Feeble. It shall suffice.

Falst. I am bound to thee, reuerend *Feeble*. Who is the next?

Shal. *Peter Bulcalfe* of the Greene.

Falst. Yea marry, let vs see *Bulcalfe*.

Bul. Heere Sir.

Fal. Fore God, a likely Fellow. Come, pricke me *Bulcalfe* till he roare againe.

Bul. O Lord! good my Lord Captaine.

Fal. What? do'st thou roare before tha'rt prickt.

Bul. Oh sir, I am a diseased man.

Fal. What disease hast thou?

Bul. A whorson cold sir, a cough sir, which I caught with Ringing in the Kings affayres, vpon his Coronation day, sir.

Fal. Come, thou shalt go to the Warres in a Gowne: we will haue away thy Cold, and I will take such order, that thy friends shall ring for thee. Is heere all?

Shal. There is two more called then your number: you must haue but foure heere sir, and so I pray you go in with me to dinner.

Fal. Come, I will goe drinke with you, but I cannot tarry dinner. I am glad to see you in good troth, Master *Shallow*.

Shal. O sir *Iohn*, doe you remember since wee lay all night in the Winde-mill, in S Georges Field.

Falstaffe. No more of that good Master *Shallow*: No more of that.

Shal. Ha? it was a merry night. And is *Iane Nightwork* aliue?

Fal. She liues, M. *Shallow*.

Shal. She neuer could away with me.

Fal. Neuer, neuer: she would alwayes say shee could not abide M. *Shallow*.

Shal. I could anger her to the heart: shee was then a *Bona-Roba*. Doth she hold her owne well.

Fal. Old, old M. *Shallow*.

Shal. Nay, she must be old, she cannot choose but be old: certaine shee's old: and had *Robin Night-worke*, by old *Night-worke*, before I came to *Clements* Inne.

Sil. That's fiftie fiue yeeres agoe.

Shal. Hah, Cousin *Silence*, that thou hadst seene that, that this Knight and I haue seene: hah, Sir *Iohn*, said I well?

Falst. Wee haue heard the Chymes at mid-night, Master *Shallow*.

Shal. That wee haue, that wee haue; in faith, Sir *Iohn*, wee haue: our watch-word was, Hem-Boyes. Come, let's to Dinner; come, let's to Dinner: Oh the dayes that wee haue seene. Come, come.

Bul. Good Master Corporate *Bardolph*, stand my friend, and heere is foure *Harry* tenne shillings in French Crownes for you: in very truth, sir, I had as lief be hang'd sir, as goe: and yet, for mine owne part, sir, I do not care; but rather, because I am vnwilling, and for mine owne part, haue a desire to stay with my friends: else, sir, I did not care, for mine owne part, so much.

Bard. Go-too: stand aside.

Mould. And good Master Corporall Captaine, for my old Dames sake, stand my friend: shee hath no body to doe any thing about her, when I am gone: and she is old, and cannot helpe her selfe: you shall haue fortie, sir.

Bard. Go-too: stand aside.

Feeble. By my troth, I care not, a man can die but once: wee owe God a death. I will neuer beare a base minde: if it be my destinie, so: if it be not, so: no man is too good to serue his Prince: and let it goe which way it will, he that dies this yeere, is quit for the next.

Bard. Well said, thou art a good fellow.

Feeble. Nay, I will beare no base minde.

Falst. Come sir, which men shall I haue?

Shal. Foure of which you please.

Bard. Sir, a word with you: I haue three pound, to free *Mouldie* and *Bull-calfe*.

Falst. Go-too: well.

Shal. Come, sir *Iohn* which foure will you haue?

Falst. Doe you chuse for me.

Shal. Marry then, *Mouldie, Bull-calfe, Feeble,* and *Shadow*.

Falst. *Mouldie,* and *Bull-calfe*: for you *Mouldie,* stay at home, till you are past seruice: and for your part, *Bull-calfe,* grow till you come vnto it: I will none of you.

Shal. Sir *Iohn*, Sir *Iohn*, doe not your selfe wrong, they are your likelyest men, and I would haue you seru'd with the best.

Falst. Will you tell me (Master *Shallow*) how to chuse a man? Care I for the Limbe, the Thewes, the stature, bulke, and bigge assemblance of a man? giue mee the spirit (Master *Shallow*). Where's *Wart*? you see what a ragged appearance it is: hee shall charge you, and discharge you, with the motion of a Pewterers Hammer: come off, and on, swifter then hee that gibbets on the Brewers Bucket. And this same halfe-fac'd fellow, *Shadow*, giue me this man: hee presents no marke to the Enemie, the foe-man may with as great ayme leuell at the edge of a Pen-knife: and for a Retrait, how swiftly will this *Feeble*, the Womans Taylor, runne off. O, giue me the spare men, and spare me the great ones. Put me a Calyuer into *Warts* hand, *Bardolph*.

Bard. Hold *Wart*, Trauerse: thus, thus, thus.

Falst. Come, manage me your Calyuer: so: very well, go-too, very good, exceeding good. O, giue me alwayes a little, leane, old, chopt, bald Shot. Well said *Wart*, thou art a good Scab: hold, there is a Tester for thee.

Shal. Hee is not his Crafts-master, hee doth not doe it right. I remember at Mile-end-Greene, when I lay at *Clements* Inne, I was then Sir *Dagonet* in *Arthurs* Show: there was a little quiuer fellow, and hee would manage you his Peece thus: and hee would about, and about, and come you in, and come you in: Rah, tah, tah, would hee say, Bownce would hee say, and away againe would hee goe, and againe would he come: I shall neuer see such a fellow.

Falst. These fellowes will doe well, Master *Shallow*. Farewell Master *Silence*, I will not vse many wordes with you: fare you well, Gentlemen both: I thanke you: I must a dozen mile to night. *Bardolph*, giue the Souldiers Coates.

Shal. Sir *Iohn* Heauen blesse you, and prosper your Affaires, and send vs Peace. As you returne, visit my houfe. Let our old acquaintance be renewed: peraduenture I will with you to the Court.

Falst. I would you would, Master *Shallow*.

Shal. Go-too: I haue spoke at a word. Fare you well.

Exit.

Falst. Fare you well, gentle Gentlemen. On *Bardolph*, leade the men away. As I returne, I will fetch off these Iustices: I doe see the bottome of Iustice *Shallow*. How subiect wee old men are to this vice of Lying! This same staru'd Iustice hath done nothing but prate to me of the wildnesse of his Youth, and the Feates hee hath done about Turnball-street, and euery third word a Lye, duer pay'd to the hearer, then the Turkes Tribute. I doe remember him at *Clements* Inne, like a man made after Supper, of a Cheese-paring. When hee was naked, hee was, for all the world, like a forked Radish, with a Head Fantastically caru'd vpon it with a Knife. He was so forlorne, that his Dimensions (to any thicke sight) were inuisible. Hee was the very *Genius* of Famine: hee came euer in the rere-ward of the Fashion: And now is this Vices Dagger become a Squire, and talkes as familiarly of *Iohn* of Gaunt, as if hee had beene sworne Brother to him: and Ile be sworne hee neuer saw him but once in the Tilt-yard, and then he burst his Head, for crowding among the Marshals men. I saw it, and told *Iohn* of Gaunt, hee beat his owne Name, for you might haue truss'd him and all his Apparrell into an Eele-skinne: the Case of a Treble Hoeboy was a Mansion for him: a Court: and now hath he Land, and Beeues. Well, I will be ac-quainted with him, if I returne: and it shall goe hard, but I will make him a Philosophers two Stones to me. If the young Dace be a Bayt for the old Pike, I see no reason, in the Law of Nature, but I may snap at him. Let time shape, and there an end.

William Shakespeare

The Second Part of Henrie the Fourth (1600)
Text from First Folio (1623)

RECRUIT

Symon Eyre, his Wife, Hodge, Firk, Iane, and Rafe with a peece.

Eyre. Leaue whining, leaue whining, away with this whimpring, this pewling, these blubbring teares, and these wet eies, Ile get thy husband discharg'd, I warrant thee sweete *Iane*: go to.

Hodge. Master, here be the captaines.

Eyre. Peace *Hodge*, husht ye knaue, husht.

Firke. Here be the caualiers, and the coronels, maister.

Eyre. Peace *Firke*, peace my fine *Firke*, stand by with your pishery pasherie, away, I am a man of the best presence, Ile speake to them and they were Popes: gentlemen, captaines, colonels, commanders: braue men, braue leaders, may it please you to giue me audience, I am *Simon Eyre*, the mad Shoomaker of Towerstreete, this wench with the mealy mouth that wil neuer tire, is my wife I can tel you, heres *Hodge* my man, and my foreman, heres *Firke* my fine firking iourneyman, and this is blubbered *Iane*, al we come to be suters for this honest *Rafe*, keepe him at home, and as I am a true shoomaker, and a gentleman of the Gentle Craft, buy spurs your self, and Ile find ye bootes these seuen yeeres.

Wife. Seuen yeares husband?

Eyre. Peace Midriffe, peace, I know what I do, peace.

Firke. Truly master cormorant, you shal do God good seruice

to let *Rafe* and his wife stay together, shees a yong new
married woman, if you take her husband away from her a
night, you vndoo her, she may beg in the day time, for
hees as good a workman at a pricke and an awle, as any is
in our trade.

Iane. O let him stay, else I shal be vndone.

Firke. I truly, she shal be laid at one side like a paire of olde
shooes else, and be occupied for no vse.

Lacie.　　Truly my friends, it lies not in my power,
　　　　The *Londoners* are prest, paide, and set forth
　　　　By the Lord Maior, I cannot change a man.

Hodge. Why then you were as good be a corporall, as a colonel,
if you cannot discharge one good fellow, and I tell you
true, I thinke you doe more then you can answere, to presse
a man within a yeare and a day of his marriage.

Eyre. Wel said melancholy *Hodge*, gramercy my fine foreman.

Wife. Truly gentlemen, it were il done, for such as you, to
stand so stiffely against a poore yong wife: considering her
case, she is new married, but let that passe: I pray deale not
roughly with her, her husband is a yong man and but newly
entred, but let that passe.

Eyre. Away with your pisherie pasherie, your pols and your
edipolls, peace Midriffe, silence Cisly Bumtrincket, let your
head speake.

Firke. Yea and the hornes too, master.

Eyre. Tawsoone, my fine *Firk*, tawsoone, peace scoundrels:
see you this man, Captaines? you will not release him, wel
let him go, hee's a proper shot, let him vanish, peace *Iane*,
drie vp thy teares, theile make his powder dankish, take
him braue men, *Hector* of *Troy* was an hackney to him,
Hercules and *Termagant* scoundrelles, Prince *Arthurs* Round
table, by the Lord of Ludgate, nere fed such a tall, such a

dapper swordman, by the life of *Pharo*, a braue resolute swordman: peace *Iane*, I say no more, mad knaues.

Thomas Dekker
The Shomakers Holiday (1600)

THE EVE OF AGINCOURT

Court, Bates and Williams, three common soldiers; King Henry V

Court. Brother *Iohn Bates*, is not that the Morning which breakes yonder?

Bates. I thinke it be: but wee haue no great cause to desire the approach of day.

Williams. Wee see yonder the beginning of the day, but I thinke we shall neuer see the end of it. Who goes there?

King. A Friend.

Williams. Vnder what Captaine serue you?

King. Vnder Sir *Iohn Erpingham*.

Williams. A good old Commander, and a most kinde Gentleman: I pray you, what thinkes he of our estate?

King. Euen as men wrackt vpon a Sand, that looke to be washt off the next Tyde.

Bates. He hath not told his thought to the King?

King. No: nor it is not meet he should: for though I speake it to you, I thinke the King is but a man, as I am: the Violet smells to him, as it doth to me; the Element shewes to him, as it doth to me; all his Sences haue but humane Conditions: his Ceremonies layd by, in his Nakednesse he appeares but a man; and though his affections are higher mounted then ours, yet when they stoupe, they stoupe with the like wing: therefore, when he sees reason of feares, as we doe; his feares, out of doubt, be of the same rellish as ours are: yet in reason, no man should possesse him with any appearance of feare; least hee, by shewing it, should dis-hearten his Army.

Bates. He may shew what outward courage he will: but I beleeue, as cold a Night as 'tis, hee could wish himself in Thames vp to the Neck; and so I would he were, and I by him, at all aduentures, so we were quit here.

King. By my troth, I will speake my conscience of the King: I thinke hee would not wish himselfe any where, but where hee is.

Bates. Then I would he were here alone; so should he be sure to be ransomed, and a many poore mens liues saued.

King. I dare say, you loue him not so ill, to wish him here alone: howsoeuer you speake this to feel other mens minds, me thinks I could not dye any where so contented, as in the Kings company; his Cause being iust, and his Quarrell honorable.

Williams. That's more then we know.

Bates. I, or more then wee should seeke after; for wee know enough, if wee know wee are the Kings Subiects: if his Cause be wrong, our obedience to the King wipes the Cryme of it out of vs.

Williams. But if the Cause be not good, the King himselfe hath a heauie Reckoning to make, when all those Legges, and Armes, and Heads, chopt off in a Battaile, shall ioyne together at the latter day, and cry all, Wee dyed at such a place, some swearing, some crying for a Surgean; some vpon their Wiues, left poore behind them; some vpon the Debts they owe, some vpon their Children rawly left: I am afear'd, there are few dye well, that dye in a Battaile: for how can they charitably dispose of any thing, when Blood is their argument? Now, if these men doe not dye well, it will be a black matter for the King, that led them to it; who to disobey, were against all proportion of subiection.

King. So, if a Sonne that is by his Father sent about Merchandize, doe sinfully miscarry vpon the Sea; the imputation of his wickednesse, by your rule, should be imposed vpon his

Father that sent him: or if a Seruant, vnder his Masters command, transporting a summe of Money, be assayled by Robbers, and dye in many irreconcil'd Iniquities; you may call the businesse of the Master the author of the Seruants damnation: but this is not so: The King is not bound to answer the particular endings of his Souldiers, the Father of his Sonne, nor the Master of his Seruant; for they purpose not their death, when they purpose their seruices. Besides, there is no King, be his Cause neuer so spotlesse, if it come to the arbitrement of Swords, can trye it out with all vn-spotted Souldiers: some (peraduenture) haue on them the guilt of premeditated and contriued Murther; some, of be-guiling Virgins with the Broken Seales of Periurie; some, making the Warres their Bulwarke, that haue before gored the gentle Bosome of Peace with Pillage and Robberie. Now, if these men haue defeated the Law, and outrunne Natiue punishment; though they can out-strip men, they haue no wings to flye from God. Warre is his Beadle, Warre is his Vengeance: so that here men are punisht, for before breach of the Kings Lawes, in now the Kings Quarrell: where they feared the death, they haue borne life away; and where they would bee safe, they perish. Then if they dye vnprouided, no more is the King guiltie of their damna-tion, then hee was before guiltie of those Impieties, for the which they are now visited. Euery Subiects Dutie is the Kings, but euery Subiects Soule is his owne. Therefore should euery Souldier in the Warres doe as euery sicke man in his Bed, wash euery Moth out of his Conscience: and dying so, Death is to him aduantage; or not dying, the time was blessedly lost, wherein such preparation was gayned: and in him that escapes, it were not sinne to thinke, that making God so free an offer, he let him outliue that day, to see his Greatnesse, and to teach others how they should prepare.

Moth] mote

Will. 'Tis certaine, euery man that dyes ill, the ill vpon his owne head, the King is not to answer it.

Bates. I doe not desire hee should answer for me, and yet I determine to fight lustily for him.

King. I my selfe heard the King say he would not be ransom'd.

Will. I, hee said so, to make vs fight chearefully: but when our throats are cut, hee may be ransom'd, and wee ne're the wiser.

King. If I liue to see it, I will neuer trust his word after.

William Shakespeare

The Life of Henry the Fift (1600). Text from First Folio (1623)

HUMOURS

Mathew, Well-bred, Bobadill, Edward Knowell, Stephen

Wel. Well, Captaine *Bobadill*, Mr. *Matthew*, pray you know this gentleman here, he is a friend of mine, and one that will deserue your affection. I know not your name sir, but I shall be glad of any occasion, to render me more familiar to you.

Step. My name is Mr. *Stephen*, sir, I am this gentlemans owne cousin, sir, his father is mine vnckle, sir, I am somewhat melancholy, but you shall command me, sir, in whatsoeuer is incident to a gentleman.

Bob. Sir, I must tell you this, I am no generall man, but for Mr. *Wel-bred's* sake (you may embrace it, at what height of fauour you please) I doe communicate with you: and con-ceiue you, to bee a gentleman of some parts, I loue few wordes.

E. Kn. And I fewer, Sir, I haue scarce inow, to thanke you.

Mat. But are you indeed, sir? so giuen to it?

Step. I, truely, sir, I am mightily giuen to melancholy.

Mat. Oh, it's your only fine humour, sir, your true melancholy breeds your perfect fine wit, sir: I am melancholy my selfe diuers times, sir, and then doe I no more but take pen, and paper presently, and ouerflow you halfe a score, or a dozen sonnets, at a sitting.

(*E. Kn.* Sure, he vtters them then, by the grosse.)

Step. Truely sir, and I loue such things, out of measure.

E. Kn. I faith, better then in measure, Ile vnder-take.

Mat. Why, I pray you, sir, make vse of my studie, it's at your seruice.

Step. I thanke you sir, I shall bee bold, I warrant you; haue you a stoole there, to be melancholy vpon?

Mat. That I haue, sir, and some papers there of mine owne doing, at idle houres, that you'le say there's some sparkes of wit in 'hem, when you see them.

Wel. Would the sparkes would kindle once, and become a fire amongst 'hem, I might see selfe-loue burn't for her heresie.

Step. Cousin, is it well? I am melancholy inough?

E. Kn. Oh I excellent!

Wel. Captaine *Bobadill*: why muse you so?

E. Kn. He is melancholy, too.

Bob. Faith, Sir, I was thinking of a most honourable piece of seruice, was perform'd to morrow, being St. *Markes* day: shall bee some ten yeeres, now?

E. Kn. In what place, Captaine?

Bob. Why, at the beleag'ring of *Strigonium*, where, in lesse then two houres, seuen hundred resolute gentlemen, as any were in *Europe*, lost their liues vpon the breach. Ile tell you, gentlemen, it was the first, but the best league, that euer I beheld, with these eies, except the taking in of – what doe you call it, last yeere, by the *Genowayes*, but that (of all other) was the most fatall, and dangerous exploit, that euer I was rang'd in, since I first bore armes before the face of the enemie, as I am a gentleman and souldier.

Step. 'So, I had as liefe, as an angell, I could sweare as well as that gentleman!

E. Kn. Then, you were a seruitor, at both it seemes! at *Strigonium*? and what doe you call't?

Bob. Oh Lord, sir? by S. *George*, I was the first man, that entred the breach: and, had I not effected it with resolution, I had beene slaine, if I had had a million of liues.

E. Kn. 'Twas pittie, you had not ten; a cats, and your owne, ifaith. But, was it possible?

(*Mat.* 'Pray you, marke this discourse, sir.

Step. So, I doe.)

Bob. I assure you (vpon my reputation) 'tis true, and your selfe shall confesse.

E. Kn. You must bring me to the racke, first.

Bob. Obserue me iudicially, sweet sir, they had planted mee three demi-culuerings, iust in the mouth of the breach; now, sir (as we were to giue on) their master gunner (a man of no meane skill, and marke, you must thinke) confronts me with his linstock, readie to giue fire; I spying his intendment, discharg'd my petronel in his bosome, and with these single armes, my poore rapier, ranne violently, vpon the *Moores*, that guarded the ordinance, and put 'hem pell-mell to the sword.

Wel. To the sword? to the rapier, Captaine?

E. Kn. Oh, it was a good figure obseru'd, sir! but did you all this, Captaine, without hurting your blade?

Bob. Without any impeach, o' the earth: you shall perceiue sir. It is the most fortunate weapon, that euer rid on poore gentlemans thigh: shall I tell you, sir? you talke of *Morglay*, *Excalibur*, *Durindana*, or so? tut, I lend no credit to that is fabled of 'hem, I know the vertue of mine owne, and therefore I dare, the boldlier, maintaine it.

Step. I mar'le whether it be a *Toledo*, or no?

    petronel] large pistol   *mar'le*] marvel

Bob. A most perfect *Toledo*, I assure you, sir.

Step. I haue a countriman of his, here.

Mat. Pray you, let's see, sir: yes faith, it is!

Bob. This a *Toledo*? pish.

Step. Why doe you pish, Captaine?

Bob. A *Fleming*, by heauen, Ile buy them for a guilder, a
  piece, an' I would haue a thousand of them.

Ben Jonson

Euery Man in his Humour (1601). Text of 1616

MASTER AND PRENTICE

Touchstone and Quicksiluer

Touch. Thou shamelesse Varlet does thou iest at thy lawfull
  maister contrary to thy Indentures?

Quick. Why zbloud sir, my mother's a Gentlewoman and
  my father a Iustice of Peace, and of *Quorum*, and tho I am a
  yonger brother & a prentise, yet I hope I am my fathers
  sonne: and by Gods lidde, tis for your worship and for your
  commoditie that I keepe companie. I am intertaind among
  gallants, true: They call me cozen *Francke*, right; I lend them
  monnies, good: they spend it, well: But when they are
  spent, must not they striue to get more? must not their
  land flye? and to whom? shall not your worshippe ha' the
  refusall? well, I am a good member of the Citty if I were
  well considered. How would Merchants thriue, if Gentlemen would not be vnthriftes? How could Gentlemen bee
  vnthrifts if their humours were not fed? How should their
  humours be fedde but by white meate, and cunning
  secondings? Well, the Cittie might consider vs. I am going
  to an Ordinary now; the gallants fall to play, I carry light

golde with me: the gallants call coozen *Francke* some golde for siluer, I change, gaine by it, the gallants loose the golde; and then call coozęn *Francke* lend me some siluer. Why —

Touch. Why? I cannot tell, seuen score pound art thou out in the cash, but looke to it, I will not be gallanted out of my monies. And as for my rising by other mens fall; God shield me. Did I gaine my wealth by Ordinaries? no: by exchanging of gold? no: by keeping of gallants companie, no, I hired me a little shop, fought low, tooke small gaine, kept no debt booke, garnished my shop for want of Plate, with good wholsome thriftie sentences; as *Touchstone, keepe thy shopp, and thy shoppe will keepe thee. Light gaines makes heauie purses; Tis good to be merry and wise*: And when I was wiu'd, hauing something to sticke too, I had the horne of Suretiship euer before my eyes: You all know the deuise of the Horne, where the young fellow slippes in at the Butte end, and comes squesd out at the Buckall: and I grew vp, and I praise prouidence, I beare my browes now as high as the best of my neighbours: but thou – well looke to the accounts, your fathers bond lyes for you: seuen score pound is yet in the reere.

Quick. Why slid sir, I haue as good, as proper gallants wordes for it as any are in London, gentlemen of good phrase, perfect language, passingly behau'd, Gallants that weare sockes and cleane linnen, and call me kinde cozen *Francke*, good coozen *Francke*; for they know my Father: and by gods lidde shall not I trust 'hem? not trust?

George Chapman, Ben Jonson & John Marston

Eastward Hoe (1605)

FAVOURITE

Mendoza speaks

Now good *Elizium*, what a delicious heauen is it for a man to be in a Princes fauour: O sweete God, O pleasure! O Fortune! O all thou best of life! what should I thinke: what say? what do? to be a fauorite? a minion? to haue a generall timerous respect, obserue a man, a statefull scilence in his presence: solitarinesse in his absence, a confused hum and busie murmure of obsequious suters trayning him; the cloth held vp, and waye proclaimed before him; Petitionary vassailes licking the pauement with their slauish knees, whilst some odde pallace *Lampreel's* that ingender with Snakes, and are full of eyes on both sides with a kinde of insinuated humblenesse fixe all their delightes vpon his browe: O blessed state, what a rauishing prospect doth the *Olympus* of fauor yeeld; Death, I cornute the Duke: sweet women, most sweete Ladies, nay Angells; by heauen he is more accursed then a Diuell that hates you, or is hated by you, and happier then a God that loues you, or is beloued by you; you preseruers of mankind, life blood of society, who would liue, nay, who can liue without you? O Paradice, how maiesticall is your austerer presence? how imperiouslie chaste is your more modest face? but O! how full of rauishing attraction is your pretty, petulant, languishing, laciuiously-composed countenance: those amorous smiles, those soule-warming sparkling glances, ardent as those flames that sing'd the world by heedelesse Phaeton; in body how delicate, in soule how witty, in discourse how pregnant, in life how wary, in fauours how iuditious, in day how sociable, and in night, how? O pleasure vnutterable, Indeede, it is most certaine, one man cannot

Lampreel's] Lampreys   *cornute*] cuckold deserue onely to inioy a beautious woman: but a Dutches? in despight of *Phœbus* Ile write a Sonnet instantly in praise of her.

Exit.

John Marston
The Malcontent (1604

HAMLET UNDER SURVEILLANCE

Hamlet, Rosencrantz and Guildenstern

Ham. My excellent good friends, how doost thou *Guylder-sterne*? A *Rosencrans*, good lads how doe you both?

Ros. As the indifferent children of the earth.

Guyl. Happy, in that we are not ouer-happy: on Fortunes cap, We are not the very button.

Ham. Nor the soles of her shooe.

Ros. Neither my Lord.

Ham. Then you liue about her wast, or in the middle of her fauors.

Guyl. Faith her priuates we.

Ham. In the secret parts of Fortune? oh most true, she is a strumpet. What newes?

Ros. None my Lord, but the worlds growne honest.

Ham. Then is Doomes day neere, but your newes is not true; But in the beaten way of friendship, what make you at *Elsinoure*?

Ros. To visit you my Lord, no other occasion.

Ham. Begger that I am, I am euen poore in thankes, but I thanke you, and sure deare friends, my thankes are too deare a halfpeny: were you not sent for? is it your owne inclining? is it a free visitation? come, come, deale iustly with me, come, come, nay speake.

Guy. What should we say my Lord?

Ham. Any thing but to'th purpose: you were sent for, and there is a kind of confession in your lookes, which your modesties haue not craft enough to cullour. I know the good King and Queene haue sent for you.

Ros. To what end my Lord?

Ham. That you must teach me: but let me coniure you, by the rights of our fellowship, by the consonancie of our youth, by the obligation of our euer preserued loue; and by what more deare a better proposer can charge you withall, bee euen and direct with me whether you were sent for or no.

Ros. What say you?

Ham. Nay then I haue an eye of you, if you loue me hold not of.

Guyl. My Lord we were sent for.

Ham. I will tell you why, so shall my anticipation preuent your discouery, and your secrecie to the King and Queene moult no feather. I haue of late, but wherefore I knowe not, lost all my mirth, forgon all custome of exercises: and indeede it goes so heauily with my disposition, that this goodly frame the earth, seemes to mee a sterill promontorie, this most excellent Canopie the ayre, looke you, this braue orehanging firmament, this maiesticall roofe fretted with golden fire, why it appeareth nothing to me but a foule and pestilent congregation of vapoures. What a peece of worke is a man, how noble in reason, how infinit in faculties, in forme and moouing, how expresse and admirable in action, how like an Angell in apprehension, how like a God: the beautie of the world; the paragon of Annimales; and yet to me, what is this Quintessence of dust; man delights not me, nor women neither, though by your smiling, you seeme to say so.

William Shakespeare

The Tragicall Historie of Hamlet, Prince of Denmarke (1604)

CRISPINELLA

Crispinella, Beatrice, and Nurse

Cris. Pish sister *Beatrice*, preethee reade no more, my stomache alate stands against kissing extreamly.

Beat. Why good *Crispinella*?

Cris. By the faith, and trust I beare to my face, tis grown one of the most vnsauorie Ceremonies: Boddy a beautie, tis one of the most vnpleasing iniurious customes to Ladyes: any fellow that has but one nose on his face, and standing collor and skirtes also linde with Taffety sarcenet, must salute vs on the lipps as familierly: Soft skins saue vs, there was a stubbearded Iohn a stile with a ploydens face saluted me last day, and stroke his bristles through my lippes, I ha spent 10. shillings in *pomatum* since to skinne them againe. Marry if a nobleman or a knight with one locke vissit vs, though his vncleane goose-turd greene teeth ha the palsy, his nostrells smell worse than a putrified maribone, and his loose beard drops into our bosome, yet wee must kisse him with a cursy — a curse — for my part I had as liue they would break wynd in my lipps.

Beat. Fy *Crispinella* you speake too broad.

Cris. No iot sister, lets neere be ashamed to speake what we be not ashamd to thinke, I dare as boldly speake venery, as think venery.

Beat. Faith sister ile begone if you speake so broad.

Cris. Will you so? now bashfulnes seaz you, we pronounce boldly Robbery, Murder, treason, which deedes must needes be far more lothsome then an act which is so naturall, iust and necessary, as that of procreation. You shall haue an hipocriticall vestall virgin speake that with close teeth publikely, which she will receiue with open mouth priuately; for my owne part I consider nature without

cursy] curtsey   *seaz*] seize

apparell, without disguising of custome or complement, I giue thoughts wordes, and wordes truth, and truth boldnes; she whose honest freenes make it her vertue, to speake what she thinks, will make it her necessity to thinke what is good. I loue no prohibited things, and yet I would haue nothing prohibited by policy but by vertue, for as in the fashion of time, those bookes that are cald in, are most in sale and request, so in nature those actions that are most prohibited are most desired.

Beat. Good quick sister, stay your pace, we are priuat, but the world would censure you, for truly seuere modesty is womens vertue.

Cris. Fye, Fye, vertue is a free pleasant buxom qualitie: I loue a constant countenance well, but this froward ignorant coynes, sower austere lumpish vnciuill priuatenes, that promises nothing but rough skins, and hard stooles, ha, fy ont, good for nothing but for nothing. ...

Nurse. ... I now will read a lecture to you both, how you shall behaue your selues to your husbands ...

Cris. Read it to my sister good nurse, for I assure you ile nere marry.

Nurse. Marry God forfend, what will you doe then?

Cris. Fayth, striue against the flesh. Marry? no fayth, husbands are like lotts in the lottery: you may drawe forty blankes before you finde one that has any prise in him. A husband generally is a careles domineering thing that growes like corroll which as long as it is vnder water is soft and tender, but as soone as it has got his branch aboue the waues is presently hard stiffe, not to be bowed but burst; so when your husband is a sutor & vnder your choyse, Lord how suple hee is, how obsequious, how at your seruice sweet Lady: once married, got vp his head aboue, A stiffe crooked knobby inflexible tyrannous creature he grows: then they turne like water, more you would imbrace the lesse you

hould. Ile liue my owne woman, and if the worst come to
the worst, I had rather prooue a wagge then a foole.

Beat. O but a vertuous marriage?

Cris. Vertuous marriage? there is no more affinity betwixt
vertue and marriage, then betwixt a man and his horse,
indeed vertue getts vp vppon marriage sometimes, and
manageth it in the right way, but marriage is of another
peece ...

    Enter *Freeuill*

Free. Good day Sweete.

Cris. Good morrow brother, nay you shall haue my lip ...

John Marston

The Dutch Courtezan (1605)

LONDON LIFE

Monopoly, Whirlepoole, Lynstock, Iudyth, Mabell and Clare

Mono. What Chamberlain? I must take a pipe of Tobacco.

3. Women. Not here, not here, not here.

Mab. Ile rather loue a man that takes a purse, then him that
takes Tobacco.

Cla. By my little finger Ile breake al your pipes, and burne
the Case and the box too, and you drawe out your stinking
smoake afore me.

Mono. Prethee good Mistris *Tenterhooke*, Ile ha done in a trice.

Cla. Do you long to haue me swoune?

Mono. Ile vse but halfe a pipe introth.

Cla. Do you long to see me lie at your feet!

Mono. Smell toot: tis perfum'd.

Cla. Oh God? Oh God? you anger me: you stir my bloud:
you moue me: you make me spoile a good face with frown-
ing at you: this was euer your fashion, so to smoake my Hus-

band when you come home, that I could not abide him in mine eye: hee was a moate in it me thought a month after: pray spawle in another roome: fie, fie, fie.

Mono. Well, well, come, weele for once feed hir humor.

Iud. Get two roomes off at least if you loue vs.

Mab. Three, three, maister *Lynstocke* three.

Lin. Sfoote weele dance to *Norwich,* and take it there, if youle stay till we returne agen? Heeres a stir, youle ill abide a fiery face, that cannot endure a smoaky nose.

Mon. Come lets satisfie our appetite.

Whi. And that wil be hard for vs, but weele do our best.

Exeunt men.

Cla. So; are they departed? What string may wee three thinke that these three gallants harp vppon, by bringing vs to this sinfull towne of *Brainford?* ha?

Iud. I know what string they would harpe vppon, if they could put vs into the right tune.

Mab. I know what one of em buz'd in mine eare, till like a Theefe in a Candle, he made mine eares burne, but I swore to say nothing.

Cla. I know as verily they hope, and brag one to another, that this night theile row westward in our husbands whirries, as wee hope to bee rowd to *London* to morrowe morning in a paire of oares. But wenches lets bee wise, and make Rookes of them that I warrant are now setting purse-nets to cony-catch vs.

Both. Content.

Cla. They shall know that Cittizens wiues haue wit enough to out strip twenty such guls; tho we are merry, lets not be mad: be as wanton as new married wiues, as fantasticke and light headed to the eye, as fethermakers, but as pure about the heart, as if we dwelt amongst em in Black Fryers.

spawle] spit   *whirries*] wherries

Mab. Weele eate and drinke with em.

Clar. Oh yes: eate with em as hungerly as souldiers: drinke
as if we were Froes: talke as freely as Iestors, but doe as
little as misers, who (like dry Nurses) haue great breastes
but giue no milke. It were better we should laugh at their
popin-Iayes, then liue in feare of their prating tongues:
tho we lye all night out of the Citty they shall not find
country wenches of vs: but since we haue brought em thus
far into a fooles Paradice, leaue em int: the Iest shal be a
stock to maintain vs and our pewfellowes in laughing at
christnings, cryings out, and vpsittings this 12 month: how
say you wenches, haue I set the Sadle on the right horse.

Both. O twill be excellent.

Mab. But how shall we shift em off?

Cla. Not as ill debters do their Creditors (with good wordes)
but as Lawyers do their Clyents when they're ouerthrown,
by some new knauish tricke: and thus it shall bee: one of vs
must dissemble to be suddenly very sick.

Iud. Ile be she.

Clar. Nay, tho we can all dissemble well, yet Ile be she: for
men are so iealous, or rather enuious of one anothers happinesse (Especially in this out of towne gossipings) that he
who shall misse his hen, if hee be a right Cocke indeede, will
watch the other from treading.

Mab. Thats certaine, I know that by my self.

Cla. And like *Esops* Dog, vnlesse himselfe might eate hay,
wil lie in the manger and starue: but heele hinder the horse
from eating any: besides it will be as good as a Welch hooke
for you to keepe out the other at the Staues end: for you
may boldly stand vppon this point, that vnlesse euery mans
heeles may bee tript vp, you scorne to play at football.

Iud. Thats certaine: peace I heare them spitting after their
Tobacco.

Cla. A chaire, a chaire, one of you keepe as great a coyle and calling, and as if you ran for a midwife; th' other holde my head: whylst I cut my lace.

Mab. Passion of me? mister *Monopoly*, maister *Linstocke* and you be men, help to daw mistris *Tenterhooke*: O quickly, quickly, shees sicke and taken with an Agony.

    Enter as she cryes Monopolie, Whirlepoole, and Lynstocke.

Omni. Sick? How? how now? whats the matter?

Mono. Sweet *Clare* call vp thy spirits.

Clare. O maister *Monopoly*, my spirits will not come at my calling, I am terrible and Ill: Sure, sure, I'me struck with some wicked planet, for it hit my very hart: Oh I feele my selfe worse and worse.

Mono. Some burnt Sack for her good wenches: or possit drink, poxe a this Rogue Chamberlin, one of you call him: How her pulses beate: a draught of Cynamon water now for her, were better than two Tankerdes out of the *Thames*: how now? Ha.

Cla. Ill, ill, ill, ill, ill.

Mono. I'me accurst to spend mony in this Towne of iniquity: theres no good thing euer comes out of it: and it stands vppon such musty ground, by reason of the Riuer, that I cannot see how a tender woman can do well int. Sfoot? Sick now? cast down, now tis come to the push?

Cla. My mind misgiues me that als not sound at *London*.

Whirle. Poxe on em that be not sounde, what need that touch you?

Cla. I feare youle neuer carry me thither.

Omni. Puh, puh, say not so.

Cla. Pray let my cloathes be vtterly vndone, and then lay mee in my bed.

Lynst. Walke vp and downe a little.

Cla. O maister *Lynstock*, tis no walking will serue my turne: haue me to bed good sweete Mistris *Honisuckle*, I doubt

    daw] revive

that olde Hag *Gillian* of *Braineford* has bewitcht me.
Mono. Looke to her good wenches.
Mab. I so we will, and to you too: this was excellent.

Thomas Dekker and John Webster
West-ward Hoe (1607)

TEMPTATION

Hellgill and Country Wench

Hell. Come, leaue your puling and sighing.
Coun. W. Beshrew you now, why did you entice me from my father?
Hell. Why? to thy better aduancement. Wouldst thou, a pretty, beautifull, juicy squall, liue in a poore thrumbd house i' th'cuntry, in such seruile habiliments, and may well passe for a gentlewoman i' th' Citie? do's not fiue hundred do so, thinkst thou, and with worse faces? Oh, now in these latter dayes, the Deuill raygning, 'tis an age for clouen creatures! But why sad now? yet indeed 'tis the fashion of any Curtizan to be sea-sicke i' th' first Voyage, but at next shee proclaimes open wars, like a beaten souldier. Why, Northamptonshire Lasse, do'st dream of virginity now? remember a loose-bodied Gowne, wench, and let it goe; wires and tyres, bents and bums, felts and falls, thou that shalt deceiue the world, that gentlewomen indeed shall not be knowen from others. I haue a master, to whome I must prefer thee after the aforesayd decking; *Lethe* by name, a man of one most admired property; he can both loue thee, and for thy better aduauncement, be thy Pandar himselfe; an ex'lent sparke of humility.
Coun. W. Well, heauen forgiue you, You traine me vp too't.
Hell. Why, I doe acknowledge it, and I thinke I doe you a pleasure in't.

Thomas Middleton
Michaelmas Terme (1607)

School for Wives

Harebrain and a disguised Courtesan

Har. Oh Lady *Gulman*, my wifes onely company, welcome! and how do's the vertuous Matron, that good old Gentlewoman, thy mother? I perswade my selfe, if modesty be in the world, she has part on't; a woman of an excellent carriage all her lifetime, in Court, Citie, and Countrey.

Cour. Sh'as alwaies carried it well in those places, sir; *(aside)* witnesse three bastards a piece. How do's your sweete bedfellow, sir? you see I'me her boldest visitant.

Har. And welcome, sweete Virgin; the onely companion my soule wishes for her. I left her within at her Lute; prethee, giue her good counsell.

Cour. Alas, she needes none, sir!

Har. Yet, yet, yet, a little of thy instructions will not come amisse to her.

Cour. Ile bestow my labour, sir.

Har. Doe, labour her, prethee. I haue convay'd away all her wanton Pamphlets; as *Hero and Leander, Venus and Adonis,* oh two lushious mary-bone pies for a yong married wife! Here, here, prethie, take the *Resolution,*[1] and reade to her a little.

Cour. Sh'as set vp her resolution alreadie, sir.

Har. True, true, and this will confirme it the more; ther's a chapter of Hell; 'tis good to reade this cold weather: terrifie her, terrifie her; goe, reade to her the horrible punishments for itching wantonnes, the paines alotted for adulterie; tell her her thoughts, her very dreames are answerable, say so; rip vp the life of a Curtizan, and shew how loathsom 'tis.

1. Robert Parsons' *First Booke of the Christian Exercise appertayning to resolution* (1582)

Cour. (*Aside*) The gentleman would perswade mee in time to disgrace my selfe, and speake ill of mine owne function.

Exit.

Thomas Middleton

A Mad World, my Masters (1608)

PRODIGAL FATHER

Merrythought (*within*).

    Nose, nose, iolly red nose,

    And who gaue thee this iolly red nose?

Mrs. Merrythought. Harke! my husband hee's singing and hoiting; and Ime faine to carke and care, and all little enough. Husband! Charles! Charles Merrithought!

    Enter *old Merrithought*

Mer. Nutmegs and ginger, cinnamon and cloues,

    And they gaue me this iolly red nose!

Mrs. M. If you would consider your state, you would haue little list to sing, I-wisse.

Mer. It should neuer bee considered while it were an estate, if I thought it would spoyle my singing.

Mrs. M. But how wilt thou do, Charles? Thou art an old man, and thou canst not worke, and thou hast not fortie shillings left, and thou eatest good meat, and drinkest good drinke, and laughest.

Mer. And will do.

Mrs. M. But how wilt thou come by it, Charles?

Mer. How? Why, how haue I done hitherto, this forty yeares? I neuer came into my dining roome, but at eleuen and six a clocke I found excellent meat and drinke a'th table; my clothes were neuer worne out, but next morning a taylor brought me a new suit; and without question it will be so euer: vse makes perfectnesse. If all should faile, it is but a little straining my selfe extraordinary, and laugh my selfe to death.

Wife. (*in the audience*) it's a foolish old man, this, is not he George?

Citizen. Yes, cunny.

Wife. Giue me a peny i'th purse while I liue, George.

Cit. I, by ladie, cunnie, hold thee there.

Mrs. M. Well, Charles, you promis'd to prouide for Jasper, and I have laid vp for Michael, I pray you pay Jasper his portion; hee's come home, and hee shall not consume Michael's stocke; he saies his maister turnd him away, but I promise you truly, I thinke he ran away.

Wife. No indeed, Mistresse Merrithought; though he bee a notable gallowes, yet Il'e assure you his maister did turne him away, euen in this place, 'twas i'faith, within this halfe houre, about his daughter. My husband was by.

Cit. Hang him, rougue, he seru'd him well enough: loue his maister's daughter! By my troth, cunnie, if there were a thousand boies, thou wouldst spoile them all with taking their parts. Let his mother alone with him.

Wife. I, George, but yet truth is truth.

Francis Beaumont and John Fletcher
The Knight of the Burning Pestle (1613)

A Puritan's Temptation

John Littlewit; Win-the-fight, his wife; Dame Purecraft, her mother and a widow; Zeal-of-the-Land Busy, a Puritan, suitor to Dame Purecraft; Solomon, Littlewit's man.

Pur. Now, the blaze of the beauteous discipline, fright away this euill from our house! how now *Win-the-fight*, Child: how do you? Sweet child, speake to me.

Win. Yes, forsooth.

Pur. Looke vp, sweet *Win-the-fight*, and suffer not the enemy to enter you at this doore, remember that your education has bin with the purest; what polluted one was it, that nam'd first the vnclean beast, Pigge, to you, Child?

Win. (Vh, Vh.)

Ioh. Not I, o' my sincerity, mother: she long'd aboue three houres, ere she would let me know it; who was it, *Win?*

Win. A prophane blacke thing with a beard, *Iohn.*

Pur. O! resist it, *Win-the-fight*, it is the Tempter, the wicked Tempter, you may know it by the fleshly motion of Pig; be strong against it, and it's foule temptations, in these assaults, whereby it broacheth flesh and blood, as it were, on the weaker side, and pray against it's carnall prouocations, good child, sweet child, pray.

Ioh. Good mother, I pray you, that she may eate some Pigge, and her belly full, too; and doe not you cast away your owne child, and perhaps one of mine, with your tale of the Tempter: how doe you, *Win?* Are you not sicke?

Win. Yes, a great deale, *Iohn*, (vh, vh.)

Pur. What shall we doe? call our zealous brother *Busy* hither, for his faithfull fortification in this charge of the aduersary; child, my deare childe, you shall eate Pigge, be comforted, my sweet child.

Win. I, but i' the *Fayre*, mother.

Pur. I meane i' the *Fayre*, if it can be any way made, or found lawfull; where is our brother *Busy?* Will hee not come? looke vp, child.

Ioh. Presently, mother, as soone as he has cleans'd his beard. I found him, fast by the teeth, i' the cold Turkeypye, i' the cupbord, with a great white loafe on his left hand, and a glasse of *Malmesey* on his right.

Pur. Slander not the *Brethren*, wicked one.

Ioh. Here hee is, now, purified, Mother.

Pur. O brother *Busy*! your helpe heere to edifie, and raise vs vp in a scruple; my daughter *Win-the-fight* is visited with a naturall disease of woman; call'd A longing to eate Pigge.

Ioh. I Sir, a Bartholmew-pigge: and in the *Fayre*.

Pur. And I would be satisfied from you, Religiously-wise, whether a widdow of the sanctified assembly, or a widdowes daughter, may commit the act, without offence to the weaker sisters.

Bus. Verily, for the disease of longing, it is a disease, a carnall disease, or appetite, incident to women: and as it is carnall, and incident, it is naturall, very naturall: Now Pigge, it is a meat, and a meat that is nourishing, and may be long'd for, and so consequently eaten; it may be eaten; very exceeding well eaten: but in the *Fayre*, and as a *Bartholmew*-pig, it cannot be eaten, for the very calling it a *Bartholmew*-pigge, and to eat it so, is a spice of *Idolatry*, and you make the *Fayre*, no better then one of the high *Places*. This I take it, is the state of the question. A high place.

Ioh. I, but in state of necessity: *Place* should giue place, Mr. *Busy*, (I haue a conceit left, yet.)

Pur. Good Brother *Zeale-of-the land*, thinke to make it as lawfull as you can.

Ioh. Yes Sir, and as soone as you can: for it must be, Sir; you see the danger my little wife is in, Sir.

Pur. Truely, I doe loue my child dearely, and I would not haue her miscarry, or hazard her first fruites, if it might be otherwise.

Bus. Surely, it may be otherwise, but it is subiect, to construction, subiect, and hath a face of offence, with the weake, a great face, a foule face, but that face may haue a vaile put ouer it, and be shaddowed, as it were, it may be eaten, and in the *Fayre*, I take it, in a Booth, the tents of the wicked: the place is not much, not very much, we may be religious in midst of the prophane, so it be eaten with a reformed mouth, with *sobriety*, and humblenesse; not gorg'd in with gluttony, or greedinesse; there's the feare: for, should she goe there, as taking pride in the place, or delight in the vncleane dressing, to feed the vanity of the eye, or the lust of the palat, it were not well, it were not fit, it were abominable, and not good.

Ioh. Nay, I knew that afore, and told her on't, but courage, *Win*, we'll be humble enough; we'll seeke out the homeliest Booth i' the *Fayre*, that's certaine, rather then faile, wee'll eate it o' the ground.

Pur. I, and I'll goe with you my selfe, *Win-the-fight*, and my brother, *Zeale-of-the-land*, shall goe with vs too, for our better consolation.

Win. Vh, vh.

Ioh. I, and *Salomon* too, *Win*, (the more the merrier) *Win*, we'll leaue *Rabby Busy* in a Booth. *Salomon*, my cloake.

Sal. Here, Sir.

Bus. In the way of comfort to the weake, I will goe, and eat. I will eate exceedingly, and prophesie; there may be a good vse made of it, too, now I thinke on't: by the publike eating of Swines flesh, to professe our hate, and loathing of *Iudaisme*, whereof the brethren stand taxed. I will therefore eate, yea, I will eate exceedingly.

Ioh. Good, i' faith, I will eate heartily too, because I will be no *Iew*, I could neuer away with that stiffenecked generation: and truely, I hope my little one will be like me, that cries for Pigge so, i' the mothers belly.

Bus. Very likely, exceeding likely, very exceeding likely.

Ben Jonson

Bartholemew Fayre (1631)

Jealousy

Lysander; Tharsalio, his brother-in-law.

Lysand. So now we are our selues. Brother, that ill relisht
speech you let slip from your tongue, hath taken so deepe
hold of my thoughts, that they will neuer giue me rest, till
I be resolu'd what 'twas you said, you know, touching my
wife.

Thars. Tush: I am wearie of this subiect, I said not so.

Lys. By truth it selfe you did: I ouer-heard you. Come, it
shall nothing moue me, whatsoeuer it be; pray thee vnfold
briefly what you know.

Thars. Why briefly Brother. I know my sister to be the
wonder of the Earth; and the Enuie of the Heauens.
Vertuous, Loiall, and what not. Briefly, I know shee hath
vow'd, that till death and after death, sheele hold inuiolate
her bonds to you, & that her black shall take no other hew;
all which I firmely beleeue. In briefe Brother, I know her
to be a woman. But you know brother, I haue other yrons
on th'anuile.

Lys. You shall not leaue mee so vnsatisfied; tell mee what tis
you know.

Thar. Why Brother; if you be sure of your wiues loialtie for
terme of life: why should you be curious to search the
Almanacks for after-times: whether some wandring Æneas
should enioy your reuersion; or whether your true Turtle
would sit mourning on a wither'd branch, till *Atropos* cut
her throat: Beware of curiositie, for who can resolue you?
youle say perhaps her vow.

Lysand. Perhaps I shall.

Thar. Tush, her selfe knowes not what shee shall doe, when
shee is transform'd iuto a Widdow. You are now a sober
and staid Gentleman. But if *Diana* for your curiositie

should translate you into a monckey: doe you know what
gambolds you should play? your only way to bee resolu'd
is to die and make triall of her.

Lysand. A deare experiment, then I must rise againe to bee
resolu'd.

Thar. You shall not neede. I can send you speedier aduertise-
ment of her constancie, by the next Ripier that rides that
way with Mackerell. And so I leaue you.

George Chapman
The Widdowes Teares (1612)

BOSOLA AND THE DUCHESS

Bosola, the Duchess of Malfi

Bos. I am come to make thy tombe.

Duch. Hah, my tombe?
    Thou speak'st as if I lay vpon my death bed,
    Gasping for breath: do'st thou perceiue me sicke?

Bos. Yes, and the more dangerously, since thy sicknesse is
insensible.

Duch. Thou art not mad sure, do'st know me?

Bos. Yes.

Duch. Who am I?

Bos. Thou art a box of worme-seede, at best, but a saluatory
of greene mummey: what's this flesh? a little cruded
milke, phantasticall puffe-paste: our bodies are weaker then
those paper prisons boyes vse to keepe flies in: more con-
temptible: since ours is to preserue earth-wormes: didst
thou euer see a Larke in a cage? such is the soule in the
body: this world is like her little turfe of grasse, and the
Heauen ore our heades, like her looking glasse, onely giues vs
a miserable knowledge of the small compasse of our prison.

Ripier] one who carries fish inland to sell

Duch. Am not I, thy Duchesse?

Bos. Thou art some great woman sure, for riot begins to sit
on thy fore-head (clad in gray haires) twenty yeares sooner,
then on a merry milkemaydes. Thou sleep'st worse, then if
a mouse should be forc'd to take vp her lodging in a cats
eare: a little infant, that breedes it's teeth, should it lie with
thee, would crie out, as if thou wert the more vnquiet
bed-fellow.

Duch. I am Duchesse of *Malfy* still.

John Webster

The Dutchess of Malfy (1623)

A MELANCHOLY MAN

Is a strayer from the droue; one that nature made sociable
because she made him man, and a crazed disposition hath
altered. Impleasing to all, as all to him; stragling thoughts are
his content, they make him dreame waking, there's his
pleasure. His imagination is neuer idle, it keepes his minde in
a continuall motion, as the poise the clocke: hee windes vp his
thoughts often, and as often vn-windes them, *Penelopes* webb
thriues faster. Hee'le seldome bee found without the shade of
some groue in whose bottome a riuer dwels. He carries a cloud
in his face, neuer faire weather: his outside is framed to his in-
side, in that he keepes a *Decorum*, both vnseemly. Speake to
him, he heares with his eyes, eares follow his minde, and that's
not at leasure. He thinks busines, but neuer does any: he is all
contemplation no action. Hee hewes and fashions his thoughts
as if hee meant them to some purpose, but they proue vn-
profitable; as a peece of wrought timber to no vse. His spirits
and the sunne are enemies, the sun bright and warme, his
humor blacke and cold; varietie of foolish apparitions people

his head, they suffer him not to breath, according to the necessities of nature; which makes him sup vp a draught of as much aire at once, as would serue thrice. Hee denies nature her due in sleep, and ouer paies her with watchfulnes; nothing pleaseth him long, but that which pleaseth his own fantasies; they are the consuming euils, and euill consumptions, that consumes him aliue. Lastly, he is a man onely in shew, but comes short of the better part; a whole reasonable soule, which is mans chiefe preheminence, and sole mark from creatures senceable.

Sir Thomas Overbury

A Wife ... Whereunto are added many witty Characters (1614)

HELL

SOME say, it is an *Iland*, embrac'de about with certaine Riuers, called the waters of Sorrow: Others proue by infallible Demonstration, that tis a *Continent*, but so little beholden to Heauen, that the Sunne neuer comes amongst them.

How so euer it be, this is certaine, that tis exceeding rich, for all *Vsurers* both Iewes and Christians, after they haue made away their Soules for money here, meete with them there againe: You haue of all Trades, of all Professions, of all States some there: you haue Popes there, as wel as here, Lords there, as well as here, Knights there as wel as here, Aldermen there, as wel as here, Ladies there, as wel as here, Lawyers there, as well as here. Soldiers march there by millions, soe doe Citti-zens, soe doe Farmers; very fewe Poets can be suffred to liue there, the *Colonel* of *Coniurers* driues them out of his Circle, because hee feares they'le write libells against him: yet some pittiful fellowes (that haue faces like fire-drakes, but wittes colde as Whetstones, and more blunt) not Poets indeede, but ballad-makers, rub out there, and write Infernals: Marrie players swarme there as they do here, whose occupation being smelt out, by the *Cacodemon*, or head officer of the Countric, to bee lucratiue, he purposes to make vp a company, and to be chiefe sharer himselfe, *De quibus suo loco*, of whose doings you shall heare more by the next carrier: but here's the mischiefe, you may find the way thither, though you were blinder then *Superstition*, you may bee set a-shore there for lesse then a Scullers fare: Any Vintners boy, that has bene cup-bearer to one of the 7. deadly sinnes but halfe his yeres, any Marchant of maiden heads, that brings commodities out of *Virginia*, can direct you thither: But neyther they nor the weather-beatenst *Cosmographicall* Starre-catcher of em all, can take his oath, that it lyes iust vnder such an *Horizon*, whereby many are brought into a fooles *Paradice*, by gladly beleeuing that either there's no such place at all, or else, that tis built by Inchauntment, and standes vpon *Fayrie ground* by reason such pinching and nipping is knowne to bee there, and that how well fauoured soeuer wee depart hence, we are turnd to *Changelings*, if we tarry there but a minute.

These *Territories*, notwithstanding of *Tartarie*, will I vndermine and blow vp to the view of all eies, the black & dismal shores of this *Phlegetonticke Ocean*, shall be in ken, as plainely as the white (now vnmaydend brests) of our owne Iland: *China*, *Peru*, and *Cartagena* were neuer so rifled: the winning of *Cales*, was nothing to the ransacking of this *Troy* that's all on fire; the very bowels of these Infernall Antipodes, shall bee ript vp, and pulld out, before that great Dego of Diuels his owne face: Nay, since my flag of defiance is hung forth, I will yeelde to no truce, but with such *Tamburlaine-like* furie match against this great Turke, and his legions, that *Don Belzebub* shall be ready to damne himselfe, and be horne-mad: for with the coniuring of my pen, al Hell shall breake loose.

Assist me therefore, thou Genius of that ventrous, but Iealous musicion of Thrace (*Euridices* Husband) who being besotted on his wife (of which sin none but Cuckolds should bee guilty) went aliue (with his fiddle at's back,) to see if he could baile her out of that Adamantyne prison; the fees he was to pay for her, were Iigs and country daunces: he payd them: the forfeits, if he put on yellow stockings & lookt back vpon her, was her euerlasting lying there, without baile or Maynprize: the louing coxcomb could not choose but looke back, and so lost her, (perhaps hee did it, because hee would be rid of her.) The morall of which is, that if a man leaue his owne busines, and haue an eye to his wiues dooings, sheele giue him the slip, though she runne to the Diuell for her labor. Such a iourney (sweet *Orpheus*) am I to vndertake, but *Ioue* forbid my occasion should be like thine; for if the Marshall himselfe should rake Hell for wenches, he could not find worse, (no nor so bad) there, as are here vpon earth. It were pity any woman should be damn'd, for she would haue tricks (once in a moone) to put the Diuell forth of his wits. Thou (most cleare-throated singing man,) with thy harpe (to the twinckling of which, inferior spirits skipt like goats ouer the *Welch* mountaines) hadst priuiledge, because thou wert a Fiddler, to be sawcy, and to passe and repasse through euery roome, and into euery nook of the Diuels wine-celler: Inspire mee therfore with thy cunning that caried thee thither, and thy courage that brought thee from thence, teach me which way thou went'st in, and how thou scapt'st out, guide me in true fingering, that I may strike those tunes which thou plaid'st (euery dinner and supper) before that Emperor of *Low Germainie*, and the brabbling States vnder him: *Lucifer* himselfe daunced a *Lancashire Horne-pipe*, whilst thou wert there. If I can but harp vpon thy string, hee shall now for my pleasure tickle vp the *Spanish Pauin*. I will call vpon no Midwiues to help mee in those Throws, which (after my braines

Maynprize] procuring the release of a prisoner by becoming surety
brabbling] squabbling

235

are fallen in labour) I must suffer, (yet Midwiues may be had vp at all howres) nor vpon any coniurer, (yet coniurers, thou knowst, are fellow and fellow-like with *Monsieur Malediction*, as Puncks are, who raize him likewise vp continually in their *Circæan Circles*) or as Brokers are, who day and night study the black Art: No, no (thou Mr of the musicall company) I sue to none, but to thee, because of thy Prick-song: For Poetry (like honesty and olde Souldiers) goes vpon lame feete, vnlesse there bee musicke in her.

And thou, into whose soule (if euer there were a *Pithagorean Metemsuchosis*) the raptures of that fierie and inconfinable *Italian* spirit were bounteously and boundlessly infused, thou sometimes Secretary to *Pierce Pennylesse*, and Master of his requests, ingenious, ingenuous, fluent, facetious, T. *Nash*: from whose aboundant pen, hony flow'd to thy friends, and mortall Aconite to thy enemies: thou that madest the Doctor[1] a flat Dunce, and beat'st him at two sundry tall Weapons, Poetrie, and Oratorie: Sharpest Satyre, Luculent Poet, Elegant Orator, get leaue for thy Ghost to come from her abiding, and to dwell with me a while, till she hath carows'd to me in her owne wonted ful measures of wit, that my plump braynes may swell, and burst into bitter Inuectiues against the Lieftennant of Limbo, if hee casheere *Pierce Pennylesse* with dead pay.

Thomas Dekker
Newes from Hell (1606)

COUNTRY LIFE

SINCE then that in the *Noblest Streames* there are such *Whirlepooles* to swallow vs vp, such *Rockes* that threaten danger, (if not ship-wracke,) and such *Quick-sands* to make vs sinke, who

1. Gabriel Harvey.

would not willingly take downe all the sayles of his ambition, and cast anchore on a safe and retired shore, which is to be found in no place, if not in the Countrie. O blessed life! patterne of that which our first Parents led, the state of Kings (now) being but a slauery to that of theirs. O schoole of contemplation! O thou picture of the whole world drawne in a little compasse! O thou *Perspectiue* glasse, in whom we may behold vpon earth, all the frame and wonders of heauen. How happy (how thrice happie) is he that not playing with his wings in the golden flames of the Court, nor setting his foote into the busie throngs of the citie, nor running vp and downe, in the intricate mazes of the law, can bee content in the winter to sit by a country fire, and in the summer to lay his head on the greene pillowes of the earth, where his sleepe shall be soft slumbers, and his wakings pleasant as golden dreams. Hast thou a desire to rule? get vp to the mountaines, and thou shalt see the greatest trees stand trembling before thee, to doe thee reuerence; those maiest thou call thy Nobles: thou shalt haue ranks of Oaks on each side of thee, which thou mayest call thy Guard: thou shalt see willowes bending at euery blast, whome thou maiest call thy flatterers: thou shalt see vallies humbled at thy feete, whom thou maiest tearme thy slaues. Wouldst thou behold battailes? step into the fieldes, there shalt thou see excellent combats betweene the standing Corne and the Windes. Art thou a tyrant and delightest in the fall of *Great ones*? muster then thy haruesters together, and downe with those proud Summer Lords, when they are at the highest. Wouldst thou haue Subsidies paide thee? the Plow sends thee in Corne, the Medow giues thee her pasture, the *Trees* pay custome with their fruite, the *Oxe* bestowes vpon thee his labour, the sheepe his wooll. Dost thou call for musick? No Prince in the worlde keepes more skilfull Musitians: the birds are thy consort, and the wind instruments they play vpon, yeelde ten thousand tunes. Art thou addicted to studie, Heauen is thy Lybrarie, the Sun, Moone, and Stars are thy Bookes and teach thee Astronomy: By obseruing them, thou makest Almanacks to thy selfe, that serue for all seasons. ... The admiration of these bewties made mee so enamoured, and so really in loue with the inheritor of them, that the flames of my affection (were in their burning) onely carried thither. So that in steade of paued streetes, I trod the vnbeaten pathes of the fields: the rankes of trees were to mee as great buildings: Lambes and skipping Kids were as my merrie companions: the cleare fountaine as my cups of wine: rootes and hearbes as the Table of an Ordinarie, the Dialogues of Birds as the Sceanes of a Play: and the open emptie Medowes as the proud and populous Citie. Thus did I wish to liue, thus to die: and hauing wandred long (like a *Timonist*) hating Men because they dishonoured their creation, at length fortune lead mee by the hand into a place so curiously built by nature, as if it had bin the pallace where she purposed none should lie but her selfe: It was a Groue set thicke with Trees, which grew in such order, that they made a perfect circle; insomuch that I stood in feare, it was kept by Fayries, and that I was brought into it by enchantment. The branches of the Trees (like so many hands) reached ouer one to another; and in their embracements held so fast together, that their boughes made a goodly greene roofe, which being touched by the wind, it was a pleasure to behold so large a seeling to mooue: vpon euery branch sat a consort of singers, so that euery tree shewed like a musicke roome. The floore of this Summer-house was paued all ouer with yellow Field-flowers, and with white, and red Dazies, vpon which the Sunne casting but a wanton eye, you would haue sworne the one had been Nayles of Gold, the other Studs of enamelled Siluer. Amazed I was when I did but looke into this little paradice, and afraid to enter, doubting whether it were some hallowed ground or no, for I could finde no path that directed me to it: neither the foote of any man nor the hoofe of any beast had beaten downe the grasse; for the blades of it stood so hie and so euen, as if their lengthes had been giuen them by one measure. The melody which the Birds made, and the varietie of all sorts of fruits which the trees promised, with the prettie and harmelesse murmuring of a shallow streame, running in windings through the middest of it (whose noyse went like a chime of Bels, charming the eyes to sleepe) put me in mind of that Garden whereof our great grand-sire was the keeper. I euen wept for sorow to thinke he should be so foolish, as to bee driuen from a place of such happinesse: and blamed him in my minde for leauing such a president behind him, because by his fall wee lost felicitie, and by his frailtie all men are now apt to vndoe themselues and their posteritie through the inticements of women.

Thomas Dekker

The Bel-Man of London (1608)

PRIDE

Euery one thinketh his owne waies best, though thei lead to destruction of body and soule, which I wish them to take heede of. And amongest many other fearfull examples of Gods wrathe agaynst Pride, to sett before their eyes the fearfull Iudgement of God, shewed vpon a gentlewoman of *Eprautna* of late, euen the 27 of Maie 1582, the fearfull sound whereof is blowen through all the worlde, and is yet fresh in euery mannes memorie. This gentlewoman being a very riche Marchaunte mannes daughter, vpon a time was inuited to a Bridall, or Weddyng, whiche was solemnized in that Toune, agaynst whiche daie shee made great preparation, for the plumyng of her self in gorgious arraie, that as her bodye

president] precedent

was moste beautifull, faire, and proper, so her attire in euery
respecte might bee correspondent to the same. For the accom-
plishment whereof she curled her haire, she died her lockes,
and laied them out after the best maner, she coloured her face
with waters and Ointmentes: But in no case could she gette
any (so curious and daintie she was) that coulde starche, and
set her Ruffes and Neckerchers to her mynde: wherefore shee
sent for a couple of Laundresses, who did the best thei could
to please her humors, but in any wise thei could not; then
fell she to sweare, and teare, to cursse and banne, castyng her
Ruffes vnder feete, and wishyng that the Deuill might take
her when she wore any of those Neckerchers againe. In the
meane tyme (through the sufferaunce of God) the Deuill,
transforming himself into the forme of a young man, as
braue and proper as shee in euerie poincte in outward
appearaunce, came in, fainyng himself to bee a woer or suter
vnto her. And seyng her thus agonized, and in such a peltyng
chase, he demaunded of her the cause thereof, who straight
waie told hym (as women can conceale no thyng that lieth
vppon their stomackes) howe shee was abused in the setting of
her Ruffes, which thyng beeyng heard of hym, he promised
to please her minde, and thereto tooke in hand the setting of
her Ruffes, whiche he performed to her great contentation
and likyng, in so muche, as she lookyng her selfe in a glasse
(as the Deuill bad her), became greatly inamoured with hym.
This dooen, the yong man kissed her, in the doyng whereof,
he writhe her necke in sonder, so she dyed miserably, her
bodie beyng Metamorphosed into blacke and blewe colours
most vgglesome to behold, and her face (whiche before was
so amorous) became moste deformed and fearefull to looke
vpon. This being knowen, preparaunce was made for her
buriall, a riche coffin was prouided, and her fearfull bodie was
laied therein, and it couered verie sumpteously. Foure men

amorous] inspiring love

immediatly assaied to lifte vp the corps, but could not moue it; then sixe attempted the like, but could not once stirre it from the place where it stoode. Whereat the standers by marueilyng, caused the Coffin to bee opened, to see the cause thereof. Where they founde the bodie to be taken awaie, and a blacke Catte verie leane and deformed, sittyng in the Coffin, setting of great Ruffes, and frizlying of haire, to the great feare, and wonder of all the beholders. This wofull spectacle haue I offered to their viewe, that by looking into it, in stead of their other looking Glasses, they might see their own filthinesse, and auoyde the like offence, for feare of the same, or worser iudgement; whiche God graunt thei maie doe.

Philip Stubbes

The Anatomie of Abuses (1583)

SHOWING OFF

ALL his humor rises vp into the froth of ostentation; which if it once settle, falles downe into a narrow roome. If the excesse be in the vnderstanding part, all his wit is in print; the Presse hath left his head emptie; yea, not only what he had, but what he could borrow without leaue. If his glorie be in his deuo-tion, he giues not an Almes but on record; and if he haue once done well, God heares of it often; for vpon euery vnkindnesse, hee is readie to vpbraid him with his merits ... Or, if a more gallant humour possesse him, hee weares all his land on his backe, and walking high, looks ouer his left shoulder, to see if the point of his rapier follow him with a grace. Hee is proud of another mans horse; and wel mounted, thinks euery man wrongs him, that looks not at him. A bare head in the street doth him more good than a meales meat. Hee sweares bigge at an Ordinarie, and talkes of the Court with a sharpe accent;

neither vouchsafes to name anie not honourable, nor those without some terme of familiaritie, and likes well to see the hearer looke vpon him amazedly; as if he sayd, How happie is this man that is so great with great ones! Vnder pretence of seeking for a scroll of newes, hee drawes out an handfull of letters, indorsed with his owne stile, to the height; and halfe reading euery title, passes ouer the latter part, with a murmur; not without signifying what Lord sent this, what great Ladie the other; and for what sutes: the last paper (as it happens) is his newes from his honourable friend in the French Court. In the midst of dinner, his Lacquay comes sweating in, with a sealed note from his creditour, who now threatens a speedie arrest, and whispers the ill newes in his Masters eare, when hee aloud names a Counsellor of State, and professes to know the imployment. The same messenger hee calles with an imperi-ous nod, and after expostulation, where he hath left his fellowes, in his eare sends him for some new spur-leathers or stockings, by this time footed, and when he is gone halfe the room, recalles him, and sayth aloud, *It is no matter, let the greater bagge alone till I come*; and yet againe calling him closer, whispers (so that all the table may hear) *that if his crimson sute be readie against the day, the rest need no haste*. He picks his teeth when his stomacke is emptie, and calles for Pheasants at a common Inne. You shall find him prizing the richest iewels, and fairest horses, when his purse yeelds not money enough for earnest. He thrusts himselfe into the prease before some great Ladies; and loues to be seene neere the head of a great traine. His talke is how many Mourners hee furnish't with gownes at his fathers funerals, how many messes; how rich his coat is, and how ancient, how great his alliance: what challenges hee hath made and answered; what exploits at *Cales* or *Nieuport*: and when hee hath commended others buildings, furnitures, sutes, compares them with his owne. When hee hath vndertaken to be the Broker for some rich Diamond, he weares it, and pulling off his gloue to stroke vp his haire, thinks no eye should haue any other obiect. Entertaining his friend, he chides his Cooke for no better cheere, and names the dishes he meant, and wants. To conclude, hee is euer on the stage, and acts still a glorious part abroad, when no man carries a baser heart, no man is more sordid and carelesse at home. He is a Spanish souldier on an Italian Theater; a bladder full of winde, a skin full of words; a fooles wonder, and a wise mans foole.

Joseph Hall

Characters of Vertues and Vices (1608)

A Witch's Prophecy

Thus ruling the realme at his will for certaine yeares, at length fortune began to shewe a chaunge of countenance after hir olde accustomed guise. For Doorus the brother of Athirco (whom as ye haue heard Natholocus supposed to haue bene dead) wrote certaine letters signifying his owne estate with the welfare of his Nephewes the children of Athirco vnto certaine Scottishe Lordes, whome hee knewe to fauour his cause. Whiche letters hee deliuered vnto a Pictishe woman, appoynting hyr how and to whome she shoulde deliuer the same, but the woman apprehended by the way, and brought vnto Natholocus, hee caused hyr secretely to be sacked and throwen into a riuer. Afterwards sending for suche of the Nobles as the direction of the foresayde letters had giuen him occasion to haue in some suspicion, he committed them first to pryson, and at length caused them to be secretly strangled. Whiche wicked deede being once notified abroade, moued so the hartes of theyr friends and alies, that they procured the people to rebell: and so gathering them togither, they raysed open and cruell warres against him.

Natholocus enformed of their determinations, withdrewe himselfe priuily into Murray lande, there to get togither an armie to resist his enimies, and for that he was desirous also to vnderstande somewhat of the issue of this trouble, he sent one of his trustie seruants being a gentleman of that countrey, vnto a woman that dwelt in the Isle of Colmkil (otherwise called Iona) esteemed very skilfull in foreshewing of things to come, to learne of hyr what fortune should happe of this warre, which was already begunne. The Witche consulting with hyr sprytes, declared in the ende howe it shoulde come shortly to passe, that the king shoulde bee murthered not by his open enimies, but by the handes of one of his most familiar friendes, in whom hee had reposed an especiall truste. The messenger demaunding by whose hands that shoulde be, euen by thine saith she, as it shal be well knowen within these fewe dayes. The Gentleman hearing these wordes, rayled against hyr very bitterly, bidding hyr go lyke an olde Witche: for he trusted to see hyr brent before he shoulde committe so villanous a deede. And departing from hyr, he went by and by to signifie what answeare hee had receyued: but before hee came where the King lay, his minde was altered, so that what for doubte on the one side that if hee shoulde declare the truthe, as it was tolde him, the king might happily conceyue some greate suspition, that it should follow by his meanes as shee had declared, and therevpon put him to death first: and for feare on the other side that if he kept it secrete, it might happen to be reuealed by some other, and then he to run in asmuche daunger of life as before: he determined with him-selfe to worke the surest way, and so comming to the king, he was ledde aside by him into his priuie chamber, where al other being commaunded to auoide, he declared how he had sped: and then falling forthwith vpon Natholocus, with his dagger he slew him outright, and threwe his body into a priuie: and afterwardes getting out by a backe doore, and taking his horse whiche he had there readie, he fledde with all speede vnto the camp of the conspiratours, and was the first that brought newes vnto them of this acte thus by him atchieued.

Raphael Holinshed

Chronicles of England, Scotlande, and Irelande (1577)

KING FERGUS

HE seemed to striue howe to passe his predessour in all poyntes of wickednesse. Hce tooke no regarde at all to the gouernment of his Realme, but gaue himselfe to exessiue gluttonie in deuouring of delicate meates and drinks, and therwith kept suche a number of vile strumpettes in house with him, whom hee vsed as concubines, that his wife was no better esteemed than as an handmayde, or rather a kitchin mayde. Who being a woman of great modestie and sober aduisednesse, coulde not yet but take sore griefe and indignation hereat: and therefore sundrie tymes assayed by waye of wholesome perswasions to turne his minde from such sinfull vsages and filthie trade of liuing. Finally when she saw there was no hope to conuert his deprauate minde, nor by any meanes to refourme him, but that the more shee laboured to doe good vppon him, the worse he was, through verie displeasure of suche iniuries as shee daylye susteyned at the handes of his concubines, shee founde meanes to strangle him secretely one night as hee lay in his bed, choosing rather to be without a husband, than to haue one that shoulde deceyue hir of the right and dutie of mariage, and that in such sort, as she must be faine to suffer the reproch dayly afore hir face, being misvsed of them whom he kept as paramours in most dispiteful maner.

The day after she wrought this feate: the bodie being

founde deade, was apparayled in funerall wise, and brought forth into the place of iudgement, where inquisition was straightly made what they were that had done so heynous a deed. For though there were but few that lamented his death, yet some of his friends were verie earnest to haue the matter tryed forth, that such as had committed the murther, might suffer due punishment.

Many were apprehended and had to the rack, but yet could none be founde that would confesse it. The Queene was voyde of all suspition, as she that had bene taken for a woman of great temperancie. But yet when shee hearde that a number of innocent persons were tormented without desart, sore lamenting (as shoulde appeare) theyr miserable case, she came hastily into the Iudgement hall, and getting hir aloft vpon the bench, there in the presence of al the company, she had these or the like wordes vnto the whole assembly. I knowe not good people, I knowe not what God moueth me, or what diuine reuengement vexeth me with sundry thoughts and cogitations, that of all this daye and morning preceeding, I haue had neither rest in bodie nor minde. And verely when I hearde that certaine guiltlesse persons were cruelly tormented here in your presence, had not wrath giuen place partly vnto modestie, whereof I must confesse there is left but a small portion in me, I had forthwith rid my self out of the way. The kings death was mine act. Conscience constrayneth me (setting apart mine owne safeguard) to confesse the truth, least the guiltlesse shoulde wrongfully perishe: Therefore vnderstande yee for truth, that none of them whom ye haue examined are priuie to the offence. I verily am shee, that with these wicked handes haue strangled this night last past Ferguse, about whose death I see you in trouble, moued so to do with two as sharpe pricks as may rest in a woman, to wit, Impacient forbearing of carnall lust and yrefull wrath. Ferguse by his continuall vsing of concubines, kept from me the due debt that the husbande oweth to the wife: whereupon when there was no hope to reconcile him with often aduertisementes, vehement force of anger rysing in my heart, droue mee to doe so wicked a deed. I thought lieffer therefore to dispatch the Adulterer, then (being destitute of my husbande, and defrauded of all Queenely honor) to liue still subiect vnto the perpetuall iniuries of such lewde women as hee kept and vsed in my steade. Loose ye therefore those that be accused of the kings death, and as for me ye shall not neede to proceede agaynst me as guiltie of the crime by order of law, for I that was so bolde to commit so heynous an act, will accordingly do execution vpon my selfe euen here incontinently in presence of you all: what honour is due to the deade, looke you to that.

Hauing thus made an ende of hir tale, shee plucked forth a knife which she had hid vnder her gowne, and stroke hirselfe to the heart with the same, falling deade vpon it downe to the grounde. All such as were present, wondered greatly at hir stoute and hardie stomacke, speaking diuersly thereof, as some in prayse, and some in disprayse of these hir monstrous doings.

Raphael Holinshed
Chronicles of England, Scotland, and Irelande (1577)

MICROCOSM

THOU seemest a World in thy selfe, containing Heauen, Starres, Seas, Earth, Floodes, Mountaines, Forestes, and all that liues: Yet rests thou not satiate with that is in thyselfe, nor with all in the wide Vniuerse (because thou knowest their defectes) vntill thou raise thy selfe, to the contemplation of that first illuminating Intelligence, farre aboue Time, and euen reaching Eternitie it selfe, into which thou art trans-

formed, for, by receiuing thou (beyond all other thinges) art
made that which thou receiuest. The more thou knowest the
more apt thou art to know, not being amated with any
obiect that exelleth in predominance, as Sense by obiectes
sensible. Thy Will is vncompellable, resisting Force, daunting
Necessitie, despising Danger, triumphing ouer Affliction,
vnmoued by Pittie, and not constrained by all the toyles and
disasters of Life. What the Artes-Master of this Vniuerse is in
gouerning this Vniuerse, thou art in the Bodie; and as hee is
whollie in euerie part of it, so art thou whollie in euerie part
of the Bodie: Like vnto a Mirrouer, euerie small parcell of
which a parte, doeth represent and doe the same, what the
whole did enteire & together. By Thee Man is that Hymen of
eternall and mortall thinges, that Chaine, together binding
vnbodied and bodilie Substances, without which the goodlie
Fabricke of this world were vnperfcct. Thou hast not thy
beginning from the fecunditie, power, nor action of the
elementall qualities, beeing an immediate Master-piece of that
great Maker: Hence hast Thou the Formes and Figues of all
thinges imprinted in thee from thy first originall. Thou onelie
at once art capable of contraries, of the three partes of Time,
Thou makest but one, thou knowest thy selfe so separate,
absolute and diuerse an essence from thy Bodie, that Thou dis-
posest of it as it pleaseth Thee, for in Thee there is no passion
so weake which mastereth not the feare of leauing it. Thou
shouldst bee so farre from repining at this separation, that it
should bee the chiefe of thy desires; Sith it is the passage, and
meanes to attaine thy perfection and happinesse. Thou art
heere, but as in an infected and leprous Inne, plunged in a
flood of humours, oppressed with Cares, suppressed with
Ignorance, defiled and destained with Vice, retrograd in the
course of Vertue; Small thinges seeme heere great vnto Thee,
and great thinges small, Follie appeareth Wisdome and Wise-

amated] dismayed

dome Follie. Freed of thy fleshlie Care, thou shalt rightlie discerne the beautie of thy selfe, and haue perfect Fruition of that All-sufficient and All-suffizing Happinesse, which is GOD himselfe; to whom thou owest thy beeing, to Him thou owest thy well beeing; Hee and Happinesse are the same. For, if GOD had not happinesse, Hee were not GOD, because Happinesse is the highest and greatest Good: If then GOD haue Happinesse, it can not bee a thing differing from Him, for, if there were any thing in Him differing from Him, Hee should bee an Essence composed and not simple. More, what is differing in any thing, is either an accident or a part of it selfe; In GOD Happinesse can not bee an accident, because Hee is not suiect to any accidents; if it were a part of Him (since the part is before the Whole) wee should bee forced to grant, that something was before GOD. Bedded and bathed in these earthlie ordures, thou canst not come neare this soueraigne Good, nor haue any glimpse of the farre-off dawning of his vn-accessible Brightnesse, no, not so much as the eyes of the Birds of the night haue of the Sunne. Thinke then by Death, that thy Shell is broken, and thou then but euen hatched; that thou art a Pearle, raised from thy Mother, to bee enchaced in Gold, and that the death-day of thy bodie, is thy birth-day to Eternitie.

Why shouldst thou bee feare-stroken? and discomforted, for thy parting from this mortall Bride, thy Bodie; sith it is but for a tyme, and such a tyme, as shee shall not care for, nor feele any thing in, nor thou haue much neede of her? Nay, sith thou shalt receiue her againe, more goodlie and beautifull, than when in her fullest Perfection thou enioyed her; beeing by her absence made like vnto that Indian Christall, which after some Reuolutions of Ages, is turned into purest Diamond.

William Drummond
'A Cypresse Grove' from *Flowres of Sion* (1623)

DEATH

FOR the rest, if we seeke a reason of the succession and continuance of this boundlesse ambition in mortall man, we may adde to that which hath been already said; That the Kings and Princes of the world haue alwayes laid before them, the actions, but not the ends, of those great Ones which præceded them. They are alwayes transported with the glorie of the one, but they neuer minde the miserie of the other, till they finde the experience in themselues. They neglect the aduice of God, while they enioy life, or hope it; but they follow the counsell of Death, vpon his first approach. It is he that puts into man all the wisdome of the world, without speaking a word; which God with all the words of his Law, promises, or threats, doth not infuse. *Death* which hateth and destroyeth man, is beleeued; God which hath made him and loues him, is alwayes deferred. *I haue considered* (saith Salomon) *all the workes that are vnder the Sunne, and behold, all is vanitie and vexation of spirit*: but who beleeues it, till Death tells it vs? It was Death, which opening the conscience of *Charles* the fift, made him enioyne his sonne Philip to restore *Navarre*; and King *Francis* the first of *France*, to command that iustice should be done vpon the Murderers of the Protestants in *Merindol* and *Cabrieres*, which till then he neglected. It is therfore Death alone that can suddenly make man to know himselfe. He tells the proud and insolent, that they are but Abiects, and humbles them at the instant; makes them crie, complaine, and repent, yea, even to hate their forepassed happinesse. He takes the account of the rich, and proues him a begger; a naked begger, which hath interest in nothing, but in the grauell that fills his mouth. He holds a Glasse before the eyes of the most beautifull, and makes them see therein, their deformitie and rottennesse; and they acknowledge it.

O eloquent, iust and mightie Death! whom none could

aduise, thou hast perswaded; what none hath dared, thou hast done; and whom all the world hath flattered, thou only hast cast out of the world and despised: thou hast drawne together all the farre stretched greatnesse, all the pride, crueltie, and ambition of man, and couered it all ouer with these two narrow words, *Hic iacet.*

Sir Walter Ralegh

The History of the World (1614)

IV

THE CRITICISM OF THE ARTS

THE UNITIES

OUR Tragidies and Commedies, not without cause cryed out against, obseruing rules neither of honest ciuilitie, nor skilfull *Poetrie*. Excepting *Gorboducke*, (againe I say of those that I haue seen) which notwithstanding as it is full of stately speeches, and well sounding phrases, clyming to the height of *Seneca* his style, and as full of notable morallitie, which it dooth most delightfully teach, and so obtaine the verie ende of *Poesie*. Yet in truth, it is verie defectious in the circumstaunces, which greeues mee, because it might not remaine as an exact moddell of all Tragidies. For it is faultie both in place and time, the two necessarie Companions of all corporall actions. For where the Stage should alway represent but one place, and the vttermoste time presupposed in it, should bee both by *Aristotles* precept, and common reason, but one day; there is both manie dayes and places, inartificially imagined. But if it bee so in *Gorboducke*, howe much more in all the rest, where you shall haue *Asia* of the one side, and *Affricke* of the other, and so manie other vnder Kingdomes, that the Player when he comes in, must euer begin with telling where he is, or else the tale will not be conceiued. Now you shall haue three Ladies walke to gather flowers, and then we must beleeue the stage to be a garden. By and by we heare newes of shipwrack in the same place, then we are too blame if we accept it not for a Rock. Vpon the back of that, comes out a

inartificially] inartistically

253

hidious monster with fire and smoke, and then the miserable beholders are bound to take it for a Caue: while in the meane time two Armies flie in, represented with foure swords & bucklers, and then what hard hart wil not receiue it for a pitched field. Now of time, they are much more liberall. For ordinarie it is, that two yoong Princes fall in loue, after many trauerses she is got with childe, deliuered of a faire boy: he is lost, groweth a man, falleth in loue, and is readie to get an other childe, and all this in two houres space: which howe absurd it is in sence, euen sence may imagine: and Arte hath taught, and all auncient examples iustified, and at this day the ordinarie players in *Italie* will not erre in.

Sir Philip Sidney
The Defence of Poesie (1595)

POETASTERS

IF I let passe the vncountable rabble of ryming Ballet makers and compylers of sencelesse sonets, who be most busy, to stuffe euery stall full of grosse deuises and vnlearned Pamphlets: I trust I shall with the best sort be held excused. Nor though many such can frame an Alehouse song of fiue or sixe score verses, hobbling vppon some tune of a Northen Iygge, or Robyn hoode, or La lubber etc. And perhappes obserue iust number of sillables, eyght in one line, sixe in an other, and there withall an A to make a iercke in the ende: yet if these might be accounted Poets (as it is sayde some of them make meanes to be promoted to the Lawrell) surely we shall shortly haue whole swarmes of Poets: and euery one that can frame a Booke in Ryme, though for want of matter, it be but in commendations of Copper noses or Bottle Ale, wyll catch at the Garlande due to Poets: whose potticall (poeticall I

should say) heades, I would wyshe, at their worshipfull com-
mencements might in steede of Lawrell, be gorgiously garnished with fayre greene Barley, in token of their good affection to our Englishe Malt. One speaketh thus homely of them,
with whose words I wyll content my selfe for thys time,
because I woulde not bee too broade wyth them in myne
owne speeche.

In regarde (he meaneth of the learned framing the newe
Poets workes which writt the Sheepheardes Caldender) I
scorne and spue out the rakehelly rout of our ragged Rymers,
(for so themselues vse to hunt the Letter) which without
learning boaste, without iudgment iangle, without reason
rage and fume, as if some instinct of poeticall spyrite had
newlie rauished them, aboue the meanesse of common
capacity. And beeing in the midst of all their brauery, sud-
dainely for want of matter or of Ryme, or hauing forgotten
their former conceyt, they seeme to be so payned and trauelled
in theyr remembraunce, as it were a woman in Chyldbyrth,
or as that same *Pythia* when the traunce came vpon her.

William Webbe

A Discourse of English Poetrie (1586)

CRITICISM OF SPENSER

In good faith I had once againe nigh forgotten your *Faerie
Queene*: howbeit by good chaunce, I haue nowe sent hir home
at the last, neither in better nor worse case, than I founde hir.
And must you of necessitie haue my Iudgement of hir in
deede? To be plaine, I am voyde of all iudgement, if your
Nine Comoedies, whervnto in imitation of *Herodotus*, you
giue the names of the *Nine Muses*, (and in one mans fansie
not vnworthily) come not neerer *Ariostoes Comœdies*, eyther

for the finenesse of plausible Elocution, or the rarenesse of Poetical Inuention, than that *Eluish Queene* doth to his *Orlando Furioso*, which notwithstanding, you wil needes seeme to emulate, and hope to ouergo, as you flatly professed your self in one of your last Letters.... But I wil not stand greatly with you in your owne matters. If so be the *Faerye Queene* be fairer in your eie than the *Nine Muses*, and *Hobgoblin* runne away with the Garland from *Apollo:* Marke what I saye; and yet I will not say that I thought, but there an End for this once, and fare you well, till God or some good Aungell putte you in a better minde.

Gabriel Harvey

Three Proper and Wittie Familiar Letters (1580)

SPENSER'S ALLEGORY

SIR, knowing how doubtfully all Allegories may be construed, and this booke of mine, which I haue entituled the Faery Queene, being a continued Allegory, or darke conceit, I haue thought good aswell for auoyding of gealous opinions and misconstructions, as also for your better light in reading therof, (being so by you commanded,) to discouer vnto you the general intention and meaning, which in the whole course thereof I haue fashioned, without expressing of any particular purposes or by-accidents therein occasioned. The generall end therefore of all the booke is to fashion a gentleman or noble person in vertuous and gentle discipline: Which for that I conceiued shoulde be most plausible and pleasing, being coloured with an historicall fiction, the which the most part of men delight to read, rather for variety of matter, then for profite of the ensample: I chose the historye of king Arthure, as most fitte for the exellency of his person, being made famous by many mens former workes, and also furthest from the daunger of enuy, and suspition of present time. In which I haue followed all the antique Poets historicall, first Homere, who in the Persons of Agamennon and Vlysses hath ensampled a good gouernour and a vertuous man, the one in his Ilias, the other in his Odysseis: then Virgil, whose like intention was to doe in the person of Aeneas: after him Ariosto comprised them both in his Orlando: and lately Tasso disseuered then againe, and formed both parts in two persons, namely that part which they in Philosophy call Ethice, or vertues of a priuate man, coloured in his Rinaldo: The other named Politice in his Godfredo. By ensample of which excellente Poets, I labour to pourtraict in Arthure, before he was king, the image of a braue knight, perfected in the twelue priuate morall vertues, as Aristotle hath deuised, the which is the purpose of these first twelue bookes: which if I finde to be well accepted, I may be perhaps encoraged to frame the other part of polliticke vertues in his person, after that hee came to be king.

Edmund Spenser
The Faerie Queene (1590)

OBSCURITY

SUCH is the wilfull pouertie of iudgements (sweet *Mathew*) wandring like pasportles men, in contempt of the diuine discipline of Poesie, that a man may well feare to frequent their walks: The prophane multitude I hate, and onelie consecrate my strange Poems to these serching spirits, whom learning hath made noble, and nobilitie sacred: endeuoring that materiall Oration, which you call *Schema*; varying in some rare fiction, from popular custome, euen for the pure sakes of ornament and vtilitie ...

But that Poesie should be as peruiall as Oratorie, and plainness her speciall ornament, were the plaine way to barbarisme: and to make the Asse runne proud of his eares; to take away strength from Lyons, and giue Cammels hornes.

That *Enargia*, or cleerenes of representation, requird in absolute Poems is not the perspicuous deliuery of a lowe inuention; but high and harty inuention exprest in most significant and vnaffected phrase; it serues not a skilfull Painters turne, to draw the figure of a face onely to make knowne who it represents; but hee must lymn, giue luster, shaddow, and heightening; which though ignorants will esteeme spic'd, and too curious, yet such as haue the iudiciall perspectiue, will see it hath motion, spirit and life ...

Obscuritie in affection of words, and indigested concets, is pedanticall and childish; but where it shroudeth it selfe in the hart of his subiect, vtterd with fitnes of figure, and expressiue Epethites; with that darknes wil I still labour to be shaddowed: rich Minerals are digd out of the bowels of the earth, not found in the superficies and dust of it; charms made of vnlerned characters are not consecrate by the Muses which are diuine artists, but by *Euippes* daughters, that challengd them with meere nature, whose brests I doubt not had beene well worthy commendation, if their comparison had not turnd them into Pyes.

George Chapman

Ouids Banquet of Sence (1595)

AGAINST RHYME

BUT there is yet another fault in Rime altogether intollerable, which is, that it inforceth a man oftentimes to abiure his matter, and extend a short conceit beyond all bounds of arte: for in

affection] affectation

Quatorzens me thinks the Poet handles his subiect as tyrannically as *Procrustes* the thiefe his prisoners, whom when he had taken, he vsed to cast vpon a bed, which if they were too short to fill he would stretch them longer, if too long, he would cut them shorter. Bring before me now any the moste selfelou'd Rimer, and let me see if without blushing he be able to reade his lame halting rimes. Is there not a curse of Nature laid vpon such rude Poesie, when the writer is himself asham'd of it, and the hearers in contempt call it Riming and Ballating? What Deuine in his Sermon, or graue Counseller in his Oration will alleage the testimonie of a rime? But the dcuinity of the *Romaines* and *Gretians* was all written in verse: and *Aristotle*, *Galene*, and the bookes of all the excellent Philosophers are full of the testimonies of the old Poets. By them was laid the foundation of all humane wisedome, and from them the knowledge of all antiquitie is deriued. I will propound but one question, and so conclude this point. If the *Italians*, *Frenchmen* and *Spanyards*, that with commendation haue written in Rime, were demaunded whether they had rather the bookes they haue publisht (if their toong would beare it) should remaine as they are in Rime, or be translated into the auncient numbers of the *Greekes* and *Romaines*, would they not answere into numbers? What honour were it then for our English language to be the first that after so many ycares of barbarisme could second the perfection of the industrious *Greekes* and *Romaines*?

Thomas Campion

Observations in the Art of English Poesie (1602)

RHYME

FOR we are tolde how that our measures goe wrong, all Ryming is grosse, vulgare, barbarous, which if it be so, we haue lost much labour to no purpose: and for mine owne particular, I cannot but blame the fortune of the times and mine owne Genius that cast me vppon so wrong a course, drawne with the current of custome, and an vnexamined example. Hauing beene first incourag'd or fram'd thereunto by your most Worthy and Honourable Mother, receiuing the first notion for the formall ordering of those compositions at *Wilton*, which I must euer acknowledge to haue beene my best Schoole, and thereof alwayes am to hold a feeling and gratefull memory. Afterward, drawne farther on by the well-liking and approbation of my worthy Lord, the fosterer of mee and my *Muse*, I aduentured to bestow all my whole powers therein, perceiuing it agreed so well, both with the complexion of the times, and mine owne constitution, as I found not wherein I might better imploy me. But yet now, vpon the great discouery of these new measures, threatning to ouerthrow the whole state of Rhyme in this kingdom, I must either stand out to defend, or else be forced to forsake my selfe and giue ouer all. And though irresolution and a selfe distrust be the most apparent faults of my nature, and that the least checke of reprehension, if it sauour of reason, will as easily shake my resolution as any mans liuing: yet in this case I know not how I am growne more resolued, and before I sinke, willing to examine what those powers of iudgement are, that must beare me downe, and beat me off from the station of my profession, which by the law of nature I am set to defend.

And the rather for that this detractor (whose commendable Rymes albeit now himselfe an enemy to ryme, haue giuen heretofore to the world the best notice of his worth) is a man of faire parts, and good reputation, and therefore the reproach forcibly cast from such a hand may throw downe more at once then the labors of many shall in long time build vp againe, specially vpon the slippery foundation of opinion, and the worlds inconstancy, which knowes not well what it would haue, and

> *Discit enim citius, meminitque libentius illud*
> *Quod quis deridet quam probat & veneratur.*

And he who is thus become our vnkinde aduersarie, must pardon vs if we be as iealous of our fame and reputation, as hee is desirous of credite by his new-old arte, and must consider that we cannot, in a thing that concernes vs so neare, but haue a feeling of the wrong done, wherein euery Rymer in this vniuersall Iland as well as my selfe, stands interressed. So that if his charitie had equally drawne with his learning hee would haue forborne to procure the enuie of so powerfull a number vpon him, from whom he cannot but expect the returne of a like measure of blame, and onely haue made way to his owne grace, by the proofe of his abilitie, without the disparaging of vs, who would haue bin glad to haue stood quietly by him, & perhaps commended his aduenture, seeing that euermore of one science an other may be borne, & that these Salies made out of the quarter of our set knowledges, are the gallant proffers onely of attemptiue spirits, and commendable though they worke no other effect than make a Brauado: and I know it were *Indecens, & morosum nimis, alienæ industriæ, modum ponere.* We could well haue allowed of his numbers had he not disgraced our Ryme; Which both Custome and Nature doth most powerfully defend.

Samuel Daniel
An Apologie for Ryme (1603)

THE NATURE OF POETRY

POESIE is a part of Learning in measure of words for the most part restrained, but in all other points extreamely licensed, and doth truly referre to the Imagination, which, beeing not tyed to the Lawes of Matter, may at pleasure ioyne that which Nature hath seuered, & seuer that which Nature hath ioyned, and so make vnlawfull Matches & diuorses of things: *Pictoribus atque Poetis &c.* It is taken in two senses in respect of Wordes or Matter. In the first sense it is but a *Character* of stile, and belongeth to Arts of speeche, and is not pertinent for the present. In the later, it is, as hath beené saide, one of the principall Portions of learning, and is nothing else but FAINED HISTORY, which may be stiled as well in Prose as in Verse.

The vse of this FAINED HISTORIE hath beene to giue some shadowe of satisfaction to the minde of Man in those points wherein the Nature of things doth denie it, the world being in proportion inferiour to the soule; by reason whereof there is agreeable to the spirit of Man a more ample Greatnesse, a more exact Goodnesse, and a more absolute varietie then can bee found in the Nature of things. Therefore, because the Acts or Euents of *true Historie* haue not that Magnitude which satisfieth the minde of Man, *Poesie* faineth Acts and Euents Greater and more Heroicall; because *true Historie* propoundeth the successes and issues of actions not so agreable to the merits of Vertue and Vice, therefore Poesie faines them more iust in Retribution and more according to Reuealed Prouidence; because *true Historie* representeth Actions and Euents more ordinarie and lesse interchanged, therefore *Poesie* endueth them with more Rarenesse and more vnexpected and alternatiue Variations: So as it appeareth that *Poesie* serueth and conferreth to Magnanimitie, Moralitie, and to delectation. And therefore it was euer thought to haue some participation of diuinenesse, because it doth raise and erect the Minde, by submitting the shewes of things to the desires of the Mind, whereas reason doth buckle and bowe the Mind vnto the Nature of things. And we see that by these insinuations and congruities with man, Nature and pleasure, ioyned also with the agreement and consort it hath with Musicke, it hath had accesse and estimation in rude times and barbarous Regions, where other learning stoode excluded.

Francis Bacon

The Twoo Bookes . . . of the Proficience and Aduancement of Learning . . . (1605)

ART AND NATURE

In some cases we say arte is an ayde and coadiutor to nature, and a furtherer of her actions to good effect, or peraduenture a meane to supply her wants, by renforcing the causes wherein shee is impotent and defectiue, as doth the arte of phisicke, by helping the naturall concoction, retention, distribution, expulsion, and other vertues, in a weake and vnhealthie bodie. Or as the good gardiner seasons his soyle by sundrie sorts of compost: as mucke or marle, clay or sande, and many times by bloud, or lees of oyle or wine, or stale, or perchaunce with more costly drugs: and waters his plants, and weedes his herbes or floures, and prunes his branches, and vnleaues his boughes to let in the sunne: and twentie other waies cherisheth them, and cureth their infirmities, and so makes that neuer, or very seldome any of them miscarry, but bring foorth their flours and fruites in season. And in both these cases it is no smal praise for the Phisition and Gardiner to be called good and cunning artificers.

In another respect arte is not only an aide and coadiutor to nature in all her actions, but an alterer of them, and in some sort a surmounter of her skill, so as by meanes of it her own effects shall appeare more beautifull or straunge and miraculous, as in both cases before remembred. The Phisition by the cordials hee will geue his patient, shall be able not onely to restore the decayed spirites of man, and render him health, but also to prolong the terme of his life many yeares ouer and aboue the stint of his first and naturall constitution. And the Gardiner by his arte will not onely make an herbe, or flowr, or fruite, come forth in his season without impediment, but also will embellish the same in vertue, shape, odour and taste, that nature of her selfe woulde neuer haue done: as to make single gillifloure, or marigold, or daisie, double: and the white rose, redde, yellow, or carnation, a bitter mellon sweete, a sweete apple, soure, a plumme or cherrie without a stone, a peare without core or kernell, a goord or coucumber like to a horne, or any other figure he will: any of which things nature could not doe without mans help and arte. These actions also are most singular, when they be most artificiall.

In another respect, we say arte is neither an aider nor a surmounter, but onely a bare immitatour of natures works, following and counterfeyting her actions and effects, as the Marmesot doth many countenances and gestures of man, of which sorte are the artes of painting and keruing, whereof one represents the naturall by light colour and shadow in the superficiall or flat, the other in a body massife expressing the full and emptie, euen, extant, rabbated, hollow, or whatsoeuer other figure and passion of quantitie. So also the Alchimist counterfeits gold, siluer, and all other mettals, the Lapidarie pearles and pretious stones by glasse and other substances falsified, and sophisticate by arte. These men also be praised for their craft, and their credit is nothing empayred, to say that their conclusions and effections are very artificiall. Finally in another respect arte is as it were an encountrer and contrary to nature, producing effects neither like to hers, nor by participation with her operations, nor by imitation of her paternes, but makes things and produceth effects altogether strange and diuerse, and of such forme and qualitie (nature alwaies supplying stuffe) as she neuer would nor could haue

extant] projecting   *rabbated*] with a piece cut out

done of her selfe, as the carpenter that builds a house, the ioyner that makes a table or a bedstead, the tailor a garment, the Smith a locke or a key, and a number of like, in which case the workman gaineth reputation by his arte, and praise when it is best expressed and most apparant, and most studiously. Man also in all his actions that be not altogether naturall, but are gotten by study and discipline or exercise, as to daunce by measures, to sing by note, to play on the lute, and such like, it is a praise to be said an artificiall dauncer, singer, and player on instruments, because they be not exactly knowne or done, but by rules and precepts or teaching of schoolemasters. But in such actions as be so naturall and proper to man, as he may become excellent therein without any arte or imitation at all, (custome and exercise excepted, which are requisite to euery action not numbred among the vitall or animal) and wherein nature should seeme to do amisse, and man suffer reproch to be found destitute of them: in those to shew himselfe rather artificiall then naturall, were no lesse to be laughed at, then for one that can see well inough, to vse a paire of spectacles, or not to heare but by a trunke put to his eare, nor feele without a paire of ennealed glooues, which things in deede helpe an infirme sence, but annoy the perfit, and therefore shewing a disabilitie naturall mooue rather to scorne then commendation, and to pitie sooner then to prayse. But what else is language and vtterance, and discourse and persuasion, and argument in man, then the vertues of a well constitute body and minde, little lesse naturall then his very sensuall actions, sauing that the one is perfited by nature at once, the other not without exercise and iteration? Peraduenture also it wilbe granted that a man sees better and discernes more brimly his collours, and heares and feeles more exactly by vse and often hearing and feeling and seing, and though it be better to see with spectacles then not

brimly] brightly

see at all, yet is their praise not egall nor in any mans iudgement comparable: no more is that which a Poet makes by arte and precepts rather then by naturall instinct: and that which he doth by long meditation then by a suddaine inspiration, or with great pleasure and facillitie then hardly (and as they are woont to say) in spite of Nature or Minerua, then which nothing can be more irksome or ridiculous.

George Puttenham
The Arte of English Poesie (1589)

PROPRIETY

THE true Artificer will not run away from nature, as hee were afraid of her; or depart from life, and the likenesse of Truth; but speake to the capacity of his hearers. And though his language differ from the vulgar somewhat; it shall not fly from all humanity, with the *Tamerlanes*, and *Tamer-Chams*, of the late Age, which had nothing in them but the scenicall strutting, and furious vociferation, to warrant them then to the ignorant gapers. Hee knowes it is his onely Art, so to carry it, as none but Artificers perceive it. In the meane time perhaps hee is call'd barren, dull, leane, a poore Writer (or by what contumelious word can come in their cheeks) by these men, who without labour, judgement, knowledge, or almost sense, are received, or preferr'd before him. He gratulates them, and their fortune. An other Age, or juster men, will acknowledge the vertues of his studies: his wisdome, in dividing: his subtilty, in arguing: with what strength hee doth inspire his Readers: with what sweetnesse, hee strokes them; in inveighing: what sharpenesse; in Jest, what urbanity hee uses. How he doth raigne in mens affections; how invade, and breake in upon them; and makes their minds like the thing he writes. Then in his Elocution to behold, what word is proper: which hath ornament: which height: what is beautifully translated: where figures are fit: which gentle, which strong to shew the composition *Manly*. And how hee hath avoyded, faint, obscure, obscene, sordid, humble, improper, or effeminate Phrase; which is not only prais'd of the most, but commended, (which is worse) especially for that it is naught.

Ben Jonson

Timber: or Discoveries (1641)

ACTING

Enter Hamlet, and three of the Players

Ham. Speake the speech I pray you as I pronounc'd it to you, trippingly on the tongue, but if you mouth it as many of our Players do, I had as liue the towne cryer spoke my lines, nor doe not saw the ayre too much with your hand thus, but vse all gently, for in the very torrent, tempest, and as I may say, whirlwind of your passion, you must acquire and beget a temperance, that may giue it smoothnesse. O it offends mee to the soule, to heare a robustious perwig-pated fellowe tere a passion to totters, to very rags, to spleet the eares of the groundlings, who for the most part are capable of nothing, but inexplicable dumbe showes, and noyse: I would haue such a fellow whipt for ore-dooing Termagant, it out Herods Herod, pray you auoyde it.

Player. I warrant your honour.

Hamlet. Be not too tame neither, but let your owne discretion be your tutor, sute the action to the word, the word to the action, with this speciall obseruance, that you ore-steppe

liue] lief   *totters*] tatters

not the modestie of nature: For any thing so ore-doone, is from the purpose of playing, whose end both at the first, and nowe, was and is, to holde as twere the Mirrour vp to nature, to shew vertue her feature; scorne her own Image, and the very age and body of the time his forme and pressure: Now this ouer-done, or come tardie off, though it makes the vnskilfull laugh, cannot but make the iudicious greeue, the censure of which one, must in your allowance ore-weigh a whole Theater of others. O there be Players that I haue seene play, and heard others prayse, and that highly, not to speake it prophanely, that neither hauing th' accent of Christians, nor the gate of Christian, Pagan, nor man, haue so strutted & bellowed, that I haue thought some of Natures Iornimen had made men, and not made them well, they imitated humanitie so abhominably.

Player. I hope we haue reform'd that indifferently with vs.

Ham. O reforme it altogether, and let those that play your clownes speake no more then is set downe for them, for there be of them that wil themselues laugh, to set on some quantitie of barraine spectators to laugh to, though in the meane time, some necessary question of the play be then to be considered; that's villanous, and shewes a most pitifull ambition in the foole that vses it: goe make you readie.

William Shakespeare

The Tragicall Historie of Hamlet, Prince of Denmarke (1604)

BIOGRAPHICAL NOTES

Adlington, William (fl. 1566). Translator of *The Golden Asse*.

Andrewes, Lancelot (1555–1626). Successively bishop of Chichester, Ely and Winchester; one of the translators of the Authorized Version (1611); theologian.

Ascham, Roger (1515–68). Reader in Greek at Cambridge; tutor to Princess Elizabeth. Chief works – *Toxophilus* (1545) and *The Scholemaster* (1570).

Bacon, Francis, Lord Verulam (1561–1626). Statesman and philosopher whose ideas had a great influence on seventeenth-century thought and led to the formation of the Royal Society. Chief English works – *Essayes* (1597), *The Advancement of Learning* (1605) and *The New Atlantis* (1627).

Beaumont, Francis (1584–1616). Popular dramatist who collaborated with John Fletcher.

Bright, Timothy (1551?–1615). Pioneer of shorthand, clergyman, psychologist, great-grandfather of William Congreve. Shakespeare's *Hamlet* was probably influenced by his *Treatise of Melancholy* (1586).

Burton, William (1575–1645). Translator, antiquary, elder brother of the author of *The Anatomy of Melancholy*.

Campion, Edmund (1540–81). Jesuit martyr.

Campion, Thomas (1567–1630). Physician, composer, writer of masques and exquisite songs, who yet in his *Observations* (1602) advocated the use of unrhymed classical metres. His best verse is contained in five collections of *Ayres*.

Chamberlain, John (1553–1627). His letters contain interesting information on the period.

Chapman, George (1559?–1634). Poet, prolific dramatist and translator. His best works are the Bussy D'Ambois plays (1607, 1613), *The Widdowes Tears* (1612), his continuation of Marlowe's *Hero and Leander* and his translation of Homer.

Cornwallis, Sir William (1579–1614). Author of *Essayes* (1601).

Daniel, Samuel (1563?–1619). Poet, historian, writer of academic and pastoral plays. His *Apologie for Ryme* (1603) was written in reply to Thomas Campion. Chief works – *Delia* (1592), *Musophilus* and verse epistles.

Day, Angel (fl. 1586). His *Daphnis and Chloe* was translated from Amyot's version.

Dee, John (1527–1608). Mathematician and astrologer; accused of being a magician.

Dekker, Thomas (1570?–1641). Prolific dramatist and prose writer. Chief works – *The Shoemakers Holiday* (1600), *The Honest Whore* (1604), *The Wonderfull Yeare* (1603) and several pamphlets describing various aspects of London life.

Deloney, Thomas (1543?–1600?). Writer of novels on bourgeois themes, including *Thomas of Reading* and *Jack of Newberrie*, and of popular ballads.

Dent, Arthur (1559?–1607). Puritan divine. His *Plain Man's Pathway* was known to Bunyan.

Drake, Sir Francis (1540?–96). Admiral and circumnavigator.

Drummond William (1585–1649). Scottish poet, who recorded an account of conversations with Ben Jonson. His prose work, *The Cypresse Grove*, was appended to a collection of his poems.

Eliot, John (fl. 1592). Disciple of Rabelais, thought by some to be an acquaintance of Shakespeare. His *Ortho-Epia Gallica* (1593) was designed to teach French conversation.

Elizabeth I (1533–1603).

Elyot, Sir Thomas (1490?–1546). Diplomatist, M.P., humanist. Chief work – *The Governour* (1531).

Erondell, Peter (fl. 1609). Teacher of French.

Fenner, Thomas (d. 1590?). Vice-admiral in 1588.

Fletcher, Giles (1549?–1611). Poet and the father of two more poets, Giles and Phineas Fletcher.

Fletcher, John (1579–1625). Dramatist. He wrote some fifty plays, many in collaboration with Beaumont and other playwrights; they are facile and theatrical, but they contain charming verse.

Florio, John (1553?–1625). The Earl of Southampton's tutor; teacher of Italian and author of an Italian-English dictionary; translator of Montaigne and possibly of the *Decameron*.

Gascoigne, George (1535?–77). One of the best Elizabethan poets before Spenser, though his prose tale, 'The Adventures of Master F. J.', is his most interesting work.

Gosson, Stephen (1554–1624). Unsuccessful playwright. His attack on poetry and drama evoked Sidney's *Defence*.

Greene, Robert (1558–92). One of the University wits; bohemian, exposer of racketeers and confidence-tricksters, author of Euphuistic and other stories, dramatist, poet. His best play is *Friar Bacon and Friar Bungay* (1594), and his novels include *Menaphon, Pandosto* and *Gwydonius*.

Grymestone, Elizabeth (1562?–1603). Writer of prose and verse, with Catholic sympathies.

Hakluyt, Richard (1553–1616). Collector of narratives of travel.

Hall, Joseph (1574–1656). Wrote verse satires in his youth, moralistic, theological and controversial works in later life; known as 'the English Seneca'; as Bishop of Exeter he was Milton's chief opponent in the episcopacy controversy.

Harding, Thomas (fl. 1566). Recusant controversialist.

Harington, Sir John (1561?–1612). Queen Elizabeth's godson, inventor of a form of water-closet which he described in the Rabelaisian *Metamorphosis of Ajax* (1596), translator of *Orlando Furioso*, epigrammatist, wit.

Harman, Thomas (fl. 1565). His *Caueat or warening for Commen cursetors* was one of the first exposures of the Elizabethan underworld.

Harrison, William (1534–93). Parson. His *Description of Britaine* was contributed to Holinshed's *Chronicles*.

Harsnet, Samuel (1561–1631). As chaplain to the Bishop of London wrote exposure in racy style of Puritan and Catholic exorcists, read by Shakespeare; afterwards Archbishop of York.

Harvey, Gabriel (1545?–1630?). A Cambridge don, Spenser's friend, who engaged in violent controversies with Greene and Nashe.

Hayward, Sir John (1564?–1627). Historian; imprisoned for dedicating his *Henry IV* to the Earl of Essex.

Hoby, Sir Thomas (1530–66). Translator of Castiglione's *Courtier*.

Holinshed, Raphael (?–1580?). His *Chronicles* (1577), based partly on Hall's and other chronicles, formed the main source of *Macbeth* and many of Shakespeare's Histories.

Holland, Philemon (1552–1637). Translator of Pliny, Plutarch, Suetonius, Camden, Livy. Known as the 'translator generall'.

Hooker, Richard (1554–1600). Master of the Temple, theologian.

The first four books of his masterpiece, *Of the Lawes of Ecclesiasticall Politie*, appeared in 1594; a complete edition in eight books was not published until 1662.

Hoskyns, John (1566–1638). Lawyer; friend of Ralegh, Jonson and Donne; author of *Directions for speech and style* (1630).

James I (1566–1625). Wrote verse in his youth; defended belief in witchcraft in *Daemonologie*, gave advice to his son in *Basil kon Doron*, and outlined his theory of monarchy in *The True Lawe of Free Monarchies*.

Jonson, Ben (1573–1637). Dramatist, poet, critic. Chief plays – *Volpone* (1607), *The Alchemist* (1612), *Bartholemew Fair* (1614). His criticism is contained in *Discoveries* and in the *Conversations with William Drummond*.

Langham, Robert (fl. 1575). Nothing is known about him except his lively *Letter*. He is usually called Laneham.

Latimer, Hugh (1488?–1555). Bishop of Worcester, 1535; resigned 1538; arrested 1539, 1546, 1553; burnt at Oxford, 1555. Popular preacher.

Lodge, Thomas (1558–1625). Writer of satires in verse, poems, novels, pamphlets; recusant; in later life a physician and the translator of Seneca's prose works. Chief works – *Rosalynde* (1590), *A Margarite of America* (1596), *Wits Miserie* and *Phillis* (sonnets).

Lyly, John (1554–1606). Novelist and dramatist. His *Euphues* (1578), influenced the prose of his generation, and his delicate prose comedies, acted by boys, influenced those of Shakespeare.

Manningham, John (d. 1622). Diarist; barrister. Some entries in his diary (pub. 1868) are possibly Collier forgeries.

Marlowe, Christopher (1564–93). University wit, poet, dramatist, heretic, spy; stabbed to death in a tavern brawl after writing the best English tragedies before *Romeo and Juliet* and the delightful unfinished poem, *Hero and Leander*.

Mar-Prelate, Martin (fl. 1588). Pseudonym of Puritan pamphleteer.

Marston, John (c. 1575–1634). Satirist, with a nose for nastiness; dramatist; afterwards a parson. Best plays – *The Malcontent* (1604), *Antonio and Mellida*, *The Dutch Courtesan*, *Sophonisba*.

Middleton, Thomas (1570?–1627). Jacobean dramatist, magnificent but uneven. His best plays – *The Changeling* and *Women Beware*

Women – are tragic; but his comedies give a vivid and realistic picture of London life.

More, Sir Thomas (1478–1535). Lord Chancellor, executed for 'treason', his refusal to acknowledge Henry VIII as head of the Church. His *Utopia* (1516) and his propagandist *Life of Richard III* were written in Latin; the *Dialogue of Comfort* (1553) was written in English when he was imprisoned in the Tower in the last year of his life.

Nashe, Thomas (1567–1601). One of the University wits; poet, dramatist, novelist, pamphleteer. Chief works – *Pierce Pennilesse* (1592), *Nashes Lenten Stuffe* (1599), and a picaresque novel, *The Vnfortunate Traveller* (1594).

North, Sir Thomas (1535–1601?). Translated Plutarch's *Lives* from the French of Amyot; his version was the main source of Shakespeare's Roman plays.

Overbury, Sir Thomas (1581–1613). Writer of 'characters' in verse and prose; poisoned in the Tower because he opposed Rochester's marriage with Lady Essex.

Pettie, George (1548–89). Translator of Guazzo (via the French) and author of short stories entitled *A Petite Pallace of Pettie his Pleasure* (1576).

Puttenham, George (1530?–90). His authorship of *The Arte of English Poesie* (1589) is disputed, but highly probable.

Ralegh, Sir Walter (1552?–1618). Courtier, explorer, poet, historian; imprisoned and executed for his anti-Spanish policy after the failure of his last voyage to Guiana. Chief works – *The Discouerie of Guiana* (1596) and *The History of the World* (1614), which was written in prison.

Rastell, John (fl. 1565). Jesuit controversialist – not to be confused with the printer and writer of interludes (d. 1536).

Riche, Barnaby (1542?–1617). Soldier, novelist, pamphleteer. His *Farewell to Militarie Profession* was the main source of *Twelfth Night*.

Rowland, David (fl. 1568). Translator of *The Pleasaunt Historie of Lazarillo de Tormes*.

Scot, Reginald (1538?–99). His chief work, *The Discouerie of Witchcraft* (1584), is pleasantly sceptical in tone.

Shakespeare, William (1564–1616).

273

Sidney, Sir Philip (1554–86). Courtier, diplomatist, soldier, poet. Chief works – *Arcadia, Astrophel and Stella, The Defence of Poesie* – all published after his death in the Netherlands campaign.

Spenser, Edmund (1552–99).

Stubbes, Philip (fl. 1580–93). Apart from his moralising *Anatomy of Abuses* (1583), his most interesting work is *A Christal Glasse* (1591), written in memory of his wife.

Tofte, Robert (fl. 1598). A bad poet and a racy prose translator.

Turberville, George (1540?–1610). Translator of Ovid and Mantuan; minor poet; traveller to Russia. Chief works – *The Book of Faulconrie* and *The Noble Arte of Venerie*.

Underdowne, Thomas (fl. 1566–87). Translator of Ovid's *Invective against Ibis* and of Heliodorus.

Warner, William (1558?–1609). Poet, novelist. Chief works – *Pan his Syrinx* (1584) and *Albions England* (1586).

Webbe William (fl. 1586). His *Discourse of English Poetrie* (1586) makes C. S. Lewis say he 'is in a class by himself, uniquely bad'. But he is rather a representative example of the feeble critics of the age.

Webster, John (1580?–1625). One of the best of Shakespeare's successors in tragedy. Chief works – *The White Diuel* (1612) and *The Dutchesse of Malfy* (1623).

Wilson, Sir Thomas (1560?–1629). Foreign intelligencer in Italy; Keeper of Records (1606–29); translated *Diana* (1596).

INDEX OF AUTHORS

ACKNOWLEDGEMENTS

FOR permission to quote extracts from their publications we are indebted to:

The Cambridge University Press, publishers of the *Complete Works of Sir Philip Sidney* edited by A. Feuillerat; The Clarendon Press, publishers of *Selections from Sir Walter Ralegh's Historie of the World, Letters etc.* edited by G. E. Hadow; and the Yale University Press, publishers of *The Life, Letters and Writings of John Hoskyns* by L. B. Osborn.